ONCE A PRIN

TO MY PARENTS RAJA MAHIPAL SINGH OF SARILA
AND RANI BHAWANI KUNWAR
AND MY SON SAMAR SINGH OF SARILA

Once a Prince of Sarila

Of Palaces and Tiger Hunts,
of Nehrus and Mountbattens

NARENDRA SINGH SARILA

I.B. TAURIS

LONDON · NEW YORK

Published in 2008 by I.B.Tauris & Co Ltd
6 Salem Road, London W2 4BU
175 Fifth Avenue, New York NY 10010
www.ibtauris.com

In the United States of America and in Canada distributed by Palgrave
Macmillan a division of St Martin's Press, 175 Fifth Avenue, New York
NY 10010

ISBN 978 1 84511 707 8 (Hb)

A full CIP record for this book is available from the British Library
A full CIP record is available from the Library of Congress

Library of Congress Catalog card: available

Printed and bound in Great Britain by TJ International Ltd, Padstow,
Cornwall.
Copy edited and typeset by Oxford Publishing Services, Oxford

Contents

Illustrations

Preface

THE WORLD into which I was born in the late 1920s as the heir apparent of a princedom in central India, Sarila, seems removed not just by three-quarters of a century but by several centuries.

The pram for my evening outings when I was a child was not the usual one with four wheels, but a huge elephant. And, as we swayed through the streets on it, people bent low and swung their right arm forward until the palm came to rest against their brow – in an obsequious salute to their future raja. Who, knowing me today, would believe that before each winter, at the end of the monsoon, which once upon a time heralded the opening of military campaigns, I was expected, as I grew up, to perform a sacrificial rite? This was the beheading of a goat by a single stroke of the sword as an offering to Kali, the goddess of war.

We had moved out of our medieval fortress to our present palace only a quarter of a century before I was born. The fortress was guarded by battlements and a moat, and on two sides by large tanks for further defence, dug at the time the stronghold was built. My grand aunt still lived in it and when I heard her reciting the heroic tales of my ancestors, who had held their own against the Moguls, I used to slip back effortlessly a century or two in time. She used to press her palms on my temples and hold them there, perhaps out of affection, perhaps to draw strength from contact with one she believed was endowed with divine right.

My father was the absolute ruler of our principality with the power of life and death over his subjects. The majority of them knew no other form of government and called him *Garib Parwar* (protector of the poor) and *Ann Data* (provider of sustenance). On festive days there were processions during which he appeared sitting in a *howdah* atop a caparisoned elephant, two officials standing behind, one holding a mace and the other a *chanwar* (silver-handled fly whisk), the symbols of sovereignty in India. He periodically held *durbars* (court sessions). At one, held during the festival of *Dussehra*, he received the fealty of our knights, senior officials and important citizens who marched backwards after each had approached the throne to salute him.

During school holidays in Sarila I shot and hunted and practised cricket and tennis. We travelled too: in 1938 we visited Ceylon, now Sri Lanka, on a P&O (Peninsular & Oriental Steam Navigation Company) steamer. Protected by a British power then unmatched east of Suez, we felt totally secure.

Who could then imagine that within a decade the princely states, including Sarila, would be swept away and their rajas and maharajas become ordinary citizens, their power and divinity passing into the hands of elected representatives, some of whom had been their servitors, retainers and vassals? And who also could imagine that the British Empire, over which the sun then never set, would collapse like a house of cards?

While memory holds the door I thought I would record what I remember of that bygone era and more. As I grew up, new currents began to swirl around me, currents that appealed to British rationalism and *savoir-faire* on the one hand and to Indian nationalism on the other.

I was sent to the Mayo Chiefs College in Ajmer – one of the five schools built by the British on the model of Eton and Harrow and run by Englishmen exclusively for the education of princes and nobles. The fledgling maharajas and their nobles – both Hindu and Muslim – were all there, reciting Shakespeare and Wordsworth and playing cricket and polo.

The great Sepoy Mutiny of 1857 had triggered a revolt by the Indian princes whose territories the British had gobbled up during their conquest of India. It proved to be a turning point in relations between the British and the Indian princes. After crushing the revolt, the British decided to conquer no more. Instead, they signed treaties with all those rajas, maharajas and nawabs who held territories not yet taken, recognized their domains and guaranteed their progeny succession to them – unless, of course, they threatened British power. Two things happened as a result. Potential British enemies became potential friends and India was divided into two: British India and Indian India – the first ruled directly by British governors and the second by autonomous rulers as the British empress's suzerains. The princely territories constituted more than one-third of the British Indian Empire and had 350 princely states, most very small, others middling and a few as large as European countries.

In the 1930s the winds of change for a democratic order had failed to disturb the feudal medieval ethos that lingered in Sarila. In the 1940s neither the war nor the rapid erosion of British strength, which turned the nationalist movement into a hurricane, disturbed the tranquillity of our existence. Indeed, this was a time when the princes in their states and in the new British capital of New Delhi constructed new palaces, several in innovative art deco style, and the capitals of princely states were beautified. Our family continued to spend several months of the burning summers enjoying the style and sparkle of Simla or Mussoorie hill stations, 6000 feet up in the Himalayas. Here, from ridges clad in pine, oak, birch and firs, one got magnificent views of the snows, the air was bracing and the travail of the people in the plains below seemed remote and ephemeral.

Before a sunset there is at times a mellow glow. Princely India in the 1930s and 1940s was bathed in such radiance, probably unmatched anywhere in the last century. These were halcyon days of bejewelled and eccentric maharajas, life in marble palaces mirrored in lakes or in mighty stone fortresses on craggy hills, tiger hunts on elephant back and elephant hunts on shank's mare, bewitching princesses hurtling on horseback or awaiting their lovers in projecting balconies trellised in stone, special trains loaded with guests shuttling to each other's domains, armies of retainers and polo, music and laughter. I partook of some of this flush.

As the princely states went under, as luck would have it, I was catapulted in a different direction. I had deputized for my father at the last meeting of the Chamber of Princes in New Delhi in July 1947 and watched with fascination how Lord Mountbatten, the new viceroy and cousin of the British King George VI, steered the maharajas to shift their allegiance from the British throne to the new Indian dominion.

In the larger neighbouring Charkhari state, whose maharaja had no heir and to the throne of which my younger brother had succeeded as ruler in 1942, agitation for representational government was raging apace, as in the other states. When my father and brother offered the agitators seats in the council of ministers and agreed to oust the *diwan,* the chief executive, they accepted me as a compromise candidate to preside over the cabinet. So, not yet 21, I became the chief minister of a state nearly a thousand miles in area with an annual revenue of about 900 million rupees or 20 million dollars on a present count. This was surely an unusual occurrence and an indication of tremulous times.

No sooner had the British departed in August 1947 than the

national government began to pressurize the rulers to give up their powers and to merge their states into larger units in which democratic governments could be introduced. In return they were offered fixed stipends, recognition of their privileges and titles, and constitutional guarantees for their personal property, including their palaces and forts. At the same time in Delhi, Mountbatten and the Indian leaders, Nehru and Patel, were ruminating on other ways to wipe away some of the princes' tears. One idea that struck them was to induct a princeling on the staff of the governor general – a show boy? I have no idea how their eyes fell upon me, but in early 1948 I found myself installed in the viceroy's house in New Delhi, right below the viceregal apartment.

It was then the largest house for a single couple in the entire world and run with iron discipline and great panache under a dynamic chief. Fortunately, I kept a diary of my experiences as an aide-de-camp to Lord Mountbatten. This gives glimpses of the life and activities of the last British governor general and his consort or HE (His and Her Ex), as we called them, as well as of the other personalities, Nehru, Patel, Rajaji, and the top civil and military leaders, British and Indian, who flitted in and out of the great house and the viceregal retreat in Simla. (Mahatma Gandhi had been assassinated before I reached Delhi.)

My book ends in August 1948 when I joined the Indian foreign service and embarked on my proper career, on which I have spent my life. Princely India had dissolved before my eyes but a new India had also started to take shape before them. The traditional vocation of the Indian warrior clans had been to defend the country and its ancient ethos. The new dispensation, the new India, afforded me greater opportunities to test that traditional calling of the Indian knights – albeit with a pen and word of mouth instead of a sword – than the small world of Sarila could ever have done.

As for what happened later, as far as Sarila and my fate were concerned, the *New York Times* published a four-column article on the subject on 4 January 1996, written by the noted journalist John Burns, under the caption 'Serenely Maharaja Strolls the Democratic Land'. This serves as the epilogue and I should like to extend my thanks to him for giving me permission to use it.

The areas in grey show the princely states that covered more than a third of the British Empire

1. Map of the British Indian Empire as it was in 1947. The areas in grey show the princely states that covered more than a third of the British Empire.

Chapter 1
An Elephant Was My Pram

THE ELEPHANT was already kneeling to receive me as I was led down the broad flight of steps of our palace for my evening outing. Her front legs were tucked away under her massive belly, her huge ears flapped gently and the end of her trunk twirled like a python on the gravel. A ladder was dangling from the *howdah* fastened to her back with ropes that went round her belly. Before stepping on the ladder I sought her eye, a watery dot embedded in coarse, chunky, dark grey skin. I thought there was a twinkle of recognition in it, which made me feel much better, for I was a bit nervous so near the huge beast.

As the elephant disentangled her front legs to get up, keeping the knees of her hind legs on the ground, the *howdah* inclined backward and the palace buildings, even the nearby tall ashoka trees, disappeared from view. I felt a mile up in the sky, ready to slip to the ground. Then a reverse movement began as the elephant straightened her back legs and I was thrown forward to the original upright position. But soon the elephant's march began, a gentle amble, and I started to enjoy the ride.

Jagdamba (she was named after a goddess) was said to be

2. The front façade of Sarila Palace, the author's home.

100 years old and with the memory that elephants have, probably remembered the clattering up of the rebel cavalry leader Tantya Tope with his troops to our fortress gate that

afternoon in 1858, to coax my ancestor Maharaja Hindupat to join the spontaneous and disorganized explosion against the raj, which the British called a mutiny, that had begun the previous year. (He got from us two artillery pieces and some cattle to provide milk for his forces.)

Before raised surface roads were built in the kingdom of Sarila, the low lying plains around our capital got waterlogged during the monsoon; horses then could not get through, and elephants were the only mode of locomotion. Consequently, my family kept several elephants. My grandfather used to ride an elephant for his morning constitutional. To make an elephant trot and turn is more strenuous than manoeuvring a horse. One straddles the elephant's neck and drives it with the pressure of one's knees and thighs and by prodding behind its ears with an *ankush* – a baton with iron spikes.

Jagdamha and her male companion Bhairongaj were 'housed' on a platform under the neem trees by the lake behind our palace, one hind leg of each fastened by a heavy chain pegged to the ground. The chains have not been removed from the spot to this day, in their memory. Elephants have an enormous appetite for leaves and greenery. I used to sneak outside the side gate to watch her being bathed and my servants told me that she trumpeted louder and squirted more water if she became aware that I was watching her.

Only after we had passed the palace's gatehouse with its massive wooden portals arched high for the passage of elephants, did the *mahout*, the elephant driver, turn and salute me – like the pilot of an airline who greets the passengers well after the aircraft is on its flight. With me sat my guardian Bassu Babba, wearing an enormous turban, who soon enough warned me to duck my head, as we were about to pass under the newly fixed overhead electric cables.

The gate faced the new road that skirted the lake and led to

3. The author's ancestor, Chhatrasal (1649–1731). He pushed back the frontiers of the Mogul Empire to form an area as large as France. This area is called Bundelkhand after the author's Bundera clan.

the open country. In the middle of the lake, surrounded by palm trees, stood our fortress, in which my old aunt, on whom we were to call at the end of our promenade, lived. My ancestor Aman Singh, whose father Pahar Singh had sent him to occupy and fortify Sarila, built this fortress between 1755 and 1760. Jaitpur was the headquarters of Jagat Raj, the second son of Chhatrasal, the warrior king who had conquered an area as large as France in central India from the weakening Mogul Empire at the end the seventeenth century. Pahar Singh was Jagat Raj's eldest son. The region has ever since been called Bundelkhand, or the land of the Bundelas, after the name of our clan. The Kshatriyas, or warriors, unlike other castes, are divided into clans and members of the same clan are regarded as blood brothers.

Sarila is situated on flat land. Its defence could only be secured with the help of water. Therefore, a 12-hectare lake was dug to the south of the town leaving an island in its middle, connected to land on one side. On this island the fortress was built. For additional defence, a deep moat was dug inside the island around the fortress's ramparts. The Sarila fortress was part of the common defence of the territories of the Bundela clan against Mogul incursions from their province of Oudh (present Uttar Pradesh) to the north. The other forts built to guard this northern frontier were at Charkhari and Ajaigarh to the east, each 50 to 100 miles from each other.

The Bundelas had fled from the rich Gangetic plains into the thick forests and hills of the Vindhya range to its south after the Turkish sultan of Kabul, Mohammad Gouri, conquered it in 1194. They had, however, survived to recover land up to the Betwa and Jamuna rivers in the north. Other clans had fled from the Gangetic plains to the deserts of Rajasthan or the forests of the Himalayan foothills and established their new domains in these less accessible areas. (The large states in the Rajasthan desert, Jodhpur, Jaipur, Bikaner, and others date from that time.)

I was perched high enough on my mount to look over the tanks' bund to the right and see masses of pink lotus flowers

4. The author's grandfather, Pahar Singh II.

floating on the blue water turning the lake to look like a garden. Further on, next to a massive banyan tree on the bund, a white domed temple glimmered. Near it was the wrestling pit where several young men were practising press-ups and sit-ups, their bodies glistening with oil. A few hundred metres away on the other side of the road, to the left, I could see another temple called Saleshwar named after a different name for Shiva, the lord of destruction and rejuvenation. This ninth century temple had given the name Salyapuri to the village once inhabited by cowherds and farmers, which got abridged to Sarila. The town had grown around it.

From the height of the elephant the people on the road looked small, the colours of their turbans so bright. They bent low to salute me, those without headgear covering their heads with the left hand as a mark of further respect. Bassu Bappa whispered the name and caste of the person saluting; and under his prompting I raised my hand perfunctorily or formally as demanded by the man's status, age and closeness to the throne.

The men wore long, collarless shirts or body fitting vests, depending on their calling. The lower garments were invariably knee-length dhotis, which from afar looked like Bermuda shorts. In Bundelkhand dhotis are worn by wrapping a piece of cloth from the waist downwards and holding it by a knot in the front, then gathering the hem between the legs from front to back and tucking it behind. The calves are left exposed. The better-off wore white dhotis of finer material; the others wore a coarser cloth. The locally made unisex, heavy shoes curled up at the toe and rose to ankle height at the rear. They looked like the hulls of the early sailing vessels of Columbus's days. Many people were barefoot. The heavy over-sized silver anklets were *de rigueur* for women in Bundelkhand. They jingled as the women walked and as I grew up I often wondered whether they made secret encounters more difficult.

I vividly remember my guardian nudging me and whispering not to return the greeting of a tall man turned out in spotless white with thick hair brushed off his forehead and a twirled up moustache, whose greeting, I noticed, had been somewhat perfunctory. Bassu Babba explained later that he was an agitator. This was my first encounter with Behari Lal, once an electrician and a carpenter in the state's service, who later was to lead the agitation against my father's rule in our kingdom. But I soon forgot the incident as we ambled on towards the open country.

The land around Sarila is as flat as a billiard tabletop; green with wheat in winter, golden as the crop matured in March, brown and barren and shimmering with mirages in the burning dry summer and waterlogged in the rainy season after July. The line of the horizon was broken here and there by clumps of trees, indicating villages. In our part of India farmers' houses are situated in villages and not in isolated dwellings near their fields. Far away to the south one could see a solitary blue hill indicating that the Vindhya ranges, where our clan had found shelter, were not too far away. The Vindhyas divide India between the northern plains and the plateau of the peninsular south.

We turned back at the canal bridge. Under it there was a small waterfall that made a gruff, but soothing sound. Into the churning waters of the pond, naked village children were diving and making merry. The many waterfalls at regular intervals in the canal indicated that the land was gently descending towards the Jamuna River. British engineers had built this 100-kilometre long canal at the end of the nineteenth century. Its primary function was to fill tanks, each anywhere between five to ten acres in size, which, with shady trees on their bunds, were a feature of our villages. The Chandela rulers (who built the Khajuraho temples) began to build these tanks in the ninth and tenth centuries; the Bundelas continued the work and, in the nineteenth century, the British built canals to feed the tanks. With the population having quadrupled since my birth, the canal water today is used more and more to irrigate the new fields, while the village tanks are getting silted and drying up.

The shred of water snaking through the flat land was an important feature of our countryside. The canal had a fair weather road running along it to facilitate its inspections and repairs. My father used to take us for car drives and strolls on this. The new fields cut a broad swathe of about 500 metres on either side of the canal in the light forest. As the sun sank, deer, chinkaras, blue bulls, sambar and wild boar would leave cover and come to slake their thirst in the canal water. If a panther had been around we would find this out by spotting its pugmarks – a soft roundish impression with five smaller round ones to the fore. Partridges and quails were aplenty in the fields. In November we looked out for ducks flying in from the north, from frozen Siberia, across the Himalayas or the Hindu Kush – big flocks, small parties, single birds and chevrons.

Often on our elephant-back strolls we would encounter a hundred or more black buck grazing in the fields. Seeing us they would stampede, hopping first to gather speed, the fawn-coloured females leading, and the majestic straight-horned black males with white bellies bringing up the rear; when disturbed, black buck have a habit of taking off to race ahead and cross your path. To clear the rise of the road they would prance two or three abreast and, as they remained suspended for a moment in midair, forelegs bent inwards, their white-circled eyes strangely calm in all the commotion, the elephant would be halted to let them pass and for me to gaze at a wondrous sight.

To meet my aunt in the fortress my elephant had to cross a bridge over the deep moat and pass two massive brick bastions before reaching the gate tower. As a safeguard against battering rams, this was angled to face one of the bastions. The heavy wooden portals the guard would swing open had iron spikes to protect them from ramming by elephants. The battlements topped by merlons rose straight from the waters of the moat. Entering this stronghold was like slipping centuries back in time.

We alighted at the main courtyard. On one side of it rose the *mahal* – a tower-like structure in brick, unadorned and severe. On the other side were quarters for officers and soldiers, stores and stables. I entered the lofty gate over a threshold made of a stout, square-cut log that Bassu would swing me over. We then passed through narrow, dark, rafted rooms with low archways. These led to an inner courtyard along one wall of which were high steps without banisters, leading to the upper floors.

My aunt blended well into the medieval surroundings. A tiny old lady with wheat coloured parchment skin, her grey hair parted severely and tied in a knot at the back, she wore saris of colours and designs preferred in an earlier century – olives and aubergines, worked with gold thread – and long-sleeved Muslim blouses and gold amulets. In other respects also she evoked a different epoch. Whenever she came to see my father or mother she travelled in a velvet draped palanquin, with the palanquin bearers walking on their heels and swinging their hips to ensure an even ride. Most of her visits to my father were made to seek money for alms and charity. My father used to complain that she could retain nothing for herself and what he gave her was immediately given away. Married to my grandfather's elder brother, she was widowed at twenty. Childless and forlorn, she had spent her entire life in the fortress.

She used to make me sit at her side on her four-poster divan (there were no chairs) and would slowly move her tiny, soft, wrinkled hand over my head and press her palms to my temples as stated above. I would grow as tall as Chhatrasal (who was six feet six inches tall) she would say. She would then recite a couplet or two in our local dialect on her above-named Bundela hero, on his valour and ruthlessness in battle and on his gentleness and philanthropy in peace. One day she presented me with a yo-yo, which I had to restrain myself from immediately starting to spring. It was from one of her sardars (noblemen) that I heard the following story of the British advent into Bundelkhand.

He told me how the British, after reaching the Indo-Gangetic plains from Bengal in the early nineteenth century, quickly spread a network of envoys and spies in the courts of the rulers of Bundelkhand, the forested area immediately to its south. In 1839 Parichat, then the ruler of Jaitpur, gathered a coalition of other rulers of the area to fight the advancing foreign foe.

Hearing of the banding together of some rulers in Bundelkhand, the British in 1840 sent a small force to show the flag. This was set upon by Parichat's forces and eliminated. Next year when a stronger force was also routed, the British, from their headquarters in Allahabad organized a pincer movement with a large force. One arm crossed the Yamuna and Betwa rivers and engaged Parichat's and the coalition forces, north of Jaitpur in Bilgain (not far from Sarila). The other marched via Banda and entered the lightly defended capital from the jungles of the southeast. Simultaneously, the British engineered the defection of Ratan Singh, the neighbouring ruler of Charkhari, a cousin of Parichat and a powerful prince in his own right. When, after a day's fighting in which he lost many men, Parichat retreated to rest for the night and recuperate in the well-fortified Mangalgarh fort of Charkhari, he was aghast to hear an 11-gun salute being fired to welcome him, which would certainly give away his whereabouts to the company's forces on the chase. Thus betrayed, Parichat immediately returned to his own capital but found Jaitpur taken by the

11

British. To instil fear among other rulers who might be inclined to continue resisting the British by force, the Jaitpur fort was razed to the ground. Thus, the kingdom from where my ancestors had come to found Sarila 90 years earlier was obliterated.

After visiting my grandmother, I would be taken to the highest terrace to enjoy the view of the tanks and the countryside beyond. As we made our descent back to our elephant, Bassu Babba pointed to a door in the outer courtyard from where, he said, an underground escape passage ran below the battlement, the moat and the tanks, into the fields beyond, but it was never used. It is a pity that this fortress was destroyed in 1962, but I have since planted hundreds of trees in its grounds and laid out walkways with views of the dark green waters of the inner moat and the shimmering blue of the tanks. On these I make my rounds – admittedly on shank's mare and not on my childhood 'pram', which passed away in the early 1940s.

On our return, we would take another route, a wide road shaded by *gulmohar* (flame of the forest) trees that led to the northern entrance of the palace. By it stood low buildings in white plaster with verandas and wide Victorian arches running along their front. These were the new state secretariat, the hospital, the school, the post office and the quarters of some officials. The road skirted the town and as we neared its houses I would see children scampering up to the flat roofs or balconies of the houses to watch the elephant – and perhaps me. Many had black lines of mascara painted around their eyes, which made them look large. The girls would watch coyly, avoiding looking straight at me.

The more important houses of the town were situated on higher ground and were double storeyed, with high gatehouses decorated with balconies, niches and archivolts – though we did not enter the town and go that far. They belonged to the higher castes. The farmers from other castes occupied houses lower down the hillock, together with blacksmiths and carpenters who were considered members of senior professions. The houses below the rise, which were likely to be flooded in the rains, were of the lower castes – weavers, leather workers, barbers, washermen and sweepers. The population of the lowest caste was infinitely smaller at that time – only 6 per cent against more than 24 per cent now. In fact, the population explosion in India in the last half century has mostly been among the lowest and other less privileged castes. The so-called upper castes have shrunk from 60 to 20 per cent in my lifetime. Demographically, India is, therefore a new country. Democracy is a game of numbers. To get elected you must have the votes of the growing lower castes and this dependence on them is loosening caste prejudices.

The few Muslim families in Sarila were distributed on higher or lower ground, according to their callings. As converts from the sultanate days, the others considered them as one of the many castes and left them to their own devices though, among themselves, they formed a casteless, if not classless, society.

We entered the palace compound by the new gate with iron portals set at the end of a 200-metre long avenue lined with eucalyptus trees imported by my father from Australia and then a novelty in India. This led to the white plastered Palladian type structure with a broad flight of stone steps that ascended from the ground level to the landing on the first floor. The three-storey building was decorated with parapets, guttae, cornices and columns, its lofty Romanesque pediment topped with a tiny *kaman* (bow), an Indian feature that blended with its European façade. From the iron gate I could clearly see our scarlet and saffron flag fluttering above the pediment. The mansion was flanked by nearly identical single-storeyed buildings protruding to the fore, creating a wide courtyard in front. In the centre of this gravel-filled square was an iron fountain set in a well-proportioned octagonal white plastered basin. Using the foundations of the nineteenth century villa on the bund of the lake, my father had created an Italian or Portuguese looking mansion.

Behind the palace lay the lake with the fortress and beyond that the open country we had roamed.

Chapter 2
My Father

M Y FATHER was born in 1898, a year after Queen Victoria had celebrated her diamond jubilee and British power in the world had reached its zenith. His father had died a few months before his birth. By then the paramount power's relationship with the Indian princes had become rigorously organized. During a prince's minority the administration was taken over by the viceroy and a *diwan*, or chief executive, was appointed to run the state. The prince was permitted to ascend the throne and assume ruling powers at the age of 19.

This was also done in Sarila and my father, when nine, was packed off to one of the five boarding schools the viceroys had established for the education of princes and nobles – the Daly Chiefs College in Indore – 400 miles away. His holidays were divided between his mother, while she lived, and the British political agent to the Bundelkhand states, stationed in Nowgong, who acted as his guardian. These were soldiers, explorers and diplomats. One of them, Colonel F. M. Bailey, had accompanied Colonel Younghusband on his expedition to Lhasa. He had also served as a secret agent in Uzbekistan during the Bolshevik revolution in Russia (as he recounted in his book *Mission to Tashkand*). Another, Arthur Lothian was to rise to become the British resident to the Nizam of Hyderabad before the end of the raj. He foretold the destruction of the Indian

5. The author's father in 1905, aged 7, in traditional Bundelkhandi dress.

princely order. Others had taken part in other adventures in the British Empire, over which in those days, the sun never set.

From the backwater of Sarila my father was thrown into contact with people who had a world-view and aplomb. And he fell under their spell.

Unlike some of the other princes, my father did not believe in the divine right of kings. On the other hand, he used to tell me that the politicians agitating for the independence of, and democracy in, India were either over idealistic or plain power hungry. Because a great country like India could not be managed by the type of leaders that the uneducated masses would choose, attention should be directed to imparting sound education to the exclusion of other issues.

He felt that, in sweeping away the inefficient and ante-diluvian medieval structures of Mogul rule in India and replacing them with a uniform administration, all-India services, an independent judiciary with proper criminal and civil codes, and building roads, railways, ports and other infra-structure, without which India could not advance, the British were performing an essential and historic task. He believed that this benign process should continue for the time being. Besides, he doubted the capacity of Congress Party leaders to organize India's defence. He did not cavil about the escalating high taxes the farmers had to pay or at the fact that much of the economic infrastructure developed primarily helped to serve British commercial interests. Because, he argued, the advantage to India was greater and the British could not be expected to do something for nothing. He also believed that the administrative reforms in British India that were being copied in the states were helping to modernize them.

He did not think that representational government was suitable for small units like Sarila. On the other hand, proposals to merge them to form larger units were impractical because the rulers would never agree to any scheme that would result in the loss of their powers. In any case, this would require the creation of new intricate structures that were beyond the capacity of most rulers to work successfully. Therefore, in his view, the only hope for Sarila's survival was continued British paramountcy.

Even when the freedom movement became a hurricane in the 1940s he continued to believe that autocracy in princely states could coexist with representational government in other parts of India and that indeed the princes, sitting in a sort of House of Lords at the federal centre, could provide checks and balances to the populist forces. He used to say that the British were merely playing with Mr Jinnah's demand for Pakistan in an attempt to put brakes on Mahatma Gandhi and the Congress Party. And he was shocked at the partition of India when it came.

His conservatism differed from that of some of the other princes I met when I started travelling with him. Some of these believed in the divine right of kings and refused to think further. My maternal grand-uncle, Maharaja Yadvendra Singh of Panna, was one such prince. A handsome man with great presence, charm and self-control, he used to tell me that kingship was the natural way of governance and, where extinguished, would emerge again one day as the sun emerges after an eclipse. He believed that British India should be brought under Indian monarchical rule, though he never clarified how. He abhorred democracy, but was a staunch patriot who wanted greatness for India, perhaps like the kings in olden days, or the kaiser or the Japanese mikado. Though he ordered his boots from Lobbs of St James's Street and his jackets from Henry Poole of Saville Row, and drove a Rolls Royce, he neither ever visited a foreign country nor evinced much interest in doing so. British officials were never absolutely at ease with him and he sometimes rebuffed them by showing exaggerated courtesy. I loved his old-fashioned manners and attention to youngsters and that he used to take me to tiger shoots. He was a great shot and one felt totally safe in the jungle with him.

Another prince with whom my father's somewhat middle-class conservatism contrasted was Maharaja Bir Singh of Orchha. The Orchha fort, which a loop in the Betwa River and dense forests protected, had become the capital of our Bundela clan in AD 1400. It was a convenient spot from which to raid Mogul caravans laden with gold and moving from the Deccan to Delhi. Emperor Shah Jahan, who built the Taj Mahal, attacked it in 1639, killing the maharaja, Jujhar Singh, but my ancestor Chhatarsal's parents escaped from Orchha and, four decades later, Chhatrasal was able to push back the frontiers of Mogul rule from our region. Maharaja Bir Singh had moved from his huge palace in his new capital Tikamgarh to a small cottage near the brown golf course he had created. The walls of this were built entirely from the bottles of the beer he and his friends had consumed, the round bases of which formed a bizarre pattern on the outer walls. The inside of the cottage was teak-panelled, lined with hundreds of books and extremely cosy. Golf, beer and books: and when it came to signing away his famous kingdom and his powers in 1948, he opted out with a shrug: 'Inevitable, inevitable, my boy,' I remember him telling me. After Orchha state disappeared, he moved to live out his life in Bombay.

Princely territories stretched from Kashmir in the north to Travancore or Kerala on the southern tip of India, and from the Kathiawar states on the western coast to Tripura and Manipur on the Burmese border. Of these Bundelkhand was a very small part. Some kingdoms, such as Hyderabad, Kashmir and Mysore were larger than many European countries. Sketches of a few Bundela princes cannot therefore reflect the diversity of views, temperaments and capacities of more than 350 princes, big and small. But it is true that they could be grouped under three headings: those who believed that cooperation with the British was their best bet, those who lived in a make-believe world and were incapable of serious negotiations on their future, and those who found the burden of statecraft a bit heavy and were quite willing to opt out if they could find the means to continue to indulge in their favoured pastimes.

Unlike many other princes, my father was neither lavish in his way of living nor interested in a fast life, which indeed he could ill afford. He remained monogamous, rare for princes at that time, though he did sow some wild oats. He used to say that one peg of scotch is medicine, two pegs irrelevant, but three poison. His moderation in all things was perhaps his chief quality. He used to drive all the way to the railway station, 70 kilometres away from Sarila, to fetch me at the end of my school terms. On the way home I would prattle away on all sorts of subjects, for example on the war raging in the deserts of North Africa, my ambition to travel one day by the Trans-Siberian Railway, the brilliant century Mushtaq Ali the cricketer had hit at Ajmer, and my ideas on religion. He would patiently hear me out but was not really interested in topics that were not of practical and immediate relevance to him; he did not set much store by religion either.

He renovated our palace, and laid out a pleasant garden with tennis courts and a swimming pool. He sent us, his five boys and three girls, to the best schools possible. In his earlier years at least he had worked conscientiously to improve the lot of his people. The administration of Sarila was reputed to be above average among the small states.

After the age of four or five, at 10 a.m. each day I would be taken to his room, which was on the top floor and enjoyed views of the park. By then he would have returned from his daily exercise – a trot on his Arab pony or a fast walk on the road leading to the canal – and had his bath. The first act I performed when ushered into his presence was to touch his feet. (I also touched my mother's feet the first time I saw her in the day.) This is a traditional Indian form of saluting elders, like bowing in Japan. However, unmarried girls and Brahmins do not touch others' feet. I used to see Pandit Jawaharlal Nehru kick about and push away people trying to reach his feet, although the people did so not because he was a Brahmin but out of reverence for him as a person. Those of the upper castes who expected the lower castes to touch their feet merely because they belonged to a higher caste invited a backlash after independence. The young in India continue to touch the feet of their elders in the family, as my son does despite having been educated in Europe.

During these visits to my father's room I used to be entranced by the foreign objects there: the weighing machine; the table clock that showed the dates; the binoculars in their leather case; the two-toned shoes with metal trees; the icebox from which he produced Schweppes ginger ale for me; his walking stick, the top of which flipped open to become a seat; and not least the stacks and stacks of English periodicals – *Spheres*, *London News* and *Country Life*, as well as the *Illustrated Weekly* and the *Onlooker* from Bombay. The pages of the English periodicals revealed strange women's dresses and hairstyles and different kinds of village houses, landscapes and art objects. There were also thick illustrated catalogues from British-run department stores in Calcutta and Bombay – Whiteways Laidlaw, Hall & Anderson, Evans Frasier, and the Army & Navy Stores. These enabled my parents to order provisions, clothes, furniture and of course toys without moving from their armchairs.

My father never left the palace in Sarila in those days, even for a walk, without his *safa* (turban). He was over six feet tall, and the *safa* added another few inches to his height. His usual semi-formal dress was tight-fitting pajamas, a shirt hanging loose over it and an open or closed-neck short coat. The open necked jackets were of European design and the closed necked ones with an upright collar, the Jodhpur coat, were the creation of a Jodhpur nobleman, Sir Pratap Singh, in the 1890s. Finding the *achkan,* the long coat worn by gentlemen, uncomfortable while riding a horse, he shortened it to the length of a normal jacket. This, with white breeches and turban, were adopted by the Mayo College, the premier college for the nobility, as its school dress in the 1910s. Thereafter, it became fashionable, first among the upper classes and then generally. After independence Prime Minister Jawaharlal Nehru, looking for an Indian equivalent to the European business suit, chose the Jodhpur coat with Western trousers – rejecting the white breeches as too fancy – as the semi-official dress for officials, though he himself stuck to the *achkan* and tight pajamas (which differ from breeches). Few of the Jodhpur coat's patrons today insist on Sir Pratap's upright collar, a shaped waist and flare and this robs it of its elegance.

Inside the house my father invariably wore a dhoti in the fashion of the area I have described in an earlier chapter. This meant that his lower calves remained uncovered; so in the cool weather he wore woollen socks. While playing tennis, of which he was very fond, he wore white ducks or flannels. His Western suits, tweed jackets and ties, were taken off mothballs only when he travelled outside the state.

He worked on state business from 10.30 a.m. to 1.00 p.m. and again for an hour or two after his siesta. Files were brought to him in black metal boxes and there was a steady flow of these boxes and officials to his office. A government of a princely state was termed a *durbar,* the nearest translation of which is the old-fashioned word 'court'. The chief executive appointed by the ruler was responsible only to him and was called the *diwan* in Sarila. He supervised all the departments of the state. In Sarila, because the state's income came overhelmingly from land taxes, the chief revenue officer was very important. The judges heard civil and criminal cases but complainants could also appeal directly to my father and receive ready justice. The police chief, the head clerk who supervised the secretariat and kept the records, the headmaster and staff of the state school, and the chief medical officer were the other officials I remember. The larger states maintained much larger establishments, even armed forces. The treasurer, a Brahmin who had been a guardian of my father in his youth, doubled up as *pujari* and presided over religious ceremonies.

My father was lucky to find faithful and prudent servants. This he used to illustrate by a story concerning his *diwan,* Pratap Narain. When young he had fallen in love with the 1932 model of the Lancia Lamda convertible, which he saw in a Bombay car showroom. It may be recalled that the back of this famous model was shaped like a boat with two spare tyres stuck to it and its front mudguards rose slender and haughty on either side of the long and squarish bonnet. He returned to Sarila with the catalogue of the car and was mulling over its possible purchase when he consulted Pratap Narain. The *diwan* immediately saw that besides its high price, the car's low-slung body might prove unsuitable for our rough roads and asked my father to give him the catalogue so that he could look at it at leisure. When after a few days my father asked him to return the catalogue, Pratap Narain promised to bring it back the next day. And when he asked the *diwan* for it again the day after, the latter replied that he had mislaid it but would certainly find and produce it shortly. My father said that in the meantime his infatuation for the car ebbed, saving him a lot of money and bother.

In many states of Bundelkhand bordering the United Provinces (now known as Uttar Pradesh) *diwan*s or chief executives were Muslims. First, because of the legacy of the old Shiite kingdom of Awadh, which the British disbanded in the mid-nineteenth century, Uttar Pradesh contained a large number of educated Muslims with administrative experience. Second, my father maintained that Muslims had more political sense than

Hindus because their faith made them politically conscious. Third, a Muslim *diwan* would not be influenced by caste and other complexities of the Hindu social structure in meting out justice. And lastly, as a member of a minority community, a Muslim would be more dependent on, and thus loyal to, the ruler.

As I have noted elsewhere there was never really a close personal rapport, or *bonhomie*, between the British and most princes. This was because of the Englishman's inherent racism on the one hand and the princes' awkwardness when mixing with those who were their overlords on the other. It was therefore remarkable that my father could develop such an easy relationship with the English, not only with those of the political department who dealt with the princes, but also with senior British officers of the government of India in Delhi and Simla. That so many of my father's English friends invited me to their clubs in London and to their homes all over the country while I was at Cambridge was proof of their friendship with my father.

My father was the type of Indian ruler the British preferred, namely pro-British and sober. He was one of the two Indian princes that Viceroy Lord Irwin (later Lord Halifax) selected to represent the 250 smaller states at the Round Table Conferences held in London in the early 1930s to chart out a new constitutional future for India. He was then 32 years old. In 1942 the political department selected my younger brother Jayendra Singh, to succeed the childless Maharaja of Charkhari in the face of stiff competition from the offspring of other princes of our Bundela clan. Charkhari was a larger state not too far from Sarila. My father thus, on the one hand, got a close glimpse of British policy towards India as it unfolded in the 1930s, as well as some acquaintance with the political elite of London, which then virtually dominated world affairs. And on the other, since my brother was a minor and my father was appointed the regent of Charkhari, he, for a while ruled two states at the same time. The chapters in the book on these two episodes have more on him.

Chapter 3
My Mother

MY FATHER spoke good English, which my mother never learnt to do. She was married to my father when she was 14 and he was 20. My grandmother had arranged the marriage before she died at an early age. My mother came from the fortress of Basela 40 kilometres away from Sarila in British India where her father was a *zamindar*. In British-led north India, lands were assigned to the local gentry, Hindu and Muslim, who were made responsible for collecting land revenue from the farmers on behalf of the British government and keeping a fixed share for themselves. My mother's father was one such *zamindar* or landlord. He belonged to the Parmar clan and had married a sister of the Maharaja of Panna, descended from Chhatarsal. As one could not marry into one's own clan, marriages between Bundelas and Parmars, the other Rajput clan in our region, were common.

My parents had no children for eight years and therefore my birth on 2 January 1927 was a considerable event for them. I am told that my arrival was announced to the people by the firing of 11 salvos from Bhawani Shankar, our biggest artillery piece, which had not been fired for 100 years. And, as was usual, Puranic hymns were chanted: 'May he be zealous in performing his duties, give in just measure, be humble in the presence of the wise, always remain in control of his emotions, temper his zeal with humanity, have a regal presence.' Half of

26

the land tax of the farmers that year was remitted and alms distributed. To the lady doctor who had helped at my birth, my father presented his Ford Model T. She was an American, Dr Longdon from California, working in the American Mission Hospital in nearby Kulpahar in British India. Thinking nothing of carrying coals to Newcastle, she took the car back to her native land when she returned home.

My mother would think nothing of carrying her children on her shoulder and walking up and down in the night to put them to sleep, or of keeping a day and night vigil if we were unwell. She prepared the choicest dishes with her own hands to please us. We children would run straight into her lap and arms on returning from outdoors. My room was next to my mother's. I remember feeling bored lying on the cot gazing at the ceiling and the light blue coloured walls of the room and hearing occasional voices and sometimes singing floating in from the courtyard. I also remember a picture that hung in the room of a blue Krishna playing the flute.

A steady flow of women from the town came to visit her so that on several afternoons of the week she had to preside over a little *durbar*. Her caring nature made her respected and popular in the entire state of Sarila. The gatherings sometimes overflowed onto the veranda and the courtyard beyond – in which case the women's crimson, rose and saffron saris made a splendid splash against the sun-washed white of the courtyard wall. Sometimes the women sang *bhajan*s or devotional songs in which my mother joined. They also sang *bhangra*s, *kajari*s, *phag*s and *gari*s in our Bundelkhandi dialect – local melodies that narrated tales of the vanity of men, the fickleness of women, the impermanence of things and the power of God's benediction. Even today these same tunes, if the wind is blowing in the right direction, come floating across the park from the town, reminding one that not all has changed in Sarila in four score years.

6. The author with mother and younger brother Jayendra Singh in the early 1930s.

One day I asked my mother why she always marked the number 74 on the top of the letters she wrote. She then told me the story of Padmini, the queen of Mewar (present-day Udaipur) in Rajasthan. Ala-ud-Din Khilji, the then Sultan of

Delhi, having heard of the beauty of Padmini, laid siege to the great fortress of Chitorgarh of the Sisodhya clan in 1303. After many months of fighting when provisions in the fortress were exhausted, the warriors wearing white and orange sallied forth from the stronghold to kill and be killed. Such a foray is called *Jauhar.* Simultaneously, Padmini and her 73 companions jumped into a well and committed suicide to prevent being taken by the enemy. (Colonel James Todd, in his *Annals of Rajputana*, however, says that Padmini and the women committed suicide by jumping into fire.) The number 74 – called *chauhatra* in Hindi – my mother said, was in remembrance of that heroic act to preserve their integrity. She was not unique among Kshatriya women of the time to use the symbolic *chauhatra* on top of the letters they wrote.

My mother could not understand why Indian political leaders advocated representational government with each person given one vote irrespective of his or her ranking in society, moral stature or capacity. She used to say that it would lead to 'mobocracy'. She distrusted the British no less. She was a patriot, because her faith made her a devotee of *Bharat Mata* – Mother India. After I grew up, she wanted me to take her to visit all the four *dhams*, sacred places situated in the four corners of India – Kanyakumari on the southern tip of the peninsula, Badrinath in the Himalayas, Dwarka on the western coast and Jagannath Puri on the eastern seaboard. This brought home to me that her faith was rooted not only in India's long history but also in its geography.

Much later my mother expressed a desire to see Mahatma Gandhi. She used the respectful word *darshan* in this context. It was a few weeks before Gandhiji's assassination when I took her to Gandhiji's prayer meeting at Birla House in Delhi in December 1947. We just walked in and stood near the dais from which he addressed the prayer meeting. There was no security. In speaking in Hindi he often got the genders of nouns wrong; many masculine nouns are feminine in his native Gujarati. My mother did not understand Gandhiji's politics. But she respected him as a person seeking to uplift *Bharat Varsha*, as she called India, and who to her was a *rishi*.

At some stage the hymn *Ishwar Allah Tero Nam: Sab Ko Sanmati De Bhagwan* was chanted. This hymn was an appeal to the Almighty that since Ishwar, in Hindi, and Allah, in Arabic, were both His (the same God's) names, he may confer benediction on one and all. To the followers of a pluralistic faith, this was perfectly understandable, but to those believing in one God to the strict exclusion of all other gods, like the Muslims, Gandhiji's message was not appealing, even sacrilegious. This did not occur to me that day, only years later.

My mother saw no contradiction in a separate identity for Sarila within India. She used to say that as each individual's soul has a separate identity but is nevertheless part of the Brahma, the godhead, so Sarila is a separate entity but an indivisible part of *Bharat Varsha*. She was in fact instinctively espousing the centripetal political system that had existed in India before the Islamic invasions wrecked it. There were numerous, separate, monarchical political units but all part of the distinct socio-cultural cum spiritual entity that was *Bharat*.

After a brother and a sister had joined the family, a governess, Mrs Floyd was appointed to look after us. She was an Anglo–Indian lady of the Anglican faith from Monghyr in Bihar who had lost her husband early in life. She was as selfless as my mother and the two got on well together. Despite my mother's prejudices against people of other religions, because of the inherent tolerance born out of her faith she came to accept the Christian lady as a member of the family. Mrs Floyd lived in Sarila until she died in 1970.

Despite her manifold duties of running the household and

looking after the children, my mother found some time each day to read the *Ramayana* and she often asked us to sit with her to hear the recitations. This epic, composed in the sixteenth century in Hindi by Tulsi Das of Banaras, is based on the earlier one composed by Valmiki in Sanskrit in antiquity. My mother used to recite the quatrains in a slightly raised voice from the verses, which broke the sameness of the recitation. The former contain the pith of the preceding verses and didactics of general significance. The Ramayana is about the trials and experiences of Rama, the heir to the throne of Ayodhya in the Ganges Valley about 1500 BC. The hero's character – upright, courageous, self-sacrificing and tolerant – is held up as the model for the perfect ruler and indeed all human beings. The *Mahabharata*, the other epic she used to read to us, is the story of the great fratricidal war between two Kshatriya clans near Indraprastha, modern Delhi, in about 1000 BC. It is a story of war and diplomacy. It contains the *Bhagwat Gita*, a longish soliloquy by Krishna on the precepts of right conduct, which is considered sacred by many.

The epics are read aloud at village gatherings, recited at village operas, and studied and memorized in households all over India. The sweep and depth of the human experience and thought revealed in the epics, and the quotable quality and beauty of their verses has throughout the centuries had a profound influence on Indians. Unlike Christians or Muslims, Hindus are bereft of a clergy, a Book, or the Final Word, or indeed a system of periodic congregations. For their spiritual education the masses depend on parental guidance and on the precepts they can gather from these popular epics. However, I am dismayed that these epics are often taken in the villages as the actual history of the period and this discourages rational historical enquiry.

Scenes from both epics are enacted in plays and operas in

7. Mother's sitting room in Sarila Palace. Now, with a new tiled floor and European furniture, it is the author's library.

many southeast Asian countries where Indian influence had permeated in the first 1000 years of the Christian era. In Thailand, the town of Ayodhya is named after the birthplace of Rama. Many Thai and Cambodian names, like the names of Indians, are taken from characters in these epics. Such was the case of the Cambodian king, Shiv Verma, who built the temple of Angkor Vat. Even in south Asian countries that later became Islamized, people continued to be named after heroes in these epics. For example, the name of the first president of Indonesia, Seokarno, was derived from that of a warrior in the Mahabharata called Sheokaran.

Of the time I am writing, ladies of the upper classes in north India did not generally mix socially with men or show themselves in public. This was a custom adopted from the Muslims, who practised *purdah* or separation of women from men. My mother followed *purdah* in Sarila but not when she was visiting towns outside the state, for example during our summer sojourns in hill stations. When it was necessary for her to talk to state officials in Sarila, a cloth curtain would be placed between her and them and she would converse through this veil. Women of the village never secluded themselves and *purdah* was not practised in south India, where Muslim influences had permeated much less. A part of the garden was fenced off where she played badminton with her maids and us. Her library was composed of Hindi books, mostly poetry and novels. The novels and short stories of Munshi Premchand were her favourite.

My mother was a traditional Indian wife. She found happiness and strength in devoting her energy to ensure the welfare of her husband and children. She tried to achieve her goals primarily by influencing them, rather than directly. The modern feminist movement would have appalled her.

Chapter 4
Life in the Palace: I

A S I GREW up there were enough nooks, corners and winding staircases in the house to play hide and seek and courtyards in which to kick a ball around. As children, my younger brother and I spent a lot of time in my mother's sitting room. The walls of this large rectangular room were decorated up to the ceiling with niches and geometrical patterns in subdued maroon, ochre, red and dark blue, with flashes of parrot green, light blue and crimson. On one side it opened onto a veranda and courtyard; on the other were my mother's rooms, including the one in which I was born. A long striped dhurrie covered the floor. For sitting, there were *takhats* (low rectangular wooden platforms) on which were spread thin cotton mattresses with spotless white cambric covers. For back support largish bolsters wrapped in white muslin were provided. A solitary armchair with cane webbing was kept for my father. The room was otherwise bare of furniture except for a large handsome black cupboard with double mirrors and cut glass handles.

My mother and I sat on the *takhat*s cross-legged. We removed our shoes before entering her rooms. This sitting room was in contrast to the large drawing room in the *mardana* (the men's part of the house), which was furnished in the European style: there were sofas and chairs in rose coloured French silk brocade, tables and consoles in mahogany loaded with

8. The back of Sarila Palace, viewed from across the lake.

photographs in silver frames and a pinkish Axminster carpet on the floor with tiger and panther skins littered over it. The light green walls were hung with large family portraits, mirrors in gilt frames and hunting trophies. A rose creeper moulding framed the doors. The high ceiling had a geometrical pattern with touches of gold leaf. A stone trellised balcony high up at one end provided a pleasant Indian motif. It could be used by the ladies to watch proceedings below or as a perch for musicians.

We had no fixed bedrooms and slept indoors only for the short winter season when the nights got cold and metal braziers with burning charcoal were used to heat up the rooms. In the summer our beds would be moved onto one of the many terraces under the stars. How brightly they shone and how near to the earth they seemed in Sarila! The Milky Way was so dense and wide that it indeed looked like the pathway of Eravat, the

35

elephant mount of Indra, the Lord of the Heavens. During the monsoon the beds were fixed with mosquito nets and placed on deep verandas. My parents' sleeping area for most of the year was a *baradari* – literally a room on the roof with 12 doors – surrounded by verandas and terraces, with its numerous doors kept open or shut according to the season. *Baradaris* were a feature of all biggish houses in Bundelkhand.

The dining place also depended on the season. We rarely dined in the large European style dining room hung with trophies of big game shot by my father – except on formal occasions. For much of the year, dinner was served on terraces under the stars. We sat cross-legged on six-inch high *pattas* (low wooden platforms) with two-foot high tables placed in front for the food. The food was served on silver *thals* (trays) with silver bowls for vegetables and meats. These we ate with hot *puris* or *chapattis* – freshly fried or roasted unleavened whole wheat bread – and rice, or a *pilau*. Rice in Bundelkhand is taken towards the end of the meal.

There was fish from the lake, partridge and quail whenever my father shot some on his evening outings, and mutton, but no beef – and of course vegetables, brinjals and potatoes being my favourites. Crushed *puris* and jaggery mixed in a bowl of milk is a favourite Bundelkhandi pudding. Buttermilk was churned in one of the courtyards. There were several kinds of milk preparations. Sweetmeats were often covered with edible flimsy real gold and silver foil. At the end we washed our hands in a silver ewer half filled with leaves with water poured from a jug held over it by a servant. The leaves prevented the water splashing. There were three Brahmin cooks for Indian food and two Muslim cooks for European dishes and meat. They had separate kitchens.

The *shehnai* is a reed instrument played from a distance to create an atmosphere or mood. Most palaces maintained *shehnai*

9. The *baradari* in Sarila Palace. The paintwork, executed in 1865, has required no retouching.

players to play in the morning and again in the evening. Ours sat on the high gate tower and the *ragas* (melodies), which included Bageshwari, Malkaus, Darbari, Eman kalyan and others, would drift in with gusts of breeze during dinner. The burbling sound of my father's hubble-bubble, which he smoked after dinner, would punctuate the music.

Breakfast was always *pukka* English: it consisted of force, a wheat cereal (cornflakes had not yet been invented) with milk, eggs, toast, marmalade and jams, home grown papayas and tea. The typical Bundelkhandi breakfast consists of *puris* left overnight and eaten with mango pickles and a glass of buttermilk. My mother was partial to this.

Bundelkhand gets very hot and dry in the summer, with the temperature during the day often shooting up to 45° centigrade. Palaces in the olden days were built on the edge of water, like ours was, with cellars for the midday siesta. The temperature was reduced in the other rooms by covering the windows with woven vetiver grass root mats that were constantly sprinkled with water from the outside. The wet mats sucked out the heat from the inside and emitted a refreshing scent at the same time. Many rooms still had *pankha*s, though electric fans had been fitted in others. The *pankha* is made of a long woven bamboo mat a couple of feet wide attached to a rod or a plank suspended by ropes from hooks in the ceiling. A long string is attached to the middle of the rod or plank and passed through a hole fitted with pulleys to another room or a veranda. There sat a servant, invisible to us, gently pulling and releasing the string alternately, to activate the *pankha* and provide a gentle breeze. Sometimes the man would doze off and the fans stop, awakening us. A sharp call to wake him up would reactivate the *pankha*.

A troop of helpers, servants and maids served us. We considered those of our clan whose forefathers had accompanied us from Jaitpur to Sarila as companions, not servants, and they sometimes joined us for meals. Their duties were akin to those of aides-de-camp in Europe. They had received grants of lands and were paid an honorarium for attending on us. The men servants were divided as follows: *nai*s (or barbers) who served as valets and masseurs; *jamadar*s, which was a superior name for those who performed the most menial tasks such as cleaning toilets and removing rubbish; *dhobi*s or washermen; orderlies, many of whom were from the Ahir or Yadav caste; traditional cowherds whose families had migrated to Sarila with us; table boys, grooms, *chowkidar*s or guards, and the cooks mentioned earlier. Qadir, a local Muslim boy, was in charge of sports and was a sort of handyman to my father. Motorcar drivers were considered superior because they had mechanical skills. None of the maids and, with one or two exceptions, the men servants had seen the inside of a school.

The most senior maid was a lady who had accompanied my

mother at the time of her marriage from her home to Sarila as part of her trousseau. She now supervised the cooking and storage of edibles. She would sit on a stool in the middle of the court-yard next to the kitchen and storerooms and, in a heavy loud voice, continuously issue orders. This sight of an elderly woman – grandmother, great aunt or whoever – directing the household operations from an internal courtyard can still be seen in many households. A widowed Kshatriya lady of middle age also lived in the palace. She would accompany my mother on outings and generally help her with household matters. Lying in my cot as a child I could identify a score of maids from the different jingling sound made by their silver anklets.

The room in the palace called my mother's *toshakhana* seemed to us children like a treasure trove because of its inaccessibility and the variety of objects stored in it. '*Of shining showrooms full of secret drawers/And the Maharani's dressing cases.*' My mother's clothes, jewellery and other valuables were kept in it. (There was another such room for my father's things.)

Each sari is a piece of silk six yard long. To store it, it is rolled round a rectangular cardboard plank and several such wrapped planks are then placed on top of one another and bound into a tight bundle with white muslin. The trunks that lined an entire side of the *toshakhana* wall were filled with these bundles. Unlike European dresses that are hung in a cupboard and are easy to see, my mother's maids had to have good memories to be able to open the right box and bundle to extract the sari she required from among hundreds. Dried neem leaves were spread at the bottom of the trunk and in between the bundles to keep insects away. The leaves, the bark and the juice of the neem tree are widely used in our countryside as an insecticide, blood purifier and cure for skin problems. Throughout my life I have chewed neem tree twigs and used the crushed end to brush my gums.

The best silks came from Surat, Mysore and Assam and the silk brocades from Varanasi. Sequin work was done on saris in Bombay. At that time chiffon saris from Lyons in France were becoming popular, for they were light, did not crush and showed off slender forms well. The French saris were in more subtle pastel hues than the generally brighter colours of the Indian silks. Itinerant salesmen used to come from Banaras or Kanpur with trunk loads of wares to display in a room of one's house, giving one a day or two to select the fabric to be made up at leisure. Chinese silk was popular for shirts and pyjamas.

Saris, which are so popular now, are of comparatively recent origin. Their inspiration came from Bengal and the fashion has not, even now, spread to the entire subcontinent. Earlier, Rajput women wore gypsy like flared skirts and blouses and draped a veil around their shoulders that could cover as much of the face, head or bulge of the breasts as the occasion or mood of the wearer demanded. The sari of north India is in essence an extension of the veil. Besides covering the upper portion of the body, the longer veil then came to be wound around the skirt and this eventually became the sari. The flared long skirt, the petticoat continues to be worn underneath, on which, indeed, the sari rests to achieve an elegant flare.

My mother kept *attar*s or perfumes in small wooden chests with inlay ivory work. The inside was divided into squares and lined with red velvet. The squares contained glass scent bottles. The scents were made from flowers, sandalwood, musk deer and the roots of plants. They were oil based as opposed to the alcohol based Western perfumes. My mother used Indian scents – khas, vetiver, rose and lemon – in the summer because they have a refreshing quality. However, when going out to parties in Delhi or in hill stations, she used French perfumes. She was convinced that 4711 eau de cologne was the best cure there was for headaches.

Throughout their history Indians have regarded jewellery as sacred, something to be cherished and preserved. Even the poorest peasant woman wears some silver if she cannot afford gold. There are pieces to be worn literally from head to toe, even something for the woman's navel. Village women wear a silver girdle round their upper hips, which enhances the seductiveness of the naked form. They also wear silver or gold nose and ear pieces, which, from my divergent viewpoint, diminish their sexual appeal. Bangles around the ankles were a must. The *hathpal* is a flat piece of jewellery worn on the back of the hand to link the bracelet with the finger rings. John Maynard Keynes, the British economist, had once spoken of 'India's ruinous love of the barbaric relic'. Nothing has changed since. Today more than 200 billion dollars, the equivalent of 29 per cent of India's gross domestic product, is locked up in gold jewellery. Though there are better ways of investing savings, this custom has protected the poor from the galloping inflation that has reduced the value of the rupee nearly 50 times since my youth.

Some of my mother's jewellery was *stridhan*, or the personal property of a married woman; other pieces that she wore for ceremonial purposes belonged to the state. Traditional Bundel-khandi jewellery was, and continues to be, made of gold with stones encrusted in gold. The emerald, the stone most evocative of India, is mined in Panna in Bundelkhand. It is combined with diamonds and rubies in necklaces, rings, armbands, *sirpenches* or *kalgis*. Armbands worn by men draw attention to their biceps and *sirpenches* topped by plumes and worn over the turban or *pugree* add to the panache of the wearer. Rubies came from Burma, sapphires from Kashmir and pearls from the Arabian Sea.

From antiquity until the discovery of diamonds in Brazil in 1725, the ancient alluvial fields of Golconda in the Deccan peninsula of India yielded most of the world's finest and most famous diamonds. Golconda lay in the kingdom of Vijayanagar before Akbar conquered and destroyed it. Later the area became part of the domain of the Nizam of Hyderabad. In fact, before the South American, Russian and South African mines were discovered India enjoyed the world monopoly of this precious stone. According to tradition, any stone larger than ten carats automatically became the property of the prince. It was, therefore, not surprising that Indian kings came to possess more diamonds than kings in other parts of the world. Diamonds, observed someone on the Prince of Wales's tour of India in 1921, seem as plentiful here as blackberries in England.

In earlier times the princes bequeathed the finest diamonds to famous temples throughout the length and breadth of India. The Orlov, which was mounted in the Imperial Sceptre during the reign of Catherine II of Russia, was one such temple diamond.

The looting of temples by Turkish and central Asian invaders from the eleventh century onwards resulted in the loss of hoards of the finest pieces. As early as the eighth century we find a 149-carat diamond from Golconda in the possession of Sulaiman the Magnificent, the Khalif of Baghdad. The treasury of the Delhi emperors held the greatest collection of jewels in history, but this Indian patrimony was lost in 1739 when Nadir Shah of Persia ransacked the Red Fort in Delhi for a whole month and carried the booty off to Persia. The 300-carat pink diamond Darya-I-Noor, the sea of light, was among the pillage, as was the 100-carat stone called the Shah of Persia. Darya-I-Noor was cut into two during the reign of the late shah and the 176-carat pink stone that shone like a torch in the centre of his crown was part of this famous stone.

This 'export' of Indian diamonds continued during the British period. The Arcots, Lal Qila, King George IV, Idol's Eye,

Star of the East, Louis XIV, Ashoka, which the Mauryan king wore in the fourth century BC, the 90-carat Nasak taken from the Peshwa, the 104-carat cushion shaped Yellow Deepdene and, of course, the dark blue Regent, now called the Hope, and the peerless Koh-I-Noor, to name only a few, were all taken out of India during this period. Indian historians considered the last two named infelicitous, and their reputation did not change in Europe. Louis XIV acquired the Regent in 1686 from the French adventurer Tavernier and the 'Sun King' died soon thereafter. The British Empire collapsed soon after the Koh-I-Noor, taken from Maharaja Ranjit Singh of Punjab, was placed in the British crown.

The dowry system among Indian princes helped to circulate the stones. I must have inherited my disinterest in jewellery from my mother, for I am more inclined to agree with Keynes's views, quoted above, than with those of a majority of my countrymen. I find diamond solitaires particularly cold and unappetizing.

Chapter 5
Life in the Palace: II

I
N THE benign shade of a 150-year-old banyan tree in the garden close to our house, my brother and I could play cricket without being scorched by the sun. Roots descend from the branches of the banyan tree and sink into the ground to become new trunks. The tree's ever widening circle enables it to support its growing weight. One famous specimen is reputed to cover an area of 600 metres so that 20,000 people can take shelter within its columned shade. The slow growing banyan tree in our garden has increased considerably in size since I used to play under it and we have now to lop off branches, along with their descending roots, every few years to protect the lawns and the house. The roots now descend into the ground nearer the trunk, which has made it sturdier.

The peepal (under which Buddha is said to have attained Enlightenment) is another big tree. It is as light and airy as the banyan is dark and enveloping. Considered auspicious, peepal trees are planted near the entrances of houses.

We also played in the mahua (*madhuka indica*) grove outside the compound, the same grove in which Tantya Tope, the Marhatta cavalry leader of the revolt of 1857–58, had camped when he came to seek Sarila's help. The mahuas with their heavy leaves and dark trunks closely planted in groves outside villages give shade and shelter to casual passers-by. A mahua grove can acquire the look of a pillared hall. Wine made from its fruit was

10. A potter's house in Sarila town.

(and is) popular in Sarila. The rubbing of its distilled spirit on joints affected by arthritis helps, as I have discovered from personal experience.

The compound contained most of the other well-known trees of Bundelkhand – tamarind, medicinal neem (*margosa*), *Imli*, *sirsa*, mango, evergreen and lofty *ashoka*, flame of the forest, which turns scarlet in spring, the tall *jamun* with the blue fruit children love, *kadam* associated with romance in ancient literature and *amaltas*, the Indian laburnum with yellow flowers that droop down in bunches. Flowering shrubs, mostly of Indian origin such as *chandni* or moonbeam, *bela*, with scented white flowers, the golden *champak,* various kinds of hibiscus, ixora, *raat-ki-rani* or the queen of the night with its sensual scent, the red-orange peacock flower, *kaner* and others, provided year-round colour in the garden. The brightest, with colours ranging from orange and purple to crimson and from brick red to pale pink, salmon, yellow and white, were the

11. A well-to-do farmer's house in Sarila town.

bougainvilleas. European summer flowers like pansies, phlox, petunias, anthuriums, sweet williams, stocks, gladioli, dahlias, hollyhocks and sweet peas, planted in October reached their full glory in mid-February but faded under the hot April sun. Roses grew well in Sarila.

There were many mongooses and peacocks in the park – both of which are great hunters of snakes. Snakes are more visible in the rainy season when their underground burrows get flooded. In the rainy season we avoided tall grass, anthills, heaps of cut grass and the spaces behind the potted plants on the veranda. The hooded and deadly cobra can scale trees, but rarely manages staircases and walls. The servants and gardeners avoided killing cobras because of the superstition that their mates would seek revenge. In fact, some people left milk outside their thresholds to pacify cobras. I suspect that they preferred to leave cobras alone because of the risk of being bitten while striking them.

If a human being gets within five or six feet of a cobra that may be lying curled up or moving, it immediately prepares to defend itself. This it does by lifting its head two feet or so from the ground, which is almost a third of its length. It then faces the suspected antagonist with its hood fully blown, its fangs bared and its breath emitting hisses. If you turn away from it, it gets back on the ground and slithers away, but if you get any closer it will lunge forward and strike like lightening and there is no escape. One should resist the temptation to take a swipe at the raised hood with a walking stick, for the snake might coil around it, reach out and bite you. The trick is to break the cobra's back by aiming the first strike on the portion of its body that remains on the ground, for then it cannot lunge forward to attack and becomes an easy target. To break its back one must use a long staff and bring it down as parallel to the ground as possible, which means bending low to deliver the blow. If you do not at one stroke break its back and render it immobile the chances are that it will get you while you are still stooping after your strike. Killing a cobra is thus a tricky operation and unless one has a long staff, discretion is the better part of valour.

One encounter with a cobra I can never forget. I must have been ten or twelve and was lightly trotting on my pony in open country when suddenly I saw a large black cobra lying in our path coiled into a bundle. I could not stop the horse that had carelessly stepped over it. I continued to trot but after a moment some instinct made me look back and I was horrified to see the black glistening reptile chasing, and indeed gaining upon, me. When cobras are enraged they can rise on their tails to considerable heights to strike animal or man, so I dug my heels into the horse and galloped away. When I told the story at the palace there was consternation and, for a few days, extra precautions were taken because of the superstition that a wronged cobra pursues its tormenter.

I once saw a cobra being chased by a peacock that was following and pecking at it. It is said that a cobra's poison does not affect peacocks. The cobra finally found a hole before the peacock could kill it. Peacocks, the enemies of snakes, are the most beautiful birds in the world. A male would sometimes fly up with a loud swishing sound and land on one of the terraces of the house. It would then spread out its long blue-green wings in the form of a semicircular fan and start to turn slowly in a dance. The spectacle of the huge multicoloured bird dancing on the white parapet with the azure sky behind it remains etched in my memory. The peacock dances to attract females. Peahens have no plumes, are smaller and much less attractive to look at. Why this reversal in gender beauty in birds and animals from us humans? But is it really so? Would not a naked male with his long hair, flowing beard, muscular, hairy and heavier body appear more beautiful to a bird or animal than a woman, smooth skinned, frail and pale?

A great variety of water birds – two thousand or more – used to fly in from Siberia each winter to the lake behind the house (as they do today), sheltering in the hyacinth and weeds. There were herons, egrets, moorhens, storks, darts, snipe and, of course, various kinds of ducks. In the park there were parrots, blue jays, woodpeckers, pigeons and green pigeons, doves, *koyals* or cuckoos, blue tail bee-eaters, kingfishers, nightingales, crows and a host of other birds. Hawk forever swept the sky. Owls sometimes hooted at night: they gave us the shivers because they were said to be birds of ill omen.

My formal education began at five with the appointment of a teacher from outside Sarila who held a Bachelor of Arts degree from Agra University. His name was Saraswati Prasad Khare. He belonged to a community of Hindu scribes called Kayasths. The community is proficient in languages and known for precision in writing and speech. (Some of the best civil servants in India

12. The author with his brother in 1942.

after independence have emerged from this community.) I did not find Master Sahib or Mr Teacher, as we called him, a great teacher of languages, mathematics or history, but I am indebted to him for something else.

49

In his university days he had been exposed to the new political currents circulating in the country from which I was totally cut off in Sarila. Even at the school I went to later, the Mayo College, my principal as well as the house masters were all Englishmen and my fellow students from among princes or their nobles, with no commoner, to use an English phrase, in sight. Though Master Sahib kept his views largely to himself, especially away from my father's ears, I was able to glean from Khare some of the political, economic and social philosophies of the nationalists and thumbnail sketches of the leading lights of the freedom struggle. He also taught me to shoot. First it was with a .22 bore fired at fixed targets, then with a 410 double barrel at birds. As I grew older we became more adventurous: sitting for boar in a concealed bunker at night and stalking deer and sambar in daylight.

Bundelkhand in those days was a sportsman's paradise. There was 86 per cent coverage of forest (now reduced to 6 per cent). Big game could be hunted from the comfort of our homes without having to organize safaris or camps, as is necessary to do in many continents. It was as comfortable as shooting pheasants in Europe, the sportsman able to return after the shoot to a hot bath and a jolly meal in his own house. There were panthers on every hill, sloth bears (these have snouts) in the more densely wooded areas, and chital, sambar and wild boar in lightly forested areas. The flat open country around Sarila abounded with black buck.

For tiger, however, one had to go about a hundred miles south to friends' or relatives' homes nearer the forests of the Vindhya hills. There was no shortage of partridge, quail, peafowl, snipe, geese or duck. Unless one saw an exceptionally fine head one avoided firing at chital, sambar or black buck. Stalking was good exercise; the approach often required crawling but always made into the wind. Khare loved hunting and I learnt much more from him about outdoor life than I did about geography or geometry.

One day during holidays from school when I was 14 or 15 he told me that we would 'sit' for a panther that night. A panther had made a kill outside the village of Parchha, a few miles away, and there was a tree nearby from which he said it would be ideal for a novice to attempt a shot. It was summer and we set out in a car at 6.00 p.m. to be in position well before sunset. We walked the last 200 yards so as not to disturb the panther if it were lying in a *nallah* (rivulet) close by; Khare and the Shikaris using sign language to communicate with each other. It was open, undulating country with dry undergrowth and few trees.

The half-eaten goat lay about 20 yards from the only biggish tree in the vicinity, a neem; it had been covered up with leaves to shield it from the attention of vultures. Our *machan* consisted of a village rope cot tied 12 feet up among the branches of the tree and camouflaged as much as possible by leaves and twigs. We climbed with the help of a makeshift ladder that was then taken away. I was to use a 16 bore with LG buckshots and Khare had his 30 Springfield. We had lozenges to keep the throat moist to prevent a cough, and a powerful torch. The men soon withdrew to the car to await our call, to be given by a sniffle.

We waited expectantly as the light faded and a hush fell over the countryside, ears cocked for sounds of birds, monkeys or other animals that might signal the panther's approach. I had been warned that a panther's approach is noiseless unless dry leaves are lying around, in which case you hear a crunch in the silent night and know he is there. A grunt of fear by a stag or the sudden scattering of monkeys or fowl alerts the other animals and the hunter to the movement of a tiger in the jungle; there is, however, no warning of a panther's approach to the bait.

About half an hour after darkness had fallen I heard the crunch of a dry leaf under our tree. Khare immediately pointed out with a downward motion of his middle finger that he was directly below us. Nothing happened for another ten minutes, though Khare was able to indicate by the movements of his chin where it had decided to sit and wait to assure itself that the coast was clear. He must have walked up silently to the prey for all I heard from one moment to another was the tearing of the flesh of the goat and the sound of munching. Khare let a little more time pass before he touched my elbow, signalling me to raise my rifle, the butt of which I then put next to my cheek, pointing the barrel in the direction of the noise and got ready to pull the trigger. Suddenly, Khare's torch, held from behind my head, was switched on, lighting up the sight of my gun as well as the scene below. The panther was half crouching next to the dead goat and as he turned his head towards us his green eyes shone. His fine spotted blue coat with yellow spots looked so precious and tidy beside the dusty yellow grass and blood soaked goat.

I aimed for its forehead, pressed the trigger and possibly shut my eyes at the same time. The panther leaped away into the dark before I could empty the other barrel. 'A miss,' Khare hissed and stood up on the *machan*, sweeping the jungle with the torch in the direction the panther had gone. He then sniffled twice and as the *shikaris* approached warned them in a low voice that the panther may be wounded and still around. *Shikaris* found no blood or spool where I had fired at him or beyond. And we carefully descended, making ample noise as we retreated to our car. My mother said it was good luck to miss one's first panther.

I later shot many panthers with the help of dead as well as live baits. For the latter a goat is secured by rope to a peg sunk in the ground. As soon as the *shikaris* disappear, the goat will start to bleat, in fear and in an attempt to call its owner. This draws the panther, but as soon as it appears on the scene the goat stops bleating and starts to pull itself as far as possible away from the direction of its enemy, gazing in terror at something that is still invisible from the *machan*. Because a panther always circles its prey, a *shikari* is able to gauge its position by looking at the goat, which always turns to face it. Then suddenly there is a scuttle and the panther pounces on the goat, but retreats after killing it to sit and wait. Only when it is sure that no one has been alerted by the aggression does it walk up to enjoy the meal. The art is to get it before it kills the goat but that means hitting a leaping target. Beginners are encouraged to wait and fire later, when it is engrossed in its meal.

To wound a panther that disappears into the night entails some risk while leaving the *machan*. Once a wounded panther charged as I was getting into our convertible Citroën to return home, but was shot down before it could do damage. A panther usually attacks by approaching in a crouching glide, keeping the intended victim to its left and making its spring from about three times the length of its own body, always aiming to knock down the human victim by its weight. A panther returns to its own kill but never to dead baits. It is slightly smaller than the leopard found in the Indian hills. In those days there were more than 100,000 panthers roaming our countryside, but that has now been reduced to 6000. (The tiger popualtion has been reduced to 3000 from 50,000 in the same half century.)

At the time Master Sahib started me on my lessons an elderly man from Sarila was appointed as my second tutor. He was called Bassu Dau. In our Bundelkhandi dialect Dau literally means elder brother. I used to call him Bassu Babba rather than Bassu Dau. Babba means venerable, more suitable to be used by a ward for his guardian. In the village people called each other (as they still do) uncle or nephew, brother, sister or son, and the elders just 'babba' or grandfather. These endearing words cut across caste and religious divisions. I particularly remember Bassu Babba for his repertoire of quotations from the epics and the *Arthashastra*,* which he used to blast into my ears as I was growing up, as his contribution to my education in statecraft. Some got engraved in my memory.

the moment to guard against is when an enemy approaches you with a smile;
* your neighbouring country is your potential enemy, the neighbour's neighbour your potential friend;
* the four ways to influence a country are – *sham* (goodwill), *dam* (offering financial incentives), *dand* (the use or threat of force) and *bhed* (creating internal divisions in order to weaken that country); and
* *bhai bin hot na preet*: without first inspiring a certain awe you cannot gain the friendship of another country (or the love of a woman).

Later, in the diplomatic service, I used to, at times, reflect on Bassu's counsel. Nehru's over reliance on 'sham' (goodwill) to influence foreign countries, to the exclusion of the coercive factors, including alliances, cost India dear, with China and Pakistan.

When I was 13 my father bought a convertible Morris Minor. This he allowed me to drive exclusively to a garden two miles away where he had built a tennis court. The idea was to harness my passion for driving a car to make me practise tennis morning and evening with our 'marker' or tennis coach. The

* A treatise on economic, political and administrative management written by Kautalya, in the third century AD for the guidance of King Chandra Gupt Mauriya.

54

trick worked and at 15 I became the school tennis champion. Cricket, tennis and squash occupied a large part of my time and effort in those early years.

Early one morning while I was asleep on the terrace, I was woken by the sound of an aeroplane flying very low. It was a biplane and I saw the pilot waving at us. The plane had come from Kanpur, about 100 miles away, to make a trial run on a rough airstrip that was being prepared for it. All this was in preparation for the *mela,* the fair, when the plane would come for a few days to give joy rides to people at Rs 5 for five minutes (the equivalent today would Rs 250–300).

The annual *mela* was an important event in Sarila. Merchandise was exhibited and sold from temporary shops set up for the occasion. These goods came from towns far off from Sarila. It was in our *mela* that for the first time I saw Japanese goods and toys. In those days Japan had a reputation for cheap and shoddy goods. Crowds milled around the shops, buying or just 'window-shopping'. My father had started plane rides during our *mela,* which none of the *mela*s in our region could boast of. It was in the early 1930s when nobody in Sarila or, indeed, large parts of India had ever seen an aeroplane. To get a ride people old and young waited in a queue. I saw that several of them covered their eyes and ears with a cloth as soon as they were ushered into the cockpit. They were terrified of what was coming. It was on this biplane that I made my first flight.

The other notable event during the *mela* was the *dangal* or wrestling tournament. Wrestling was then one of the most popular sports in our area. The *dangal* was held in an *akhara*, a square piece of ground (about twice the area of a boxing ring) dug up with a shovel and the ground softened further with loose earth poured over it. The wrestlers wore short tight trunks in either chintz or bright colours. Whoever could force his opponent to a position in which both shoulder blades

13. *Dangal*, wrestling tournament, Sarila, 1938.

touched the ground would win the bout. There was a referee in the ring to judge whether this had happened. He would then shout '*Ho Gaya, Ho Gaya*' – 'it is done, it is done.' The victor would immediately run to my father, who would be sitting on a platform by the side of the *akhara*, and touch his feet. To those who had wrestled really well my father would make cash awards. The wrestler would then wave his hands to the crowd and the next match would begin.

Wrestlers from fairly far off districts and towns would come to the Sarila *mela*. They would strut round the *akhara* announcing how much they would pay the wrestler who would take them on and beat them. I enjoyed those bouts in which wrestlers were frisky, quick and willing to take risks. Thousands gathered to watch – some climbing trees for a better view, but no woman was ever seen in the crowd.

The monsoon comes to Sarila at the end of June or early July. The heavy movement of dark clouds and strong winds precede a deluge. Just before it starts to pour, the sky flashes and thunders and huge drops start to descend. I used to run onto the terraces to enjoy their splattering on my body and would get thoroughly drenched. It is a moment for nature to reawaken – birds sing, frogs croak, cows moo, dogs yelp and my elephant would sound a long trumpet. According to miniature paintings, this is the moment when maidens stretch up with raised arms and lifted breasts, and yearn for love.

The breaks in the monsoon were the time to fly kites. There was usually a breeze and the clouds, white, grey and menacing blue, chased each other in the sky. One team led by my brother and the other by me would be stationed on two different terraces of the palace. The team that downed most of the other side's kites won. This was done by cutting the string of the enemy's kite with the string of your own. The art was to tug, tighten and give edge to your string at the moment of contact with the string of the other. We used to see many kites flying in the town at the end of the park. Sometimes we would be allowed to play with the boys outside or invite them to strengthen our teams.

Later I learnt that in cities, kites flown from rooftops of packed houses were used for flirtatious purposes. As custom did not permit boys to meet unmarried girls, the strings of the kites enabled them to caress by proxy the bodies of their beloveds, even rupture them – the parents below none the wiser.

As soon as the temperature began to rise in earnest in May – 45° C plus – we usually migrated from Sarila to a hill station in the Himalayas 6000 feet up, for four solid months. This made me miss that wondrous moment of the coming of the monsoon for many a year.

Chapter 6
The Round Table
Conferences in London

I REMEMBER, though hazily, the return of my father from the second Round Table Conference in England in January 1932. I was escorted to the welcoming *pandal* that had been put up on the road a few miles outside Sarila. All our sardars and officialdom were there, as well as a large crowd. Crossing the seas was then rare and considered a hazardous undertaking. It was also their ruler's return from an important conference, at which he had represented the princes of India. (I cannot recall his return from the first conference.)

I also remember a ceremony that took place in the palace soon after. At this, water from the Ganges was sprinkled on him from a ceremonial ewer. My guardian Bassu Bappa told me that properly he should have gone for a dip in the holy Ganges to wash away the impurities of contact with foreigners across the seven seas. I was then too young to note the contradiction between his being given a rousing reception on his return from England and the atonement he had to make for the same. At that time I did not understand that shunning contact with people of other lands was one of the reasons why India had been repeatedly and successfully invaded by the Turks, the central Asians, the Afghans and then the Europeans. How can you organize a defence against people when you care to know nothing about their creeds and mores, strategies and tactics, or strengths and weaknesses? How can you fight enemies blindfolded?

My father also attended the third Round Table Conference the following year and later served on a consultative committee of the conference. Therefore I heard a lot of talk about England and these conferences as I grew up. What I have written below is based on that. It was a peep into the larger world – unfamiliar and exciting.

My father was accompanied on his trip by his valet Bhappa and Pandit Pratap Narain, the *diwan* of Sarila. For the second conference, on the recommendation of the British Resident to the central Indian states, a man called Mathews, an Anglo–Indian, was taken on as secretary. The idea was that Mathews could help him in the drafting of speeches and with his correspondence. Mathews was, by all accounts, a young man with an engaging tongue and pleasing manners.

On the opening day of the conference a large crowd had gathered at the entrance of St James's Palace. Wearing turbans, the princes made a splendid splash as they alighted one after the other from their chauffeur driven Humbers or Daimlers. Never-theless, the crowd's loudest cheer was reserved for Mahatma Gandhi who descended from the car wrapped in a white shawl and in sandals without socks. I remember my father telling us that he was surprised that the British should applaud loudest a person who wanted to snatch from them their most precious jewel, the Indian empire. The princes' delegation to the confer-ence consisted of 16 rulers. My father and the Raja of Sangli from Maharashtra represented the 250 smaller states.

The British government's purpose in summoning the confer-ence had been to snatch the initiative from the Indian nationalists who under the leadership of Mahatma Gandhi were strength-

14. Father alighting from his car for a meeting of the Round Table
Conference, London, 1932.

ening and widening their agitation in favour of early Indian
independence. Lord Irwin wanted to influence Mahatma Gandhi
in two ways. First, by confronting him at a conference with
moderate Indian opinion, which favoured a gradual withdrawal
of British power from India; and second, by dangling before him

the possibility that the princely states – one-third of the country – would join a future federation of a united India. Because the presence of the Indian princes in any future central legislature in Delhi would automatically serve as a break against the Congress Party, the viceroy saw this as a distinct advantage for Britain.

At the first conference Maharaja Ganga Singh of Bikaner, a veteran of the Versailles Peace Conference, and the young polo playing Nawab Hamidullah Khan of Bhopal, had taken the lead among the princes to support the participation of the princes in the proposed All India Federation. Their positive attitude at the first All India Federation had indeed persuaded Gandhiji to attend the second conference.

My father used to say that Pratap Narain had predicted at the beginning of the second conference that it would fail because of Gandhiji's participation. Mahatma Gandhi spoke at the second conference in favour of a transfer of complete control of defence and external affairs even before the All India Federation with dominion status was proclaimed. This demand hardened the British attitude and the British then turned to Muslim leaders led by the Aga Khan to block what they termed the radicalism of Gandhi and his party.

Once the conference got bogged down, the initiative passed to the British. The princes, who were once convinced that nothing was likely to come out of the effort, became cautious about making offers that might prejudice their powers and the integrity of their families. They sank back in their thrones, relieved that the viceroy would be making no more efforts to push them towards a different future. On the other hand, the nationalists became even more convinced that direct action was more likely to ensure that they kept the initiative in their hands than such conferences in which, according to them, unrepresentative opinion could be given weight. They thus resumed the civil disobedience movement in India.

My father's visits to England convinced him that no power on earth could shake British rule over India, and least of all the Indian agitators. He used to tell me, as I grew up, that the best thing that had happened to India was to have been occupied by the British. The Indians were 50 years behind the advanced countries and continued British rule over India would help us to catch up. I heard people in Sarila asking my father whether the streets of London were paved with gold. He said no, but England had wealth beyond their imagination and that the British lords lived better than most maharajas. He talked of the discipline, civic sense and patriotism of the masses and of the strength of the middle class, which then hardly existed in India. He recounted the story of a cab driver who returned to his hotel to deliver the wallet that he had left behind in his taxi. He also described the well-kept countryside and the neat, gabled, raftered houses with bow windows, surrounded by hedges, in villages.

I remember some of the other glimpses of the British scene he gave us. In England, he said, ordinary people were less arrogant in their dealings with Indians than the British sahibs were in India. British lords rode buses and carried their mackintoshes on their shoulders, although commoners always addressed them as 'Mi Lord'. Below the lords came the gentlemen class and the common people addressed them as 'sir'. Class divisions therefore prevailed, he said, but they did not prevent the chauffeur of his car entering the same café as himself during an outing in the countryside and sitting down at a different table, though at a distance. The thought of a driver having a snack in the same café as my father caused disbelief and amazement in Sarila.

He told them that the British were not as clean as the Indians. He gave two instances of this. The British delegate sitting next to him had not changed his shirt save for its white collar during the entire conference, the same pencil mark on his cuff showing throughout. (The wearing of under garments from neck to feet in fact made changing shirts less necessary.) Second, they bathed in tubs, namely in their own washed filth, instead of under flowing water or showers and did not wash their bottoms. He said that to impress them you had to talk back looking straight into their eyes. The subtle pleadings employed in India would be mistaken for weakness or cunning. There was much more money mindedness there than here. And he was appalled that children left the homes of their parents as soon as they became adults and did not care much for them thereafter. People were judged successful by their capacity to generate wealth rather than by their capacity to fulfil the required obligations to their family, cast and deity, as in India.

He recounted that one day he found Ranji, the famous cricketer and Maharaja Jam Sahib of Nawannagar, ordering beef in a restaurant and Ranji's explanation to him of this: 'Damn it, the English cow is not sacred.'

He talked about the Aga Khan and his latest Begum. The two fascinated him. Coming from a family of horse traders in Bombay he had risen to acquire considerable influence among the English establishment. He admired him for the way he functioned: never pressing his point too assertively and always being seemingly at ease. My father found the Begum, who was much taller than the Aga, both charming and intelligent.

My father said that the Aga's elegant suite at the Ritz Hotel had become the venue for informal discussions between the various Indian groups to which Gandhiji also came. The Aga Khan had built up his position in the first quarter of the century by ensuring that the Ismailia sect of Shia Muslims, of which he was the head, remained loyal to the British imperial cause. The Ismailias were spread over British East Africa, the Persian Gulf and Hunza bordering Sinkiang, besides of course western India. Simultaneously, he became a spokesman for the

Indian Muslims and a bridge between them and Britain. His leadership role among the Muslims helped to submerge the Sunni Muslims' antagonism to the Shia Ismailias. He was periodically weighed in precious stones, gold and diamonds, which his grateful followers then offered to him, so it was to his distinct advantage that he was so stout. He lived on the French Riviera, raced horses in England and married one English woman after the other, though the Begum my father met, his last wife, was French.

Sir Paul Patrick, who had dealt with Indian princely affairs in the India Office in London, told me in the 1950s about a letter the Aga Khan had written to him shortly before his death. Sir Paul said that in this he had bitterly lamented the sorry state in which the Muslims had found themselves, and had recalled with emotion that period of history when they controlled a very large part of the old world. Sir Paul then asked whether I was not surprised that the worldly Aga Khan's last thoughts should have been about happenings of a thousand years back.

To avoid pollution through physical contact with foreigners, the Maharaja of Alwar had acquired the habit of wearing gloves if he felt obliged to shake hands with them. My father described to us the crisis that erupted at the time of Alwar's presentation to George V at an outdoor reception for the Indian delegates to the Round Table Conference held in the gardens of Buckingham Palace. British protocol officers had warned Alwar that he would have to take off the glove of his right hand to shake the emperor's hand. As the guests lined up to be presented to the king, he still had his gloves on, so K. M. Panikkar, who was attached to the princes' delegation, was asked to go and speak to him to avoid a crisis that might cost him his throne. Tension mounted as the British monarch moved down the line of guests and approached Alwar with the latter having done nothing to remove the offending garment. Only a moment, a second, before George V extended his hand to greet Alwar did the maharaja solve his problem by dramatically bowing deeply, almost touching the ground, and saluting the king with folded hands in Indian fashion, a salutation more obsequious than shaking hands but nonetheless avoiding physical contact. The maharaja had clearly got a kick out of the suspense he had caused, for he later chuckled about it to my father.

My father told us, to our astonishment, that Buckingham Palace was not as large as the Viceroy's House in Delhi, though its interior was opulent. The king did not appear to him as bright as the viceroys and senior British officials in India. I might add that in those days a picture of the king and queen was printed on the covers of Indian children's textbooks, so I remember very well how they looked – he, somewhat diminutive, with a neat beard and parted hair and she tall, imperious and bosomy.

To us children the most interesting tale about the conference was about Mathews's activities in London. Pratap Narain told us that within a few days of arriving in London, Mathews started turning up in expensively cut suits and smart ties and shoes. His diffidence gone, he became exultant, even bossy.

Never wear black shoes with a blazer, or tie the knot of one's tie too tight, the English gentlemen never do that, he advised. Never say 'beg your pardon' but 'what', if you want your interlocutor to repeat what he had just said, and don't use the word 'ill' but 'sick'. Manners maketh the man, Diwan Sahib – that is the motto of Winchester, the school my father went to.

In society one is often judged first by one's clothes and last by one's character. So beaux Mathews made a lightening entry into London's salons, where elderly ladies were seen to swoon

15. Armistice Day, Whitehall, London. The British Cabinet is ranged in front.

over him. He was also seen to attend parties wearing pretty young ladies on his arm. Mathews told my father tales of his wealthy English family somewhere in Yorkshire, though he never introduced any of them to him.

Nemesis struck Mathews when after some weeks my father received his bank statement. From this £800 was missing – a more important sum in those days than now, when a Saville Row suit cost 10 guineas or £11 and a handmade shoe less than a pound. When my father consulted the manager of the hotel – the Savoy – he was put in touch with an officer of the London police posted at the hotel. The very next day the officer produced a cheque for £800 on which my father's signature had been forged.

When Mathews was confronted with the forged cheque, he collapsed. He fell at my father's feet in typical Indian fashion,

16. Armistice Day detail. To the right of the Prince of Wales (the future King Edward VIII) and the Dukes of Kent and Gloucester are standing four Indian princes. The author's father is the tall one in the second row.

his English flamboyance gone, and asked to be forgiven. He told my father that while living in a cubbyhole of a room by the railway lines of Mhow cantonment, he had fantasized about the high life in England. Indeed, his life's ambition had been to savour that life at least once in his lifetime, at any cost. For this he had carefully prepared himself by cultivating English manners and the language of 'us', the English upper classes. Since my father had left the chequebook with him, yielding to temptation was the only way he saw of realizing his dream. He had run through only £250 and gave back the rest.

The India Office in London, which dealt with the delegation to the conference, advised my father to send

Mathews back by the next available boat. This was to avoid the possibility of newspapers getting hold of the story and turning it into a scandal. His new acquisitions were not seized partly to ensure that he kept quiet and partly because my father had started to half like the man. 'A bounder but an engaging one,' he said. He was a very different type of Anglo–Indian from the solid Mrs Floyd, about whom I have written in an earlier chapter.

The Anglo–Indian community was fairly prominent in India in the 1930s. They mostly dated from the eighteenth and early nineteenth centuries when British officials came out to India unaccompanied by their women. The British trusted the Anglo–Indians and employed them in services of strategic importance, such as railways, post and telegraphs and intelligence, but they refused to mix freely with them. Sir Kenneth Fitze of the Indian civil service was political secretary to the Viceroy of India in the early 1940s. He had married an Anglo–Indian woman of great beauty and charm, but had to leave her behind in England during his four-year tenure in an important post in Delhi because the other sahibs in the capital would not accept her. Indians also looked down on the community. This double social ostracism forced the Anglo–Indians to create and live in a somewhat make-believe world. For example, although 99 per cent had never been there, they invariably referred to England as home and assiduously studied British geography to be able to talk familiarly about the Scottish moors or white cliffs of Dover. The Anglo–Indians had two great virtues. They knew English, which was becoming indispensable for modernization, and they did not shirk routine but indispensable tasks, which both the British and the Indians tended to do.

My father brought back an overcoat from Harrods and toys from Gooches for me, and several gifts for my mother who was happy at his safe return from across the seas. With him back, life in Sarila recaptured its rhythm, everyone reassured that British policy to effect constitutional reforms would pose no threat to Sarila. However, the winds of change had started to blow from another quarter nearer home.

Chapter 7
A Tiger is Shot in Sarila

I N THE EARLY 1930s, where we are at present in our story, I was too young to hunt and shoot. My father gave me my first rifle when I was nine, which was in 1936 shortly before I was sent off to school. It was a .22 bore Winchester. But I had started occasionally to accompany my father and his guests on shoots and hunts. Around Sarila we found black buck, *chinkara*, the sneezing deer, blue bull, sambar, the Indian horned stag, wild boar and most interesting of all, panther, which lifted goats from the edge of villages. What we absolutely did not have was tiger – the king of the Indian jungle.

Therefore, you can imagine the general astonishment when one day in the summer of 1933 Mrs Floyd the governess excitedly announced that a tiger had been sighted a few miles from Sarila towards the Betwa River and that my father was shortly setting out to hunt it. I ran outside to see what was happening and saw drawn up in the forecourt our convertible Citroen and a half truck, with several servants dressed in khaki loading them. It was blindingly hot, for the hot loo wind was howling and I was pulled back into the house. A little later I heard that, despite the weather, the hunting party had left.

I sought out my mother who said that when a report was received the night before that a tiger had been seen, it was dismissed as the tale of someone who had seen a large hyena or panther. Then, that forenoon a reputable *shikari* (huntsman) had come running all the way to announce that he had with his own eyes seen the animal and that it was a huge male tiger. He said he had seen it in the early morning moving in open country and then entering a thicket in a depression where, unless someone disturbed it, it was likely to lie until the evening. Since it was bound to move away from our relatively open country at the earliest opportunity, the time to get it was now. Also, our villagers knew nothing about tigers and one might inadvertently surprise it and invite an attack.

Only the year before I had seen a tiger in the jungle for the first time and my excitement knew no bounds. We had been driving in an open car in the tiger infested forests of Panna when my grand uncle, the maharaja, had suddenly pointed ahead. A hundred yards away I could see a tiger was crossing the road walking slowly in the same weary way as cats do, turning its head right and left. Then, noticing our car, it started to trot and as our car got nearer, it broke into a gallop. I was awestruck at the sight of the huge yellow and black muscular body with the large whitish head, bounding through the jungle at a speed faster than a galloping horse, before disappearing from view. A mature tiger is almost three yards in length, the tail another three yards. It can consume as much as 40 kilos of meat in one feeding. His roar can be heard two miles away. My grand uncle told me that a heavy double-barrelled rifle should be used to shoot a tiger so that the two shots can be fired in rapid succession; there may be no time to move the bolt to reload a single-barrelled rifle if the beast charged.

Tigers are generally shot from *machan*s in trees at least 20 feet high with baits of buffalo fastened to thick staffs below. Sometimes a group of hunters lined up on a *machan* will hunt together. In places with high grass, they can be hunted from the back of an elephant. Since an elephant's back slopes the tiger is often tempted to leap from behind and may reach two-thirds of the way up and then remain clinging: this is the moment to turn in one's seat, press the rifle barrel into its snarling mouth, and fire.

The most risky way to shoot a tiger is by stalking it on foot, which was what my father decided to do on that hot afternoon in Sarila. He told me later that he had no alternative: the villagers were not trained to beat and there were no high trees in the area in which to place a *machan*. He, of course, had a crack shot with him to help stop the animal if it charged. If a tiger charges in thick jungle all that you see is an enormous head coming straight at you and a headshot may then fail to stop it before it reaches you. Fortunately, my father was standing in open country with no chance of the tiger taking him by surprise.

A tiger is generally frightened of human beings – until one day, by chance it kills one. Then it discovers what a paper tiger man is, and how easy it is to kill him and how tasty is his flesh. Old or wounded tigers that cannot chase game also turn into man-eaters and start to lurk near human habitations and stalk men and women entering the forest.

On reaching the depression, which the tiger was said to have entered, my father sent a hunter to creep up to see if it was still in it. The man soon returned to signal that he could not see the animal from the distance he had thought safe enough to approach. And the feeling spread that the tiger had slipped away, contributing to the general carelessness that followed.

I was told what happened in much detail in the days ahead. The oblong depression where the tiger was supposed to be resting was about four or five metres deep and fifteen metres across with fairly steep sides. During the monsoon water must be collecting in it, for bambul trees and fairly thick undergrowth covered its floor. The land sloped towards the nearby river and because of soil erosion the ground was hard with a lot of gravel, thorny scrub here and there hugging the furrowed ground. The loo was raising dust squalls and the sun a ball of fire in the sky.

The party now advanced to a few yards from the edge of the ditch and some people were sent round to the farther side. At a given signal they were to try to disturb the tiger so that it emerged at the near end. My father in the meanwhile took up a position near a gully that ascended from the thicket below and from where the animal – if it were still there – might walk up. When the ballyhoo produced no result, one of our older *shikaris*, Priti Pal Singh, moved to the edge of the depression and threw a large stone into the thicket below. In doing so, he slipped on the gravel and disappeared from view. Simultaneously, there was a sound of cracking branches, a roar and a human cry. And within the time it takes to blink an eyelid, the tiger was atop, trotting away in the open country to the right from where my father stood.

It was about 30 metres away and perfectly placed for a broadside shot on the shoulder that would pierce the heart. My father brought his 375 Holland and Holland magnum double barrel to his shoulder and pressed the trigger. The bullet ripped through the tiger's stomach missing the shoulder. The next moment all hell broke loose. The tiger stopped, spun round and with a mighty roar charged the shooting party. The tiger uses the roar to petrify and paralyse its assailants or the game it is chasing. My father now fired his second and last shot. It tore into the tiger's chest as it bounded towards him with its paws and claws outstretched and its fangs bare. The *shikari* at his elbow then emptied his two barrels into the charging beast. The impact of the three bullets arrested the forward movement and the tiger swerved to one side and fell on the ground, a bare three or four metres away from where my father and his party were standing. Another bullet was then put in its head to dispatch it for sure.

17. The author with his younger brother, Jayendra Singh, by the tiger that was
shot in Sarila. Poles prop up the dead beast's head.

Priti Pal Singh's accident marred the jubilation. He was found
lying unconscious in a pool of blood, his shoulder torn away by
the tiger's blow. Although rushed to the Sarila hospital gangrene
set in and he died a few days later. When my father returned to
the palace, darkness had fallen but we were all up to hear about
the day's events. But besides announcing that the tiger had been
shot no one talked much that night. Since a tiger had never in
living memory been seen in Sarila, its shooting attracted considerable attention and people from far off villages came to see
it the next morning. Two photographs of the tiger lying on our
lawn with a forked stick propping up its head, one of my father
standing with a foot on it and the other of me and my younger
brother standing near it, still hang in my office in the house.

Chapter 8
The Political Department

J ARDINE WAS a very tall Englishman with brown hair, moustache and a cocker spaniel that invariably accompanied him. The dog was an expert at retrieving downed ducks from bush or water. Jardine was a British government officer in India's political department and I remember him because he was the first Englishman I ever saw at close quarters; this was while he was a guest at our home in Simla.

The functions of this department were to control with a mixture of courtesy, panache and menace, the princes whose territories occupied one-third of the British Indian Empire. The states were autonomous but subject to British paramountcy. They paid no tax or tribute to Britain. When once asked to define paramountcy in the House of Commons, the secretary of state for India's reply was short: 'Paramountcy is paramount.' Nevertheless, the iron fist was concealed in velvet gloves. Political agents were reminded that often the most valuable part of their work was what they left undone.

The personnel of the political department were handpicked officers from the Indian Civil Service – the cadre that administered British India – and from the British Indian Army. The head of the service, the political secretary, worked directly under the viceroy. Jardine's headquarters were at Nowgong, 70 miles from Sarila where a British military garrison was also stationed. He came under the Resident of central India, a senior

British officer stationed in Indore 400 miles to the southeast, and who, besides Bundelkhand, dealt with the states of Malwa and such larger ones as Gwalior, Indore, Rewa and Bhopal.

I remember my guardian Bassu Babba talking to me about Englishmen, who were a rarity in our state and whom the locals called red-faced monkeys. He told me that if an Englishman's polo pony was injured, he would wake up several times in the night to see how it was getting on, while an Indian owner in similar circumstances would leave the nursing to his groom. On the other hand, as soon as an Englishman's polo pony got old and outlived its utility, the British owner would shoot it, whereas the Indian would put his old pony to pasture in an enclosed grassy area until the end of its natural life. Bassu's other story concerned a bad tempered Englishman in Nowgong who used to abuse his bearer. Then, one day he slapped the servant, who in uncontrollable anger slapped him back. After that the two got on perfectly well.

My father used to visit the British political agent in Nowgong fairly often for a chat and to play tennis. Once I reached the age of seven or eight he would take me along with him and I loved the political agent's house. It had a thick thatched roof and deep verandas with wide Victorian arches on which flowering creepers would climb. The inside of the house was cool and airy; it had local grey stone floors, cream coloured plastered walls, large fireplaces (in winter the temperature at night would dip to near freezing point), waxed teak tables and chairs, faded chintz sofas and curtains, water colours on the walls and flower pots everywhere. A large garden with old trees and acres of lawns, great masses of cannas and curving lines of phlox and gleaming golden nasturtiums surrounded the bungalow. There were also two tennis courts and a swimming pool, which my brother and I were invited to use as we grew up. Though the house looked like a large cottage in comparison with the princes' palaces and forts, it was infinitely more inviting than many of them. The Residency in Indore was grander, with an impressive pillared façade and a vast herbaceous border along the long drive to it. Whatever the pros and cons of the British Empire, its builders around the globe left behind imaginative gardens and comfortable houses, as I was to observe on my travels in the foreign service.

The British government in those days worked in Delhi in the winter months and in Simla in the summer. The Delhi political department was housed in the new secretariat that Herbert Baker had designed and that had been built of red Dholpur stone. It bore a resemblance to the two-winged Louvre, although the far side, occupied by Edwin Lutyens's massive Viceroy's House, is distinct and stands well back. The political department was more splendid than the other parts of the secretariat. The ascent to the first, the main floor, was by a broad flight of stairs that led to the princes' waiting room. This round room had walls and floors of green and white marble, tall mahogany doors and a painted dome depicting the four stages of life in ancient India. The foreign secretary occupied the corner room of immense size next door. He advised the viceroy on matters relating to India's frontiers: Afghanistan, the Persian Gulf, Sinkiang and Tibet. The political secretary, who advised the viceroy on matters relating to the princely states, sat in another equally stately corner room with teak panelled walls, leather chesterfields, a Persian carpet, marble fireplace and a huge desk. Most officers in the department were British; only the clerks were Indian.

After independence, Prime Minister Jawaharlal Nehru chose this end of the secretariat for his office, as well as for the Ministry of External Affairs, and he took over one of the corner rooms for himself. Today a bloated prime minister's office has pushed the foreign office further down the corridors.

Simla, a very English town 6000 feet up in the Himalayas, surrounded by deodar and oak forests and with snow peaks shimmering in the distance, is quite different. There the viceroy lived and worked in a Scottish-looking gable-windowed turreted stone castle surrounded by acres of lawns at descending levels and with views of the snows to the north. His officers lived up and down the sides of the ridge in bungalows that might well have come straight out of the Lake District in England. The town also offered fashionable shopping on the Mall, first-class hotels, an amateur theatre and, in Anandale valley, a polo ground. From here the affairs of the teeming millions in the hot plains of India seemed remote and unimportant.

Early in the summer of 1937 my father received a letter from Sir Arthur Lothian, a senior officer in the political department, asking him to meet him in Simla at an early date. It may be recalled that Lothian had been posted in his earlier years as the political agent in Bundelkhand and that during my father's minority he had acted as his guardian. Since my father had not yet decided to which Himalayan hill station we should go to for that summer, Sir Arthur's letter helped him to make up his mind in favour of the summer capital of the British raj.

When the Marquis of Linlithgow appointed Lothian as the new viceroy it was with a view to him heading a team of political department officers who were to open negotiations with the princes on their accession to the All-India Federation, which had been proposed following the Round Table Conference. Under this scheme, the 11 British provinces were to have elected governments, while the princes would nominate one-third of the members at the centre of the federal legislature from their states and in this way, with the support of the more conservative elected members, possibly control the government of India. Furthermore, unless a certain percentage of princely states acceded to the federation it would not be launched, so the princes acquired a veto over the federal scheme. It was much later, as part of my education, that my father explained the scheme to me and recounted his conversations with Lothian.

Sir Arthur told my father that once a 'popular' government had been installed in a next-door province, pressure on princely states to grant representational government within them was expected to grow. When asked whether such a prospect was more likely to induce the princes to enter the federation and try to obtain control of the central legislature as an insurance against Congress Party mischief or merely to turn their backs on the federal scheme, my father told Lothian that the chances of the latter were greater. When Sir Arthur then asked my father how the Bundelkhand princes reacted to the proposal, he explained that none gave it much thought and that in his view the Bundelkhand rulers were likely to wait and watch. My father told me that he came away with the impression from this talk that the viceroy was unsure whether to push the princes to join the scheme or to use their veto to abort it.

The general feeling among the British officials in Simla with whom he played tennis and dined was that the states' entry into the federation would help kick-start it, but whether this would be in the interest of the princes was a moot point. Sir Kenneth Fitze, the former Resident in central India, and my father's best friend among the British officers, held the opposite view. He told my father that the best way to counter Congress Party pressure was to enter the federal legislature where they would have a strong voice and try to become a political force to be reckoned with. 'Jump into the saddle and gather the reins in Delhi before those against you get into the saddle in the British provinces next door to you,' he had said. But this was not to be. The princes continued to dither and the political department made no serious effort to induce them to join the federation.

I know nothing about the talks the political department held with princes in other parts of India; I only know about Bundelkhand and that the British Resident for the central India states at that time was a Scotsman called Campbell. He was a short man with a moustache who always wore chalk-striped worsteds and a brown porkpie felt hat. The political agent in Bundelkhand was Major Poulton, who was a tall soldierly man with a bushy black moustache. The only concrete move made to encourage the Bundelkhand rulers to take a view on the federation was to stage the Bundelkhand week, a series of cricket, tennis and squash tournaments in Nowgong between Christmas and New Year 1938 in which the rulers and their close relatives were invited to participate. The idea was that bringing princes together on the playing fields of Nowgong might help them harmonize their position on the federal scheme and give thought to political reforms in their own states.

The games were unremarkable because the participants were not young and most were out of practice. For example, in cricket several only batted but did not field. My uncle, the ruler of Garrauli, tried to relive his youth by trying to bowl fast with a long run and suffered a heart attack. During the Bundelkhand week there were no serious discussions among the princes or between them and the Resident on the All-India federal scheme and no meeting was arranged for such a discussion.

In retrospect, the only way to push the rulers of small states like Bundelkhand to join the federation was to tell them that in the future they would get no British protection in the event of agitations in their states. This, the Resident had no authority to do. Rather, the general mood was to escape from tiresome subjects like groupings, democracy and the abridgement of princely powers and get back to the familiar routine, including the New Year's duck shoot at nearby Isanagar lake in Charkhari state – the best duck shoot in Bundelkhand. In any case, this shoot stands out more vividly in my memory than the Bundelkhand week, so let me describe it to my readers to give them an idea of how these things were done in those days.

I remember leaving with my father for Isanagar very early in the morning with the temperature hovering around two or three degrees centigrade and driving on an unmetalled road through scruffy bush and boulder-strewn hills. After some miles a stone wall running up and down on the spine of the ridges looking from far like a poor cousin of the Great Wall of China came into view. Then we skirted the village of Maheba, where the robe and sword of Chhatarsal, the conqueror of Bundelkhand, are preserved. Unlike in flat Sarila we were now in the heartlands of the Bundela clan.

On arriving at the lake we found, spread out below its bund, a township of khaki coloured tents and much hustle and bustle. Groups of tents were pitched in rectangular blocks divided by pathways lined with potted plants and coated with red *murram*. We drove up to our tent, which had an awning in front of it. One raised a cloth-covered flap to enter the tent, which consisted of a squarish room with walls lined with a pleasant pale yellow cotton cloth spotted with tiny brown prints. Furnishing the room were two cots laden with thick quilts, collapsible tables, a couple of folding chairs, a mirror hung up with a table below for dressing, clothes hangers on a rope suspended along a wall of the tent and a bright *durree* spread on the floor. With the sun now beating down on the canvas outside, the interior was pleasantly warm, though I had been told that coal braziers would need to be placed on the floor to make it warm enough for our comfort in the evenings.

Another flap door at the far end led to the bathroom. Its

floor consisted of loose red bricks placed close to each other and covered with a jute mat. It was equipped with a china basin, jug and soap dish on a table, and a tin bath tub that a *bahishti* (water carrier) could fill with warm water when necessary. In the far corner stood a stool with a lid on it that concealed a ceramic toilet pot – 'thunder boxes' as they were called – to be evacuated by the camp sweeper as many times as required.

Electric bulbs were attached to the ceiling, meaning that a generator had been temporarily installed for our convenience. Behind the tent were two smaller conical tents to house our staff. These three tents made up the Sarila enclosure. There was such an enclosure for each prince or senior British officer. For the Resident, however, the tent was larger with two adjoining rooms and a dressing room.

Soon after our arrival breakfast was served on a long table under a large *shamiyana*, a flat-topped marquee stretched over poles pegged to the ground and open on all sides. The Resident had by then arrived and he sat at the head of the table. Breakfast consisted of Force, with milk, buttered eggs on toasted bread, jams and fruit. Our host, the Maharaja of Charkhari, was nowhere in sight and we were told that he was 'sick'. As a very shy man, however, he generally avoided meeting new people, particularly Europeans, and the whole British contingent from the Bundelkhand week was there, plus British army officers and their wives from the military cantonment in Nowgong along with their holiday guests from England, besides of course several rulers and their guests.

After breakfast we were directed towards a chart fixed to a board on which was indicated the butt (or hide-out) each guest was to occupy for the shoot. Though my name was not on the chart, I was to accompany my father. There were about 20 butts. Butts are made of straw mats and placed at the edge of the water so that the *shikaris* can remain invisible to the birds as far as possible. Each *shikari* was provided with a helper who carried his guns, two per person – and pouches bursting with cartridges – the approach to the butts made as silently as possible. In the butt were two rough stools on which to sit and rest when not firing.

The lake at Isanagar was said to be more than a kilometre in diameter, though tall grass in the marshy wooded islands in it made it difficult to see all its banks. According to the helper, there were about ten thousand birds on the lake, though from my hide-out I could only see about three to four hundred floating on the water – teals, pochards and coots. No doubt grey legs, bar-headed geese, spoonbills and others would be hiding among the reeds and marshes that covered almost half the lake. In the distance I could also see some storks and cranes. Like in our small lake in Sarila many of these were migratory birds that flew in from the frozen lakes of Siberia through the Hindu Kush and Himalayan passes. Their encirclement did not appear to alarm them.

After the shoot began the birds started to rise in groups and as they came over the butts, the guns blazed. I was too young to shoot, though I carried a 410-bore gun with me. Each time he emptied his 12-bore, the loader placed the second gun fully charged into my father's hands so that he could maintain a continuous barrage. The birds that were hit fell in the lake and on shore and the helpers would make a note of where they had dropped. As the birds rose beyond the range of the guns there were lulls in the shooting, but as soon as they swept back towards the water the firing would start once again. So the game went on, each bird the *shikari* brought down giving him a 'kick' of exhilaration, which is the essence of the sport. By the end of the shoot my father must have dropped two dozen birds, which was not a good score. The ladies and gentlemen emerged from the hide-outs flushed and excited, anxious to ensure that the ducks each had shot were retrieved. Unlike duck shoots in other countries where dogs are used, here humans retrieved all the dead birds.

The lunch was more elaborate than the breakfast: there was plenty of gin and beer to begin with, followed by red wine with venison. Meanwhile, all the shot birds had been collected and placed in rows on the ground before the large tent – there were about 600 of them. This was no match to the great shoots at Bharatpur and other places in India where a morning's bag might reach 2000 or 3000. Since the Resident had to return to Nowgong and there was to be no duck shoot that afternoon, many drifted into the hills and surrounding jungle to get the spotted deer that were plentiful in the valleys. At night, campfires were lit and drinks and dinner served around them. I, however, was sent to my bed fairly early.

The work of a political officer or Resident in the states was far less onerous than that of his colleagues in British-administered provinces, who were engaged in the nitty-gritty of day-to-day administration and had, besides, to face the brunt of political agitations. Few services in the British Empire at that time provided the opportunities the political department offered its officers for a pleasant existence: elegant bungalows or mansions, pomp and ceremony, hunting and shooting in the maharaja's preserves, tours to exotic locations, and varied entertainment and festivities. No wonder a majority of these officers – and their wives – were loath to rock the princely boat, especially as their country and the viceroy's team were divided on the federal scheme.

The war broke out soon afterwards and the British priority shifted towards obtaining the help of the princes in men, money and material rather than spending time trying to persuade them to join the federal scheme. After the Congress ministries in the provinces resigned (to put pressure on the British to make a declaration to grant independence to India after the war), the viceroy, the political department and most princes heaved a sign of relief. Neither London nor the Congress Party would now push them for some time to change the status quo. This drew the curtain on the federal experiment for a united India conceived in 1935 in which the princes were given an opportunity to become major players in the affairs of their country.

Sir Paul Patrick, who had been a secretary in the India Office and was a friend of my father, used to invite me for lunches at his club in London – The Travellers – in 1949–50. I remember him telling me that the Conservative diehards in London derailed the 1935 scheme that would have resulted 'in the emergence of a free, united India under a conservative Indian leadership'. He asked me how only a few years later Lord Mountbatten and Sardar Patel had, between July and August 1947, obtained the accession of all the Indian princes, except Hyderabad and Kashmir, to the Indian dominion, which the British political department had been unable to do for the federal scheme between 1936 and 1939. The short answer, had I known it then, was 'because you did not crack the whip, the political department in India did not show any enthusiasm to the federation scheme.'

One day in 1949 Sir Cecil Griffin, the last political secretary before independence (who in retirement spent his mornings transcribing books into Braille for the blind) invited me to lunch at his tiny house in Henley-on-Thames. I was rather surprised to see the towering (six foot six inch) Lord Halifax (earlier Lord Irwin) as the only other guest. Perhaps Halifax was curious to see an entrant into the new Indian foreign service, especially one whose father he had chosen for the Round Table Conference in 1931 when he was the viceroy of India. There

18. Sir Kenneth Fitze,
political secretary in Delhi.

was some discussion about the demise of princely rule, Halifax expressing no opinion at all. But I remember Griffin saying that the political department never had its heart in encouraging the princes to join the 1935 federal scheme, for which the ball was set rolling by none other than Halifax 'because we believed that they could get better terms outside it'. Lord Halifax gave me a lift back to London, managing to drive with his only hand – and rather fast.

This view of the political department did not change until 1947. As the negotiations for Britain's departure intensified after 1942, the British government, on the department's advice, repeatedly announced that British paramountcy over the princes would lapse when the British withdrew, making the princely states legally independent. If the lapse of paramountcy would liberate them from Delhi it would also liberate the future free India's new rulers from any obligation to protect them. The viceroy at that time was Field Marshall Lord Wavell. Did he not see that the proposed lapse of paramountcy might help the bigger states – like Hyderabad, Kashmir, Travancore and Mysore – to stake claims for independence but that it would leave in the lurch 95 per cent of the states, which were not viable units and too dependent on the surrounding provinces and the central government's support to survive?

British policy changed a couple of months before the British withdrawal from India. Mountbatten closed the political department in July 1947, and the Attlee government thereafter worked with the Congress Party to end princely rule.

Sir Kenneth Fitze, political secretary in Delhi before Griffin, and my father's friend, had always been more high spirited and talkative. He and his Anglo–Indian wife had retired to a lovely cottage, Teal Hatch, near Crawford Forest, in Sussex. They used to invite me from Cambridge to spend weekends with them and would pull my leg about being unable to arrange for a valet to unpack my luggage or a *dhobi* (washerman) to launder overnight my soiled clothes thrown on the floor, as was done in old England. A form faithfully adhered to in the Residencies in India. Fitze once told me that the Indian princes could not complain too much since they escaped the fate that befell most European rulers.

He was then writing his memoirs, *The Twilight of the Maharajas*. In this he vents his frustration at his department's near-sightedness, and failure to perceive the winds of change in India:

> It was with strangely mingled emotions that we, who had for so long scrupled to lay sacrilegious hands upon the guaranteed prerogatives of the most unworthy of pygmy principalities, witnessed the release of new forces which caused great states like Baroda and Kolhapur to drop like ripe plums into the lap of the nearest [Indian] province and which launched an army of people raised and trained for the service of the King Emperor, against the Nizam of Hyderabad, who valued most among all his resounding titles that of 'Faithful Ally of the British Government'.

87

Chapter 9
Mayo: The Eton of India

I WAS SENT to school when I was nine-and-a-half years old. This was to the Mayo Chiefs' College situated in Ajmer in Rajputana (now called Rajasthan). I joined Mayo on 7 July 1936 and spent ten years there, the last four in its college section where boys studied to take the Agra University Bachelor of Arts degree. I was among the last boys to study at Mayo before, following the end of princely rule, the college was opened up to pupils other than princes and their nobles.

As my father and I drove up from the Ajmer railway station to the school, a tall marble tower soon came into view. This was the school's 108-foot clock tower, and the chimes emanating from it were to govern my life for a decade. After passing an impressive iron gate and the school building in unpolished marble with Lord Mayo's statue in front of it, we drove straight to the principal's house. The grounds were spacious and extremely well kept; the roads were decorated on either side with a spread of red *murram* and, further back, with low *mehndi* (henna leaf) hedges. Beyond were the buildings and gardens of the boarding houses and the playing fields.

V. A. S. Stow had been the principal of the school for a decade. It was he who had persuaded my father to send me to Mayo College. Normally, I should have gone to Daly College at Indore, which was my father's Alma Mater and the college to which the princes and nobles of the central Indian states were

19. The Mayo College main building with the Taragarh mountain in the
background.

normally sent. In the 1870s the British had founded five
schools for the education of princes. Besides the Mayo and Daly
colleges, these were Aitchsen College in Lahore, Princes College
in Rajkot in west India, and a similar college at Raipur for boys
from the eastern states. Stow had convinced my father that
Mayo College was the grandest of them all and, indeed, it was
referred to as the Eton of India.

After crushing the great revolt of 1857–58 the British
decided to stop conquering and to make peace with, indeed
win over, the princes and chieftains who held sway in the still
unconquered territories of India, which was more than one-
third of the total area. What better idea could there be than to
resuscitate dispirited Indian aristocrats into playing a role as
partners of the British by giving them a British public school
education? As the preamble of Mayo's charter read, the aim of
the school was 'to guide the sons of the aristocracy of India in
liberal and enlightened education, to keep pace with the ever

advancing spirit of the age'. Special emphasis was laid on teaching English, which was then hardly spoken in the princely states. Speaking at the Mayo College in 1888, Viceroy Lord Dufferin declared: 'Already in the counsels of providence the edict has gone forth that English shall be the language chiefly prevalent upon God's earth. Within another hundred years the English speaking races of the world will number upwards of a thousand million.' (These words are a good illustration of the confidence the British had started to feel in their invincible destiny by the nineteenth century.)

Stow received my father and me at the footsteps of his large grey stone bungalow. It was here that I committed a *faux pas* I have been unable to forget all my life. Stow asked me a simple geographical question: 'where was the Deccan?' I merely gazed at him, for I did not know the answer. 'In peninsular India, of course,' Stow said sharply.

Another problem I faced on my first and subsequent days was difficulty pronouncing my name. I used to stammer badly, especially when pronouncing words that began with the letter 'N'. When asked my name, the tip of my tongue would get stuck to the pallet and I would stumble out with something like 'N-n-n-n-n Narendra Singh'. I had never faced this problem in either Sarila, where no one ever asked me my name, or in other places because under such circumstances my father would always introduce me. Mayo College was not as bad as most English public schools, where new entrants are often treated quite roughly, but with my stammering some teasing was inevitable and this did nothing to improve my stutter. At Mayo College most people called me Sarila. The other boys were similarly called by the name of the principality or domain from which they came, so when asked our name we would give it in full, in my case Narendra Singh Sarila. Before the tenth and eleventh centuries 'Singh' was never added to the name of the warrior clans. However, when Turkish and central Asian invaders began to defeat them, we see 'Singh', which means lion, added to their names. Was it to boost their falling morale? The Sikhs also add 'Singh' to their names. They started to do that when the Mogul emperors of Delhi persecuted them and they took to the sword to defend their faith. From that moment onwards they classed themselves as warriors or Singhs. In other words, all Sikhs are Singhs but not all Singhs are Sikhs. The word 'Singh' has given birth to a city and country outside India, namely Singapore or the town of lions.

I might mention that I overcame my stammer when I started learning French in France at the age of 22. Indians have difficulty pronouncing three sounds in the French language – the French 'U', 'EW' and 'R'. So my French teacher used to make me do certain exercises, *'pour la formation de la bouche'*, she would say. These exercises helped me not only with these sounds but also mysteriously cured my stutter. After the first few months in Mayo the boys left me alone, but throughout my school days I was never asked to read aloud passages of prose or poetry from text books in the class, as other boys were asked to do. On the other hand, the essays I wrote started to get high marks. I was asked to write a daily summary of the news from the war fronts for posting on the college notice board.

Notwithstanding the bad impression I had made on my first meeting with the principal, he invited me to take breakfast at his house every Sunday, which was a special favour. Joining us would be his three boarders, Bahadur Singh, the Maharaja of Bundi, Bahadur Singh's brother Kesri Singh, and Jai Singh, a prince from Manipur, the princely state on the Burmese border. The principal's house had a large garden with old trees, flowering shrubs and the best tennis court in the school, on which the annual tennis championship would be played. Inside the house I had to be very careful not to slip on the highly

20. Mayo College, aerial view.

polished teak floors and knock down one of Mrs Stow's precious cut glass rose bowls. Tall, silver haired Mrs Stow would preside over the mahogany breakfast table and its gleaming silver. With silver dishes of scrambled eggs, sausages and bacon on burners on the sideboard, the coffee percolator on a table with wheels by the side of the hostess and the principal's Labrador licking our feet, the only sound to break the awe-stricken hush was of a sewing machine on the veranda where a *darji* (tailor) repaired the *Memsahib*'s garments.

Stow ran the school with an extremely firm hand: the staff and boys' lives revolved around the programme he set and that the clanging of the tower clock proscribed. He never rode a bicycle as the boys and masters did and either walked, with his baton in hand and his two fox terriers sprinting ahead to alert the unwary of his approach, or rode his maroon and black highly polished car. (I gathered later that he earned Rs 2000 a month, which today would be close to Rs 100,000 or US$ 2000. The Rs 1200 (today about Rs 55,000) he received from his three boarders supplemented his basic salary. The British teachers earned a quarter of his salary and the Indians, on average, one-tenth.)

The house master of Jodhpur House (and of the two neighbouring houses, Bikaner and Tonk) was W. H. Bradshaw. He lived in a stone bungalow situated in its own grounds, not far from our house. He had been a fast bowler at Oxford and used to play for the Europeans in the all-India pentangular tournament that was then held in Bombay each year. (The other teams in the pentangular used to be of Hindus, Muslims, Parsis and Anglo–Indians.) Because of his prowess in cricket and a very fine bowling action, we held him in awe. But it was not he but our Indian coach (and groundsman) G. R. Naidu, who spotted my talent as a natural late-in swing bowler.

The school was built on a glorious site in a forested valley at an altitude of 600 metres. To the north of the campus towered the Madar hill, which from the school looked rather like a pyramid, and to the west some miles away, stretched a higher mountain with the ancient Taragarh, 'the fort among the stars', built around 1218, occupying the crest. The prevailing west wind had to rise above the 3000-foot Taragarh ridge, and then descend over a large lake, the Ana Sagar, which acted as a natural coolant for the valley in summer. The view across the Ana Sagar, with the pink light of the setting sun playing on Taragarh and other surrounding hills, was captivating. It was on the bund of the Ana Sagar that Emperor Jehangir received Sir Thomas Rowe, the first British envoy to India, in 1615. Georges Clemenceau, who led France in the First World War and visited Ajmer after the war, was impressed enough with the view to declare that this was the place on earth where he would most like to die when the time came.

The main school building in Indo-sarsenic style and in white marble stood on a slight rise in the middle of a 300-acre compound. The boarding houses were situated on either side of a horseshoe shaped road. The central cricket ground with its handsome red stone pavilion donated by Bikaner state occupied the central space in the campus. A broad mall with marble fencing and lawns connected the central ground and the college building. Since each state had tried to compete with the other on the beauty of the boarding house it built, the school got endowed with some very fine buildings. The planning was on a grand scale. By the time I arrived there in 1936 there were two polo fields, two full-sized and three other cricket grounds, several football and hockey fields, seven tennis and three squash courts, a gymnasium and a swimming pool.

The Mayo coat of arms was based on a design by Rudyard Kipling's father, an art teacher called Lockwood. A fully-armed Rajput warrior wearing a steel helmet and chainmail and a Bhil tribal warrior with a string bow and quiver of arrows support a five-coloured (*pachranga*) shield. The symbols of the Rajput lineage are mixed with a cross and quarterings, a lion rearing, an open hand and an ermine. The badge is a dancing peacock, the sacred bird, poised on a *khanda* (a two-edged sword) and the motto reads: 'Let there be light.' Being awarded college colours gave one permission to wear the five-coloured blazer. The riding ponies in Mayo had *pachranga* martingales.

The central hall of this building is one of the finest in India for size and beauty. Its colours are light greenish-blue, white and gold. The skylights near the high arched ceiling light up the gold work and the portraits of the maharajas who founded the school and of the principals who ran it. In the circular eastern end is a marble dais, with an intricate marble railing at each of its two ends. It was on to this dais that those who won prizes in academia or sports walked up in *achkans* and turbans in stiff military style on the annual prize giving day to collect their prizes from the presiding prince that particular year. The personages of the board who ran the college – mostly the rulers of Rajasthan – sat on either side. The principal in a gown used to stand to call out the names of the boys to come up to collect their prizes. Books given away as prizes were always leather-bound and the sports cups and silver shields were huge. It was to this dais that I marched up to collect the viceroy's medal for all-round merit in 1944.

Each state of Rajputana had, at its own expense, built a boarding house for boys of all ages from that state and they were given individual rooms. Stow had promised my father to put me in the most recently constructed house, the new wing of the Jodhpur House, and in so doing had ignored the usual practice.

My room had a desk, two easy chairs, a bookcase, a small dressing space and an attached bathroom. The chillied food served in the Jodhpur House mess was too hot for me, so Stow permitted me to be accompanied by a cook from Sarila. It was customary for each boy in the Mayo College to have a valet, but in my case, besides the cook, a water carrier was added to my staff to help the cook and to carry hot water to my bathroom because no geysers then existed.

Three servants for one boy at boarding school would appear preposterous to most people today, but looked at from a different angle, namely that of the norm at Mayo at that time, my entourage would be considered modest. In a report at the end of the nineteenth century Colonel Lock, the principal of the school, wrote: 'One boy joined Mayo College with 190 followers but left with 19,' alluding to the progress he had achieved. I had merely joined the school with three servants and had left in 1946 with one.

In its early days the school had been somewhat disorderly, reflecting the princely decomposition of the nineteenth century. The situation academically at that time was far from satis-factory. 'One of the causes of the comparative low standard was undoubtedly the tendency to idleness among the students who were free from the stimulus of poverty and the necessity to employ education as the means of livelihood,' states a college report written in the 1880s.

Before the layout of the school campus and its buildings were completed it was actually quite a jungly place. The records show that the boys hunted jackals on horseback and panthers prowled the grounds (though there is no record of a boy being lost). Cricket was then played in the full school regalia, namely with *achkan*, the long coat and turban, the ends of the *achkan* secured around the waist. The turban or *pugree* helped to prevent head injuries on bumpy pitches.

By the time I joined the college the situation was much less despairing academically, menacing physically and unseemly sartorially. Boys prepared for an examination called the Chiefs' College diploma, which was equivalent to the standard set for passing the high school examination in other schools. We certainly learnt to speak English better than boys in normal schools. 'A person influences you not so much by any particular words or deeds of his,' Stow used to drum into us, 'but by what you call the tone of his character, that is to say the general impression made upon your sentiment by his habitual manner and conduct.'

In deference to our future perceived responsibilities, the rudiments of law, the Evidence Act and procedures governing land revenue and land records were included in the syllabus. But some shortcomings from the old days lingered. For example, even if you got nought in one paper you could still pass if you secured an aggregate of 45 per cent, which may have been contrived because so many Rajput boys got ducks in mathematics.

The routine of half an hour of physical training first thing in the morning and an emphasis on sports of all kinds was a feature of the school. Riding was considered a part of technical training because no large landowner in those days could get about quickly and comfortably to supervise things for himself without a horse. Polo was played twice a week besides football, hockey, rounders, tennis, squash and of course cricket. Cricket was considered not only a game but also an education in its own right, which it is. Given that one's actions are less automatic or instinctive in cricket than in fast moving games that last a short time, it makes one apply one's brain much more than usual. Also, acting in cold blood helps to train the nerves, for one cannot either bat or bowl successfully without maintaining an even temper and being patient. And again, more than in any other game and in life, so much depends upon chance, so one learns to take the rough with the smooth.

Cricket was not played in the monsoon season, which was when I joined the school, but after Dussehra, namely from October when the dry and cool season begins. I loved cricket from the very first day I played it and practised bowling relentlessly, even during the lunch break between classes. Some of my most memorable moments in Mayo were of captaining the cricket team (which I did for three years while in the college section) and with fastish late inswingers knocking down off stumps while the batsmen shaped for late cuts. My later selection to play in the interprovincial cricket tournament called the Ranji Trophy, first for Rajputana and later for the United Provinces is attributable to my concentration on the game at Mayo.

My proficiency in tennis, squash and shooting gave me opportunities to make social contacts in various lands, which helped my diplomatic career. When posted in The Hague (1951–54) I played squash for the Netherlands against Belgium and when in Accra (1954–58) I represented the Gold Coast (later Ghana) in tennis against Nigeria. Invited to shoot and hunt in the presidential estates in France when I was ambassador there brought me close to two of the fastest friends of the then president of France, François Mitterrand. (The most important duty of an ambassador after all is to get close to the fountainhead of power in the country of accreditation; merely pussy footing with the local foreign office, the prescribed channel, does not get one very far.)

On our way from Sarila to Ajmer to join the school, my father had bought me a Knightsbridge bicycle in Delhi. The distances in the school between the boarding houses and the school building, the playing fields and other places of activity were so vast that every boy had to equip himself with a bicycle. Our school dress consisted of a white Jodhpur coat, white breeches and a turban, the white coat replaced in the winter by a black woollen one. We played games without having to wear the turbans but no boy could leave his boarding house without having one on, even on his way to the sports field. We removed our turbans while playing games in such a careful manner that its folds did not become undone and the turbans could be replaced on the head for the return journey to the boarding house. The starch on the turbans' muslin helped.

One of the picturesque sights in Mayo was of groups of boys on bicycles peddling furiously to their chores, with the tails of their multicoloured headdresses flying in the wind like kites. There was no fixed colour or design for turbans worn by boys, which added to the colourfulness of the sight, though school colour holders had a distinctive coloured turban for formal occasions. This was the *pachranga* consisting of red, deep green, white, light blue and gold stripes – the five holy colours of Rajputana as well as the school colours. School monitors also had a distinctive pink and white striped turban. The designs of multi-coloured turbans all have distinctive names: *mothra* is the name given to checks; *leheria* to straight stripes; *bhopali leheria*

21. The author aged 17 wearing a traditional turban called a *safa*.

to zigzag stripes; *bandhni* to tie-dye designs; *dobli* to tie-dye designs with larger squares; and *lahesia* to those with shaded colours that merge into one another.

99

The college principal and house masters were Englishmen, but the college also had a large Indian staff. Most of the English teachers were drawn from Cambridge and Oxford universities. The principal selected the Indians for their scholarship and loyalist views. They came from all parts of India. Teachers who entertained pro-Congress Party sentiments, like Ashfaque Hussain in my time, were eased out. The *Hindustan Times*, which was then the mouthpiece of the Congress Party fighting for India's independence was not allowed in the school; only the *Statesman* and the *Times of India*, both of which had English editors. These restrictions did not prevent boys from feeling the stirrings of nationalism. Some of the old patriotic fire that had made their ancestors resist invaders had not been entirely extinguished among them.

In the late 1930s there were 350 boarders among whom were included the future rulers of a score of princely states. By then the school had acquired most of the characteristics of a British public school, except that entry was still restricted to princes and nobles of whatever religion.

Though the elephants and carriages were gone, several senior boys kept chauffeur-driven cars, which the principal or house masters would requisition to take boys on shooting parties and picnics. We would wait for sand grouse at the water's edge and take them as they dived, stalk black buck around Ajmer and try to get school friends with properties in the deep desert to invite us for a shoot of the rare bustard.

One episode concerning an Arab boy in our school stands out in my memory. He was Fahr bin Taimur, a boy from Oman who later became the defence minister of his country. Unknown to the teachers or boys, this huge, dark, curly-haired boy used to carry a cutlass strapped to his waist under his garments. One day during the school recess he quarrelled with a boy, lost his temper and, pulling out his cutlass, chased after the boy who ran for his life while the other boys rushed to report the matter to the principal. The result was that Stow confiscated Fahr's weapon and gave him a warning, but there were clearly no ill feelings because, in 1970, now a minister in Oman, Fahr donated a boarding house to the school, which is called 'Oman House'.

By the time I passed the diploma examination and reached the college section I was in my sixteenth year. There were now fewer subjects and only 50 to 60 students. I joined the classes for English literature, history, economics and civics. Because we were few in each class, personal attention could be paid to each student. We wrote weekly essays on subjects given to us, and the teachers discussed our work with us, as is done in European universities, a practice that had disappeared in Indian universities by the 1940s because of the large sizes of the classes.

ೲഝ

One day our history teacher told us that the origin of the word India was Greek. When Alexander reached the Sindhu River (its correct name in Sanskrit) in 327 BC the Greeks called it the Indus, and the people of the area Indians. These words became popular in Europe and then in the rest of the world. At that time Bharat Varsh was the most usual name for this land. Thereby also hangs the tale of how the word Hindu arose, another word of recent foreign origin. When Arab sailors started to trade with India, they turned the European word India into Hind or Al Hind, and Indians into Hindis; in fact these names are still used in Arab countries. When the English came to India, they described anyone they could not identify with Islam, Christianity or Judaism and who had no definite Gospel, Book or Final Word, as Hindus, thereby using a word with essentially geographical connotations to describe the faith or faiths of a people. The word Hindu cannot be found in any book in the Indian languages before the mid-seventeenth century.

A shy Englishman, J. A. M. Ede, headed the college section. He loved poetry and philosophy and introduced us to writers of all descriptions, including the agnostic C. E. M. Joad, whose books *God and Evil* and *The Future of Morals* were popular in England at that time. I remember Ede complimenting me on an essay I had written in which I speculated on life after death. I argued that when we died all the physical elements dissolved and merged in the five elements of which the body is composed; I asked whether there could be some abstract element, perhaps some psychic phenomenon formed as a result of our mental activity during our lifespan, some spirit that did not dissolve with the five physical elements and did not perish like the rest? Was I trying to find a rationale for rebirth? In any case, by this time I had started to turn towards agnosticism, which I felt, and feel, does not mean rejecting our *sanatan dharma*, our ancient ethos.

The brightest boy I came across at Mayo was Kesri Singh from Mundiar, a *jagir* in the deserts of Jodhpur state. With his sharp retentive memory he could remember and recite several stanzas of poetry or long passages from Shakespeare's plays by going through them only two or three times. It was absolutely amazing. He came from a family of *barats*, who traditionally recite epics or other lore to audiences without ever referring to the text. Mundiar's prodigious memory was no doubt the result of his genes. The essays Kesri wrote got him high marks. Our teachers used to say that there was no better test of a boy's intellectual fibre than the clarity of his writing. After college he went back to Mundiar and in 1962 was elected to the Rajasthan assembly.

Kesri wrote the best book I know on the famous battle of

Haldighati, fought on the morning of 18 June 1576 between the army of the great Akbar, commanded by his foremost military commander, Prince Man Singh of Jaipur, and Maharana Pratap of Mewar. The description of the fighting is detailed and vivid and Kesri shows that it was a sally from mountainous terrain by Pratap to give a bloody nose to the much larger Delhi–Jaipur forces and to kill Man Singh, whom he considered a traitor. The Maharana's charge on Man Singh's elephant failed and he lost his beloved mount Chetak, but he did, however, manage to spread panic in the imperial army's ranks and successfully retreat into the narrow defile of Haldighati to defy Akbar for another two decades. Al Badayuni, the Mogul chronicler who had seen the battle from close quarters, says that when he asked Commander Asaf Khan Mirbakshi: 'how are we to distinguish between friendly and hostile rajputs?' the reply he got was: 'whichever side they may belong, their being killed will be a gain for Islam.'

There was a good-looking temple with a covered pillared terrace for Hindu boys, which we all attended for prayers once a day. On Sunday mornings the college *shastri* would speak to us on some spiritual subject for about half an hour. Among the Rajputs the worship of Durga, the deity of the warriors was popular. In my boarding house, the Jodhpur House, on Ram Navmi day the senior boy was expected to slice off the head of a goat with a bold stroke of the sword and offer it to the deity; the boys who had gathered for the ceremony would mark their foreheads with a spot of the sacrificial blood. Since *sanatan dharma* is pluralistic, namely it incorporates different beliefs and worships without necessitating the selection or elimination of any, it was relatively easy for Hindu boys to be doctrinally tolerant of whatever form of worship, practice or non-practice, within or outside the *dharma*, suited them best. For example, for me, the *shivalinga* (a ribbed stone) in the ninth-century

Shiva temple in Sarila, has little to do with the Supreme Being but serves to remind me of our home, Sarila, the history of our family, which went there in 1755 to defend that part of India, and indeed to reinforce patriotism.

The Muslim boys had a mosque. I never saw any one of them praying five times in the school premises. Not one Muslim Mayo old boy, including the Arab Fahr bin Taimur of Oman, is known to have turned into a fanatic. The tolerant and pluralist ethos had had its effect on the Muslim boys too.

In 1945 the winds of change started to swirl around even our conservative citadel. The new principal, M. A. McCanlis (who had once captained Oxford in cricket) invited Jawaharlal Nehru, then recently released from his long incarceration in British prisons and touring the region, to speak to the senior boys. This was the first glimpse I got of our future prime minister. He was dressed in a grey short *kurta* and knickers, as worn by prisoners. He looked very relaxed, no doubt enjoying the order and elegance of his surroundings, which were so different from his habitual noisy undisciplined political meetings. Mayo probably took him back to his Harrow days. In any case, he spoke to us as he would to Harrow boys, addressing us as 'gentlemen'. Later in his remarks he gave a definition of one, which has stuck in my memory: 'A gentleman is one who gives more to society than he receives from it,' he said. He also said that whenever he came to Rajasthan he felt suffocated by the sight of huts alongside palace walls. These words of his came to mind when even worse shantytowns sprang up in Delhi during his prime ministership, especially given that some of these were next to the prime minister's residence.

In retrospect, I feel that the Mayo College was defective in some respects. Its atmosphere was too inbred and it cut the boys off from the new emerging classes. Because most of the boys did not have to exert themselves to make ends meet after they left school, they did not work hard enough on their studies. There was little inclination to compete aggressively with each other in the academic field; the desire to dazzle was reserved for the playing field. Some of the degradation affecting nobles in those days seeped into the school. Mayo did not concentrate on the sciences at that time. On the other hand, the school did teach moderation, tolerance, discipline, team spirit and the value of physical fitness. It made boys into jacks of all trades and gave them a worldview that was sorely lacking among Indians. Also, we developed pride in our Indian heritage while imbibing the many good aspects of Western *savoir-faire* and culture. The splendid buildings and grounds left a lasting beneficial impression, for handsome is that handsome does.

The boys emerging from these chiefs' colleges could not change the course of Indian history, as Britain had hoped they might. The princely states that the old boys of these schools ruled went under in the 1940s, but largely because of the education they had received at these schools, these old boys did not go under individually. In the tolerant ethos that is a feature of our country, this group gradually emerged to serve the republic as legislators, cabinet ministers, military commanders, civil servants, diplomats and businessmen. In the 1950s Mayo and the other chiefs' colleges became public schools, or more accurately private schools that anyone who could afford to pay the fees could enter. Mayo is popular today because, among other things, people are enamoured of its aristocratic traditions, which, to an extent, linger on.

Chapter 10
The Dussehra Durbar

THE ORIGINS of Dussehra are obscure, but, as Tulsidas described in the epic Ramayana, many people relate it to the victory of Rama, the heir apparent of the kingdom of Ayodhya in the Ganges Valley, over Ravana, the king of Lanka, around 1500 BC.

During this festival the people in our region burn huge effigies of Ravana and of his sister, Sarupnakha, who played a villainous role in abducting Rama's bride Sita, which was what provoked the war. It is a time for holidays, fairs, operas and merry making for young and old alike. The most notorious Dussehra festival in India was held in the princely state of Mysore in South India, the centrepiece of which was the parade of hundreds of the maharaja's decorated and caparisoned elephants and the fireworks thereafter. This attracted tourists from far off places.

The forests of Mysore contained hordes of elephants and, each year on a designated day, beats were organized with the help of domesticated elephants to drive as large a number of them as possible into a stockade (so that they could be domesticated). This operation was called a 'kheda'. It was attended by the maharaja and his guests, who sat on wooden stands erected around the arena. It was a major annual event for princely India.

Dussehra falls after the monsoon. In the olden days this was a convenient moment to take stock of arms and men before the cool dry season, the most appropriate time for campaigning in India. It also gave dignitaries an opportunity to pay homage to their chiefs at a ceremonial *durbar* and for the chiefs in turn to pay homage and offer sacrifices to the god and goddess of war. With the establishment of British hegemony the princes' days of campaigning ended, but Dussehra, the Kshatriyas' most important festival, continued to be celebrated in all Hindu princely states.

The ceremonies in Sarila started a day before Dussehra with a *puja* (worship) to the goddess in the town's conical-roofed Bhawani temple. Her benediction was sought by performing a sacrifice. Originally, a buffalo was slain, but my father modified the proceedings by introducing the slaying of a goat instead. Once I became old enough, the ritual goat-slaying became my duty and I used to be in a constant panic in case I either brought down the sword too hard, so that after beheading the animal I hit the stone floor and damaged the blade, quite apart from making an ugly clang, or used too feeble a stroke thereby failing to sever the head and bringing ignominy. Finally, I learnt how to do it. The art is to pull the sword inwards at the point of contact with the goat's neck, thus letting the slide accomplish the task. I used to thank the *devi* (goddess) that the days of buffalo-slaying were over.

Then came the rite of the veneration of arms when, after my father's charger had been anointed, turmeric and flowers would be thrown in the direction of the other horses ranged in a line along with our guns, swords, spears, daggers and artillery pieces. During the procession or parade, which took place in the evening, my father and I would ride on an elephant, followed by horses and attendants on foot.

Behind us on the elephant stood attendants holding a red and gold velvet canopy and waving a mace and silver cone with a white yak's tail falling from it – the erstwhile symbols of sovereignty. The umbrella-like royal canopy held over the monarch represented the vault of the sky with direct access to God. Royal heralds holding silver tipped staffs and wearing long white robes and red turbans marched ahead of the elephant. The elephant's head was decorated with paint and placed on its back was a velvet and gold embroidered caparison on which the *ganga-jamuni* howdah (seat) was tied. *Ganga-jamuni* is the name given to the blending together in handicrafts of gold and silver, a name inspired by the confluence of the waters of the two famous rivers, Ganga and Jamuna, in Prayag (Allahabad) in the northern plains. People packed the streets, the women on balconies, to cheer and see their ruler pass.

We dressed in white muslin *angarkhas*, long flared coats, white breeches and a turban, invariably consisting of 12 metres of slightly starched muslin wound round the head in different ways in different parts of India. The Rajputs' ceremonial turban is traditionally in bright colours with dazzling designs and cockily tied, one end left sticking up as a plume, the other forming a two-foot long flowing tail. A servant used to tie my turban in those days but after I went to school, where it was part of the daily school dress, I learnt to do it blindfolded.

A turban is described in a book by Patnaik as an all-purpose garment. It protects the traveller from the scorching sun in the summer; by drawing the floating end across the face and nose, one can keep out the dust and sand (of which there is plenty of both in India); the thirsty traveller can use it as a rope to draw water from a well; and at night it becomes an agreeable pillow. In an assault, the turban cushions the head and in case of injury strips from it can be used to bind the wound. The floating end serves another purpose – that of a disguise: if by chance you are caught *in flagrante delicto*, drawing it across the face helps to cover one's shame, as various Indian miniatures of lovemaking scenes so vividly illustrate. Also, in defeat, it can save one's head because laying it before the victor is an acknowledgement of one's defeat and a plea for clemency.

The *durbar* ceremony took place in the evening under a *shamiyana* that was the size of a tennis court and supported by gilded poles. A snow white cotton cloth was spread over the cotton dhurries on the floor. A seat made up of large cushions covered with red velvet was placed at one end of the rectangular sitting area. It has been said that a simple cushion is the traditional throne of an Indian monarch, rather than the more elaborate throne that is popular in other countries. Electric bulbs suspended from the ceiling of the *shamiyana* provided the illumination. *Shamiyana*s are traditionally used in India for large assemblies that cannot be accommodated indoors.

The descendants of all the Bundela warriors who had helped Aman Singh found the state in 1755 and had been given land (for which they paid no taxes) were ranked the highest in the *durbar*. I was taught to address all those knights who were older than me, however humble they might be, as *Dau* or elder brother. It was also customary to grant lands to certain Brahmin families. The Brahmins either helped us perform religious rites on appropriate occasions or were assigned to temples where they conducted religious ceremonies on behalf of the state or the public. They recited the verses of the Vedas parrot-like at rituals. I doubted, however, that they exercised any influence on the spiritual development of the devotees. The Brahmins were seated with the elite in Sarila. Into this circle were also incorporated the more reputed and wealthier businessmen. These three estates, and the state officials (some senior ones among them recruited from outside the state), formed the *durbar*, namely the consultative court or assembly.

The invitees, dressed in white with coloured turbans and some carrying swords, sat two or three deep on the floor on both sides of the throne facing each other. The knights sat on the right-hand side and the Brahmins and senior officials on the left. The royal herald would announce my father's arrival by thumping his silver-headed staff on the ground and in a loud voice recite the various attributes of a good ruler – protector of the people, provider of food, dispenser of justice, and gentle and moderate in manner. These words were flattering in one sense but they were also a reminder of what qualities were expected of him. The assembly rose as he entered and saluted him by bending and swinging their hands forward to touch their heads.

A smaller throne would be placed on his right for me, as heir apparent. For the occasion my mother would place a necklace of precious stones around my neck and a *serpetch*, a crown-like ornament also of precious stones, on my turban. A sash was tied to my waist as a mark of dignity. On all formal occasions I carried a sword with a silk handkerchief tied to its bejewelled handle. To complete the outfit my mother put a tiny black new-moon-shaped mark on the side of my forehead, to blemish my looks and deflect the evil eye. My father, as far as I recall, wore no jewellery. Correctly, the warrior clans had to dress simply and remain unornamented in accordance with their spartan ethos. Princes came to wear jewellery to draw attention to their wealth and power, but many princes in my youth did not wear jewellery. Was not carrying a sword studded with jewels a bit like carrying a gem-encrusted AK 47 rifle today?

The ceremony would open with the assembled guests coming up to the throne one by one to pay homage to the ruler. This they did by placing a silver or gold coin on a handkerchief on the upturned palm of my father's right hand, with the left palm supporting the right from underneath. The offering was only a symbolic gesture. After my father had touched it, the courtier would withdraw the offering, take out a rupee, hold it over my father's head and throw it down on the floor in a gesture that symbolized his willingness to sacrifice everything for the ruler. He would then retrace his steps, marching backwards, and the next person would rise and come up as soon as the earlier one had retreated. The Brahmins did not make offerings but anointed my father instead. The servants of the barber caste would collect the money that had been thrown on the floor.

The audience would greet my father's short statement wishing the assembly and people of Sarila good cheer by rising to their feet and saluting him. For the *attar-paan* ceremony, which then followed, the assembled guests would once again troop up to the throne to receive *paan* leaf and be anointed with the Indian perfume *attar* in a thanks-giving gesture by the ruler. Those not participating in the ceremony collected outside the *shamiyana* to watch the proceedings.

Finally, the assembly would be entertained with a dance, colloquially referred to as a *nautch*. The proper Indian word for dance is *kathak*, which comes from the Sanskrit word *katha* (story), the *kathak* being the storyteller. Since time immemorial dance in India has been used to tell a tale. *Katha* necessitated the development of a complex vocabulary of mime, gestures and movements of the feet. The aim of *kathak* is to induce in the audience the desired emotional mood and sentiment, the *rasa*. The epic Mahabharata contains the earliest literary reference to *kathak*.

Sarila is situated at the southern edge of the Indo–Gangetic plains, alongside Oudh, a former Mogul province that became more or less independent when Delhi's authority shrank and which Nawab Wajid Ali Shah had ruled in the nineteenth century. He was a great patron of dance and *kathak* was introduced into active urban life once it had started to become known through its appearance on temple walls. When Islamic invaders destroyed most Hindu places of worship in the Indo–Gangetic plains, many of the dancers dispersed to seek the patronage of rajas and nawabs. Then, as the British armies advanced from the coast and the princes' position became more hopeless, dancers in courts provided a sort of escape from the realities of the developing situation. In fact, the British noted with glee that dance had supplanted serious business in the assemblies of the principalities upon which they were about to pounce. Once the British established their paramountcy over the princes, the *durbars* become purely ceremonial, with no serious business of state being transacted and some entertainment helping to breathe life into these ritualistic proceedings.

The Oudhi dance renaissance influenced dance in our area. One of the most enthralling dances to develop in the court of Oudh was a sort of tap dance, with jingling ankle bells rather than tap shoes providing the beat. A dancer usually wore between 100 and 200 such bells, or *ghungroos* as they were called, tied onto a long blue string wound around each ankle. The artiste's make-up was accentuated by painting the lips, putting *kajal* (mascara) round the eyes to magnify the dancer's every glance and decorating the hands and feet with *alta,* a red washable fluid, to highlight the *mudras*, or gestures used in the dance. In the Oudhi tradition, *kathak* dancers wore gypsy-like white skirts embroidered with gold borders, brocade bodices and pastel coloured veils on their shoulders, appropriate jewellery and a brocade velvet cap.

The dance would begin languidly, with some darting movement of the hands and head and an occasional whirl while the crescendo of the feet built up. As the frenzy mounted, the sounds of the 200 bells on the dancer's anklets would descend to the clear echo of a single bell, the body above the hips becoming as still as a statue, only the breasts slightly quivering. Arms akimbo the dancer would then survey the audience and brag with her flashing eyes. Occasionally, she would let herself go and spin like a top, her skirt flying high to reveal pajama-clad legs with the crotch buried in folds, which was even sexier than the bare thighs revealed in a Western whirl.

Dussehra is a festival devoted to honouring martial valour and the *nautch* in it symbolized the altered state of affairs. My father did not stay too long with the merriment, but the dance continued when I left with my father and joined my mother and the ladies on the terrace to watch the proceedings for a while longer. I could see from my perch that the courtiers, more relaxed in the absence of their chief, began to eye the dancers more appraisingly, some throwing coins at their feet in appreciation. The music lovers alone stayed as the others gradually drifted away.

The Dussehra festivities in India date back to before elephant parades and *nautch*es in *durbar*s, and they have survived the disappearance of the princely courts. Rama of Ayodhya remains a sacred symbol of righteousness and valour; and the people now have more money with which to organize the celebration of his triumph without the need for official patronage.

Chapter 11
The Princely States of Rajputana

A S I STATED earlier, my school was in Rajputana, a land of princes and their feudal lords, which had a very special flavour, albeit it one that has largely disappeared since the end of princely rule. The Aravalli Hills run north to south in Rajputana. The Thar or Great Indian Desert lies to their west and flatter forested country to their east. This was the impenetrable outback of India to which the various Kshatriya clans – the Rathors, Kachhwahas, Chauhans and others fled after the rich Indo–Gangetic plains they ruled came under the sway of Turkish invaders in the eleventh and twelfth centuries. Only the Sisodhya clan of Mewar (Udaipur), in the south, had been there all along. From the beginning these kingdoms were organized as feudal military states, the feudal lords supplying the foot soldiers and cavalry to the prince, in return for grants of land.

Each state capital had a distinctive character but all the orderly planning of thoroughfares, parks and some fine buildings in local architecture, in which the firm hand of the autocrat was visible, had some features in common, namely tanks that doubled as water reservoirs in this dry region; ancient forts and battlements, mute sentinels of past battles; as well as new palaces and parks. Camel carts, horsemen and an occasional elephant could be seen plodding their roads. With the density of population low, traffic scarce and even poor people's houses generally built of stone blocks with stone-chip roofs, one did not get the same sense of over-crowding, chaos and poverty that one gets today, even though people were poorer then and the middle class was practically non-existent. The mere sight of the multi-coloured turbans that all the men wore over their white shirts and dhotis, the women's gypsy-like bright patterned skirts and upper garments, the murals on the walls of many houses and the *havelis* (town houses of feudal lords and merchants) dotted around the old parts of town, were enough to lift anyone's spirits.

The princes of Rajputana had not crossed swords with the British, who had mostly battled with the semi-independent governors of Turkish, Afghan and Mogul descent of the tottering Mogul Empire, and the Indian Maratha warriors who had advanced from the western coast in the eighteenth century to fill the political vacuum left by the Mogul collapse. Nor were they involved in the revolt of 1857 against the British, rather serving as a bulwark against the tide. Rajputana's hilly and under-populated territories were not commercially attractive enough to interest the East India Company. The writings of Colonel Todd, the British agent, had built up an extraordinarily romantic image of the Rajputs, depicting them as a race apart and not unlike the knights of medieval Europe. The British were content to forge alliances with them, place political agents and spies in their midst and leave their kingdoms alone.

Indian languages have two words for 'you' – one for people who are senior and higher in society and the other for those below. In Rajputana the better placed addressed most people with the more deferential word and were answered in return with courtliness. This reminded the visitor of Rajputana's continuing feudal ethos. The maharaja made tax free grants of land to barons called Jagirdars, on condition they provided three horsemen and three foot soldiers for every Rs 1000 (the equivalent today of Rs 50,000 or $1000) of the revenue they derived from such land annually, and attended the ruler's court for some months. In Udaipur state, for example, 50 per cent of the land was in *jagirs* or fiefdoms of the barons, the chief directly exploited 25 per cent and the remaining 25 per cent was reserved for charitable purposes. Thus, on average, the prince received about a quarter of the land revenue from his dominion for running the civil administration and his personal expenses. The amount of rent on land varied from a quarter to half the yield and was payable either in cash or in kind, with the Brahmin and Rajput cultivators paying less.

The nobles or barons, also called sardars, were therefore powerful entities and were divided into three categories. To give expression to these different statuses the chief would rise to receive the highest grade. The sardar would then place his sword in front of him, bow and touch the hem of the chief's garment, with the chief acknowledging the salutation by placing his hand on the noble's shoulder and then drawing it back to his chest. The form was the same as above for the second grade except that after touching the sardar's shoulder the chief would not draw his hand to touch his chest. For the third grade the chief would merely rise.

During the holidays I visited many of my schoolmates' homes, which were mostly forts. In fact, there were several forts near Ajmer town in the area surrounding the school. When there were heavy floods in 1942 the senior boys were sent out to the countryside to supervise the distribution of government relief. Each evening after the exertions of the day we could go to the fortress of a local *thakur* or baron, invariably an old Mayo boy, to rest for the night. These forts, situated on heights with commanding views, were comfortable and tastefully furnished. At dinner, musicians the lords maintained, would sing *thumries* (light classical music), or typically Rajasthani tunes like the haunting *mand*, or play ragas on sitars or sarangis, with the sound of the flute floating in from a distant tower.

Each fort produced its own variety of fiery liquor called *arak*, distilled from fruits or flowers with rose, orange or saffron flavours. This, of course, the boys were not allowed to touch; nor were they allowed to eye too closely the *kumaris*, the young girls of the *thakur*'s household who flit sylph-like in chiffon saris behind trellised screens – though the *thakur* might eye prospective matches for them from among the Mayo boys. On the other hand, because of the rocky soil, agriculture was poor and the only industry consisted of weaving dhurries and cloth in bright colours. Even so, the men and women held their heads high.

With its sheer drops, Bhinai fort near Ajmer appeared impregnable. The Thakur of Bhinai told us how his forefathers had captured it from the Bhil tribesmen, whose stronghold it had been. Failing to starve out the Bhils, a huge cauldron filled with brimming liquor was placed within sight of the defenders and, after a mock drinking party, the attackers withdrew behind rocks. The Bhils, unable to resist the temptation, soon came out to drink the brew and were slain. It is said that half the foot soldiers and archers of the Rajput army that faced Akbar in the battle of Haldighati in 1664 had been Bhils.

Jodhpur, the capital of the Rathor clan, was situated in the desert. The massive Mehrangarh Fort, which towered over the town on a 200-metre sheer rock cliff with menacing ramparts, was begun in 1245, 'Only giants could have built it' wrote Rudyard Kipling. The view of the city from the Mehrangarh is extraordinary. A tinge of indigo is invariably added to the white lime coat on houses in Jodhpur. There are no tall buildings and

22. Mehrangarh Fort, Jodhpur. 'Only giants could have built it' (Kipling).

the squarish flat roofed dwellings on undulating surfaces are each in a slightly different shade of light blue, with paler roofs. The view from the fort recalls the chunky brushwork of a Cézanne and one can only imagine how the city might look when bathed in the light of a full desert moon.

Jodhpur, the biggest state of Rajputana, had the most powerful feudal lords who had forts in the desert and handsome mansions surrounded by parks in the capital city. The Umaid Bhawan Palace, situated on a rise and visible from all parts of the town, had then just been completed. Its art deco interior and furniture in honey and brown were quite striking – though the exterior in sandstone, a squarish building with a central dome and four short minarettes at each corner – looked like a half-hearted *taj*.

The Jodhpur Rathor is a bold horseman who in the afternoons could be seen performing on Jodhpur's two grass polo grounds on either side of a rocky rise that resounded with the loud calls of players, the thunder of the hoofs of horses and the sharp clicks of mallets on balls. Their ladies, posed very much like the señoras one saw at *corridas* in Andalusia half a century ago, would watch them from the upper reaches of a pavilion. A mixed Jaipur–Jodhpur polo team, captained by Maharaja Mann Singh of Jaipur at that time, had three nine and eight handicap players in it and was a world-class championship team.

Hanumant Singh, the heir of Jodhpur, who was a few years senior to me at school, was a fat, rambunctious boy whom the sons of the nobles of Jodhpur at Mayo treated like a demigod. He made waves as soon as he succeeded his father, Maharaja Umaid Singh, shortly before the British departure. I shall relate in the appropriate chapter how he scared Nehru and Patel out of their wits by entering into negotiations with Mr Jinnah to join Pakistan. He also surprised Mountbatten when, during the negotiations for Jodhpur's accession to India in the governor general's house in August 1947, he whipped out a revolver concealed in a pen and threatened to shoot V. P. Menon, the Secretary of the Ministry of States, if, after having signed the Instrument of Accession, Delhi failed to provide wheat to the famine stricken people of Jodhpur.

Once he lost his kingdom in 1948 Hanumant Singh, now hellbent on proving his popularity in a democratic election, threw down the gauntlet before his 'chief enemy', the Congress Party leader of Jodhpur, Jai Narayan Vyas. In the first election held for the assembly of the new Rajasthan state into which Jodhpur had been merged in 1952, his nominees won 25 of the 33 seats he contested against the Congress Party and J. N. Vyas lost his deposit. Unfortunately, before he could hear the news of his dazzling victory, Hanumant Singh was killed in a plane crash that very day. Today, his son, Gaj Singh, is one of the most respected ex-rulers of Rajasthan.

Jaipur was the second largest state of Rajputana. During my time in Mayo, its nine-handicap polo-playing maharaja, Mann Singh, was in his thirties. He was a dashing figure who had just married – his third marriage – Ayesha of Cooch-Behar, one of the most beautiful women in India and the princess of a state in eastern India. On his visits to the Mayo College, his style was to land his self-piloted biplane on the college polo ground. The maharaja and maharani were at the centre of a dizzying social whirl in their capital, which included foreign royalty. Tiger hunts during the day at nearby Ranthambhore forest would help raise the guests' adrenalin for the festivities at night.

They had wide contacts in Europe and America and were close to the British royal family, near whose Windsor Castle they had a country estate. In 1948 after the princes of Rajputana gave up their powers and merged their territories into the new state of Rajasthan, Mann Singh was chosen to be the new state's *rajpramukh* or constitutional governor. Later, in the 1960s, Prime Minister Indira Gandhi appointed him as the first Indian ambassador to Spain. To me, who followed him in this post a few years later, it was obvious that he had succeeded in arousing in General Francisco Franco, the fountainhead of all power in Spain at that time, an interest in India, about which Franco knew next to nothing. It was a help that he used to invite Franco's only daughter, Villaverde, to shoot tigers in Jaipur.

In the late 1960s Maharani Ayesha joined the Swatantra, a newly founded conservative party for which Indira Gandhi felt deep distrust. When Ayesha swept the polls in her former territories with the highest majority in any democratic election in the world (157,692 votes from a total of 190,909, making it into the *Guinness Book of Records*) and some other princes who had followed her into the opposition also won convincingly in their former domains, the prime minister became alarmed. Whether this had anything to do with the registration of a case against the Maharani for possessing undeclared gold and for which she was briefly imprisoned, I do not know. Nor do I know to what extent Indira Gandhi's dislike of Ayesha influenced her decision to deprive the princes of their permanently guaranteed stipends and privileges, though leaving their private properties untouched.

Indira Gandhi did this in 1971 by using the two-thirds majority the Congress Party had won in the general election just before the Bangladesh war (a khaki election) to amend an article in the constitution protecting the princes' stipends and privileges. Once she had helped East Pakistan break away from Pakistan – the first decisive victory of Indian arms in a thousand years – Indira Gandhi's popularity in the country soared to such a peak that no one questioned this funky act. On a visit to Mountbatten at his home, Broadlands, soon afterwards, the former viceroy showed me a letter from Indira Gandhi that contained an oblique suggestion that he explain her action suitably to his niece, the Queen. Mountbatten said, 'So, Indira did develop some qualms. It was naughty of her to break her father's promise given to me to uphold the princes' privileges if they delivered their territories to him.'

Bhawani Singh, or Bubbles, the present Maharaja of Jaipur, was a child when I was in Ajmer. In 1971, at the time of the war with Pakistan, he was a lieutenant-colonel in the parachute regiment of the Indian Army and won the Maha Vir Chakra (MVC, the equivalent of the British Military Cross). For four days he led his commandos across the Rajasthan desert border and deep into enemy territory, thereby facilitating the capture of a large number of Pakistani soldiers as well as territory. In the citation accompanying the presentation of his MVC, there was mention of 'his personal courage, exceptional leadership and devotion to duty' in this operation. There were two maharajas in that war; the other was the Sikh prince, Sukhjit

Singh of Kapurthala, who was also awarded an MVC for his exemplary leadership and courage. He had been commanding an armoured regiment on the Western Front when Pakistani armour attacked it in strength. His battalion repulsed the attack and then, with him standing with the dupola of his tank open and exposed to fire, he guided a flanking movement that closed in with the enemy and succeeded in destroying eight tanks and capturing several Pakistani officers and other ranks.

When I first set eyes on Jaipur city in the late 1930s it still retained its original architectural purity. Maharaja Jaswant Singh built it in 1728 in a wide valley near the Kachhwaha clan's earlier capital of Amber. The geometrical pattern of its layout, enclosed by walls and gate towers, was like the now destroyed old city of Peking. Though there was no Forbidden City there was the walled compound of the city palace with massive stone gates leading from one flagged courtyard to the next until one reached the prince's residence, behind which stretched a park up to the city walls and the Aravalli hills beyond. In the days before today's traffic congestion, neon lights and billboards, it was a magical experience to drive in the moonlight through Jaipur's broad streets flanked by pink stone double-storey buildings, all of identical design.

The imposing Maharaja Ganga Singh of Bikaner (who died in 1942) was the most distinguished ruler of Rajputana at the time. The British appointed him as a delegate to the Versailles Conference in 1919 and, through the 1920s and early 1930s, he canvassed for the princes to play a more active role in India's constitutional development, as described in an earlier chapter. On one occasion we were taken to see his most outstanding achievement; this was the Ganga canal, which brought water from the rivers of the Punjab in British India to make a portion of his desert kingdom bloom.

The rare bustard was found in the desert around Bikaner.

We heard in school how the maharaja shot these large birds while at the wheel of his convertible Rolls. (There were no jeeps then.) As soon as a bustard was sighted, he would turn the car in its direction and approach it as noiselessly as possible. When the bird took wing – bustards fly slowly – he raced towards it, taking ditches, sand embankments between fields and minor irregularities on the ground in his stride. As he got near enough to fire, an attendant sitting in the back seat would hand over a gun to him and he would let go of the steering wheel as he aimed, with the car tossing and turning until the bird came down. Bikaner was as famous for its sandgrouse shoots as Ganga Singh was for the care he took of his guests. The memoranda he gave them setting out the agenda to the last possible detail ran into scores of pages.

My classmate Maharana Bhagwat Singh of Mewar (Udaipur) belonged to the most highly respected clan among the Rajputs, the Sisodhyas. They had produced such heroes as Rana Sanga who faced Babar in 1526 and Rana Pratap who defied the great Akbar later in the same century, preferring exile to sub-mission.* Even during the period of British overlordship they maintained a certain reserve by not coming to the capital and avoiding the British lord's Delhi *durbars*.

We used to tease Bhagwat Singh at school for placing earth and tufts of grass under his mattress – a symbolic gesture that was supposed to suggest that they were still campaigning and resisting Delhi. Jawaharlal Nehru did not, however, see this as a foible. After he became prime minister of independent India, he travelled to Udaipur and escorted Bhagwat Singh to the capital to proclaim that the campaigning was over. The maharana later joined the Congress Party.

---

* Some members of the Sisodhiya clan during their exile reached Nepal and sought service in the Nepal army. In the mid-nineteenth century they took over the government of Nepal through a coup, making the king a mere figurehead. They ruled Nepal until the middle of the twentieth century.

Queen Elizabeth II paid a visit to Udaipur in Bhagwat Singh's time and, according to Brian Masters, when he asked the Queen to proceed ahead at a function, she demurred, saying: 'Please lead the way. You come from a much older family that I do.'

Having heard my mother's stories about it, I was keen to see Chitorgarh, the old Sisodhya stronghold. Here the rite of *Jauhar* (described in Chapter 3) had been performed on three different occasions by the besieged defenders; in 1403 to defy the Sultan of Delhi, Alauddin Khilji, in 1535 against the Sultan of Gujrat and in 1567 against the great Akbar, during which thousands of warriors and their consorts perished.

Udaipur, the post-Chitor Sisodhya capital, nestles in hills surrounded by lakes. The walls of its main palace, as Andrew Robinson described them in his book *Maharajas*, 'are tremendously long, sheer and undecorated, rising straight out of the waters of the [Pichola] lake'. From its lofty marble terraces the views are spectacular. Across the wide waters, beyond the boat-like pleasure palace in the middle (today the Lake Palace Hotel), one could in those days watch wild animals come down from the forested hills to slake their thirst on the opposite bank at sundown. Below the palace on the other side of the lake lay the city, its bazaars chock-a-block with *havelis* with oversized entrances. Many Mewaris still then wore long close-fitting coats with Mewari *pugrees*, a beret like headdress of varied colours, their moustaches and whiskers flowing, the gentry carrying swords or cutlasses strapped to their waists, as if ready for campaign.

Havelis, or courtyard houses, are a feature of India and particularly of Rajputana. In 1943 a school friend of mine invited me for a weekend to his *haveli* in Udaipur. It was situated in the old congested part of the city, below the old palace. We alighted from the car before a high gate with metal studded doors shaded by a longish stone balcony above. Entry to the house was through a right-angled passage to prevent a direct view of the interior from the street. The passage led to the main courtyard, about ten by ten metres. On its three sides were verandas with cusped arches, above which rose double-storeyed buildings with windows and balconies and drooping eaves. A neem tree grew in the courtyard, its bunchy dark-green leaves and dark bark contrasting with the white plastered walls. Neems are planted in courtyards or near houses because they purify the air.

Behind the verandas on either side were long rooms with rafted ceilings: on one side there was a European style drawing room and on the other an office in which scribes sat on dhurries writing on low, sloping desks. The drawing room, used for receiving guests, had Victorian sofas and chairs, hunting trophies and portraits of my friend's ancestors wearing Udaipur *pugrees*. The far side wall of the courtyard had a door that led to an inner courtyard. Although we were in the middle of a crowded city, it was peaceful and quiet in the house. It was also fresher than elsewhere in the city because as the hot air rises in a courtyard house, the cooler air sucked in from above then circulates in the verandas and adjoining rooms.

My host's father, a tall elderly gentleman with a white upturned moustache, soon joined us. He wore a khaki closed-collar tunic with military like flap pockets and khaki breeches. He had not been out riding or hunting as one might imagine from his habit; this was his habitual daytime dress. He told me that the house had been built around three courtyards; the innermost courtyard was for the ladies and the outermost for the servants. He said courtyards had to be narrow enough to leave an area for year round shade and wide enough to receive the winter sun. If you wanted more floors, you had a larger courtyard.

I was given a corner room on the second floor. It had a *jharoka* (balcony) that protruded over the street with a finely worked stone screen that acted like a one-way mirror. From there I could watch the hustle and bustle of the street below yet remain invisible. If I remember correctly, the room was square and domed, with no curtains, but doors fitted with coloured glass – deep green, yellow, blue and red. On the cement floor was a beautiful square dhurrie with a red and gold border and a luminous light green interior, the like of which I had never seen before. I later learnt that it was a piece that had been woven for the temple in the village of Nathdwara in Jodhpur state, and that it was rather rare. There was an adequate cement-floored bathroom attached, but only shelves and wooden pegs for one's clothes.

My friend took me to the inner courtyard for the midday meal, where there was more ornamentation on the walls and windows than in the outer one. I particularly remember a dancing peacock motif repeated on many wooden doors. And there was the inevitable white carved pedestal with a *tulsi* plant growing out of it. Whatever its spiritual qualities, chewing a few leaves of *tulsi* each day is said to keep cancer away.

In the dining room I met my friend's mother, a stout lady dressed in a long full skirt with a short chiffon scarf draped over the bodice. The traditional Rajasthani dress is not unlike what gypsies wear. She appeared meek and deferential but I was told that she ran the household with an iron fist. The entire family joined us for lunch – a dozen people. These were my friend's two elder brothers with their wives, his sisters and one or two aunts, all of whom lived in the same house. Each couple or single person had separate rooms in which to dress and rest but no individual rooms in which to sit and eat.

We sat cross-legged on low, flat wooden platforms and the food was placed on slightly higher wooden tables. In this part of the house, the lifestyle was totally Rajasthani or traditional. The sitting room had carpets to sit upon and bolsters against which to rest one's back. There was a minimum amount of furniture. As in the traditional part of our palace in Sarila, few areas of this *haveli* were rigidly defined. One sat, ate, slept and worked where it was coolest or warmest according to the season. This included the flat terrace at the top of the house, which was an ideal place to sleep in the summer months and to have massages under the sun in the winter. Sitting places could be converted into sleeping quarters within minutes by placing mattresses on the floors and there were enough maids and men servants to accomplish such tasks.

In the evening we joined my host's father and some of his friends on the terrace of the *haveli*. From our perch we could get a glimpse of Lake Pichola turning melon pink with the glow of the setting sun. They were drinking *arak* that had been manufactured in the *thakur*'s desert fortress 70 or 80 miles away. It had a saffron base and was said to be very potent. The guests were *thakurs* from other feudal estates in Udaipur, but there was a merchant there too, who did not drink and was conspicuous in his different dress – white *dhoti*, long brown coat and a black boat-like cap. The different states of Rajputana have distinctive colours: Jodhpur, blue; Jaipur, pink and Jaisalmer, honey; Udaipur's colour is white, supposedly to signify the purity of the Mewar rulers for never having offered their princesses in marriage to the Delhi sultans.

My friend's older brothers would periodically get up and disappear for a few minutes. This was to take a few puffs on their cigarettes because it was considered impolite to smoke or drink in front of one's elders. When any of them left they would touch their father's feet to say goodnight if they were not going to be seeing him until the next day. We, the younger lot, soon took our leave to go to the club for a game of squash and then on to dine at another *haveli*.

Bharatpur, a state ruled by a Jat prince, had then perhaps the finest duck shoot anywhere. Jat tribes inhabited the area west of Agra right up to Lahore further north. Many Jat farmers and warriors had accepted the Sikh gospel, though not the Maharaja of Bharatpur, whose kingdom was close to the old Mogul capital of Agra. The Jats repeatedly looted Agra in the eighteenth century when Mogul power was declining and Maharaja Surajmal even went so far as to dig up Akbar's grave. These forays gave them the wherewithal to build palaces like the beautiful one at Dig, which, with its latticed façade and surrounded by ornamental pools and water fountains, appears to float on water.

The duck shoots date from 1890 when a lake was created for the purpose out of marshlands on the periphery of the capital. The annual Bharatpur duck shoot, with the Viceroy as the main guest, was a feature of princely India. Between 1907 and 1946 there were nineteen shoots in each of which more than 2000 birds were shot in a day and five in which the bag numbered more than 3000. In 1938, while I was at the Mayo College, 4217 birds were bagged by 50 guns in a single day's shoot, which the Maharaja had organized for Lord Linlithgow. Today, the lake is a famous bird sanctuary in which some 130 species can be found, many of which fly in from Siberia for the winter.

The then frolicsome Bharatpur prince once invited senior Mayo boys to celebrate Holi, the spring festival, with him. On alighting from our bus we were ushered into an open-air *durbar* (or rather ceremonial gathering) where we found the Maharaja sitting on a dais with his nobles and officials seated either side of him. Just behind the dais there was an antiquated fire engine with hand pumps and two large barrels filled with red coloured water. Whenever His Highness wished to show special favour to anyone he would direct the nozzle of the fire engine in his direction. Fortunately, no special favour was shown to the Mayo boys. Later we moved to the nearby palace garden and the delights of a large square pool coated with slippery clay, which made it difficult to get out if you slipped or were thrown in. Merriment was provided to onlookers as their friends clawed, wriggled and slithered in the mud as they tried to get out. In the meanwhile, *sharbats* and sweets laced with *bhang* (Indian hemp) were being passed round. We heard that a similar ceremony was taking place in the *zenana* (women's) garden, but had no way of watching the slithering and panting going on there.

In his *Annals of Rajputana*, Colonel Todd describes Holi in Udaipur in the previous century and claims that:

> The most brilliant sight is the playing of Holi on horse-back ... each chief who chooses to join has a plentiful supply of missiles, formed of thin plates of mica or talc, enclosing crimson powder, called abira, which with most graceful and dexterous horsemanship they dart at each other, pursuing, caprioling and jesting.

In towns and villages across India Holi provides men and women with an opportunity to make merry by directing jets of coloured water on each other with syringes, mugs or even their hands. It is a time to give vent to repressed urges – for revelry, sexuality, benevolence or sadism.

On crossing a wooded pass 100 miles along the road east from Ajmer one suddenly comes across a white multi-storeyed balconied palace clinging to a barren dark grey rock with a large tank mirroring it from immediately below, which Rudyard Kipling called 'the beehive palace'. This is Bundi, the stronghold of the Hara-Chauhan clan, whose prince, Bahadur Singh, was my senior at school. A little farther east is Kotah, another Hara state, whose present prince has been a member of parliament and is the president of Mayo's board of governors.

The fort of Jaisalmer, built on a three-kilometre long outcrop deep in the Thar Desert near Pakistan's border, dates from 1156. Its round protruding bastions in close proximity to each other make it look redoubtable. Looking at it from afar, an English writer once compared it with 'an enormous tawny lion crouching in the desert sand'. A bustling town surrounds the maharaja's citadel inside the fort; it is the only fort in India today that has a flourishing township within its battlements.

The fort is built of hard sandstone, but Jaisalmer also has softer sandstone, which lends itself to intricate carving. The old houses of Jaisalmer have wonderfully carved lace-like traceries in lieu of windows. Jaisalmer was built in medieval times when it was a thriving and prosperous trading centre on the old caravan route between India and the Middle East. Once, when staying with the prince of Jaisalmer, I asked why the eyes of some of their maids were so green and was told that they were probably the progeny of the green-eyed Circassian houris who once used to pass through the Jaisalmer bazaars to the harems of the Delhi nobles.

There were other rulers in Rajputana who remain imprinted in my memory. The Maharaja of Dholpur, a short, wiry man with a ramrod straight back who always wore a long coat and *pugree* was, among other things, memorable for his beautiful manners. He could even charm wild animals, for I have watched him whistling up to his car spotted deer, sambars, black buck and other species in his jungles. Believing firmly in the divine right of kings and considering himself a trustee of his subjects he was totally opposed to representational government because, he argued, it would place intermediaries between him and those placed in his trust. He was one of the last to accept a democratic India in 1947.

Then there was the Maharawal of Dungarpur who captained the Rajputana cricket team and whose sizzling cover drives we loved to watch. One day, in the mid-1940s, I was with my father when Dungarpur, whose views were diametrically opposite those of Dholpur, spoke about the future of small states. He believed that, apart from Hyderabad, Mysore Kashmir and a few others, most states did not constitute units of a sufficient size to survive in the modern world. Further, without grouping themselves into larger, viable units that equalled British provinces, he told my father, a beginning could not be made with representational government, the demand for which was bound to gather force.

A descendant of the first boy to enrol at the Mayo College in 1871 was then the naughtiest maharaja of Rajputana. He was Sewai Jey Singh of Alwar, the same person who created anxious moments at a Buckingham Palace garden party during the Round Table Conference in London in 1931 by refusing to remove his gloves as George V advanced to shake his hand. While I was in Rajputana a rebellion was raging in his state; at the time a British officer summed Alwar up as follows:

He could not endure being outclassed in any way by the other princes. This led him ever deeper into debt. The condition of his state grew progressively worse. ... Stories of his cruelties, perversions and sadism were legion and the atmosphere in the state was sinister. One Viceroy called him 'a modern Caligula'. But the Maharaja was shrewd. On his visits to England he cultivated Secretaries of State and Prime Ministers and bluffed them into thinking of him as a philosopher prince, for, when he chose, he could be an amusing and interesting conversationalist.

Alwar, by all accounts, had an enquiring and sensitive mind, was well-read and an excellent extempore speaker. Where from then came the wickedness? Perhaps his extreme vanity, reverse racism and sadism were a reaction to frustration at having to bow down to the English, though he might have been clinically slightly mad too. One day, while in a rage, he poured petrol over and burnt a polo pony and this, more than any other of his misdemeanours, made the British decide to remove him from his throne.

I have not yet dealt with racism in British times and how it affected people like the Rajputs who believed they were descended from the Sun and Moon; it certainly would enrage people like Jey Singh of Alwar. To a large extent the princes were protected from the phenomenon because of the care the political department took and because, except for political officers, there was very little contact between their subjects and the British. However, in railway trains crossing British India one had to be careful of British army personnel who might refuse to allow you to enter a compartment they were occupying even though you had a valid ticket for a seat in it, and would bully the station master if he intervened. As Field Marshal Auchinleck explained:

Supposing you were on leave in the Himalayas and riding along a mountain track. If an Indian came along the other way riding his pony, he was supposed to get off. Similarly an Indian carrying an open umbrella was supposed to shut it. It sounds ridiculous but that attitude was still being imbibed into the newcomer to Indian Services when I went out [to India].

This was before the First World War. In my youth we heard of clubs in the larger towns that excluded Indians, but I can recall no first-hand experience of discrimination. In one of his earliest weekly top secret reports to the secretary of state in 1947, Lord Mountbatten wrote about having to address the governors of British provinces about some English women who had talked offensively within the hearing of his daughter (Lady Pamela) about his Indian guests at a reception at the Viceroy's House and requiring them to ensure that such practices ceased forthwith. So it had remained until the end.

There were many causes for this attitude, which by all accounts was very strong just before my time. In the seventeenth and eighteenth centuries the struggle had been between British and Indian forces of not dissimilar strength; and equality in battle breeds mutual respect, even fraternity. By the nineteenth century, however, one side had achieved absolute ascendancy in industry, science, arms and organization; so the Indians were pushed into an inferior position and weakness invites contempt. The impression that had remained fixed in the European mind for so long of India as a rich country with a great manufacturing capacity (20 per cent of world production until the seventeenth century) was destroyed and, with it, respect for India and Indians.

Furthermore, to face the onerous challenges of a worldwide empire the British needed to believe in their own supremacy and supereminence. Hence the coining of slogans like the 'white man's burden'. Christian missionaries who came to India in the nineteenth century were sustained by donors back home and, to obtain funds, it was only human for them to paint the worst possible picture of those to be redeemed. And then sex, the great equalizer, lost its humanizing influence when faster ships made it possible to bring British women out to India. To protect them too the race card had to be played to the hilt. By the time I grew up, however, things had improved. Perhaps, with the rising strength of nationalism, the forces poised against each side had again become more even.

The princes of Rajputana were thus rather a mixed bag, though we did not realize that at school. It is debatable whether the people of these Rajputana states were less happy in those days than the people of British India who had started to enjoy limited representational government. Direct taxation was lower overall than in British India, but land revenue rates were higher, though mitigated in practice by the accumulation of arrears and greater leniency in collection, not least because of administrative inefficiency. Under-administration rather than maladministration may have been their chief weakness. None of the states of Rajputana could compete with states like Baroda, Travancore and Mysore, where literacy levels and social legislation were of a higher standard than in British India; nor were they on a level with Gwalior and others where industries were being installed despite the objections of the British government, which wanted to protect British manufactured goods. The larger states of Rajputana did, however, employ distinguished Indian and English administrators. Also, the princely states gave Indians opportunities to rise to top positions in political and administrative affairs, which they could not do in British India.

Many of the famous industrial and trading houses of today, like the Birlas, Singhanias, Jalans and Khaitans, to name but a few, hail from the desert areas of Strekharati and Marwari in Rajputana. In days gone by these Marwari businessmen advanced money to traders plying the desert routes between Persia and Delhi. In the nineteenth century, when Britain began to monopolize trade through ports, they migrated to Calcutta where, as distributors of British imported products and money lenders, they gradually built up the commercial houses and later, under the exigencies of the two world wars, were given licences to set up industries. The Birlas financed the Congress Party during the struggle for independence, also paying stipends to individual leaders who were too busy agitating and going to prison to earn a living. Interestingly, none of the Marwari businessmen started up their enterprises in their own homelands in Rajputana which was probably because commercial prospects there were too bleak. Vast stretches remained parcelled out to feudal lords, mostly old Mayo College boys, who did little to attract the talent of these enterprising sons of the soil.

Rajputana, however, scored in one respect over British India. Relations between castes and religious groups were more harmonious than in the British-ruled territories and the society was more relaxed and tolerant. In the absence of political parties or elections, demagogues had no occasion to seek votes from uneducated people by appealing to their emotions and baser instincts. Hence the absence of communal antagonism between non-Muslims and Muslims in Rajputana and in the princely states in general. Unlike in a democracy, in a monarchy it is unnecessary for the various religious or ethnic groups to reconcile their political or other differences before giving their loyalty to the head of state and thus to the principality or country. The followers of Islam in any case find hierarchical systems more congenial. One may indeed wonder whether Spain or Belgium, each of which contains sub-nations within its boundaries, could have survived as single units in the last century without being monarchies, or whether Russia or Yugoslavia would have broken up had they retained their tsars and kings as constitutional heads. That the Indian princes were great patrons of the arts and sports, which recognize no distinctions of faith, greatly contributed to communal harmony within their territories.

By the mid-1940s the question of whether the Indian princes' rule was enlightened or not and their subjects happy or unhappy was, however, not the point. The plain fact was that in the changing situation the princes and their kingdoms were fast losing their relevance; they were being bypassed by history. As the nationalists, mostly from the Western-educated middle-class started to organize themselves politically, the traditional leaders, the princes, stood aside, so much so that as the time approached for the British to quit India, many Indians began to see the continuation of the princely order and the Indian states as a threat to the country. By a cruel irony the traditional guardians of the country's integrity had become suspected of threatening its unity.

I passed my youth in Rajputana bathed in the mellow glow that preceded the sunset of princely India and was bewitched by its beauty and panache: the stone palaces made feathery and floating by trellised façades; the mighty forts and their awesome ramparts, indeed the work of giants; huge moons floodlighting marble domes and falling on still waters; the colours of men's turbans and women's skirts and bodices – magentas, blues, parrot greens, sharp yellows and deep browns; the sound of the flute of a shepherd playing *mand* of a sleepy afternoon; the scent of desert flowers on a night of *shikar*; and of course boasting and singing round a campfire, right out of *The King's Jest*:

> And the talk slid north and the talk slid south
> With the sliding puffs from the hookah-mouth;
> Four things greater than all things are –
> Women and Horses and Power and War.

Chapter 12
Turmoil in Sarila

D URING May 1939, I was in Sarila, my father having delayed going to the hills because of the brewing agitation in the state. I used to hear shouts of *Inqalab Zindabad* (Long Live the Revolution!) – coming from the town. The palace staff told me that seditious meetings were being organized. On 13 May three blue truckloads of armed police arrived at the palace. The British political agent in Nowgong had sent this elite force at the request of my father, who wanted to reinforce the state police in dealing with the developing situation. The central government maintained this force, the Crown Reserve Police, for the purpose of aiding princes in the event of any threat to their rule.

The next day, 14 May, I heard louder shouts of *Inqalab Zindabad* and, when they sounded as if they were coming nearer, I climbed up to the terrace to see what was happening. From there I could see a procession coming from the direction of the town and pouring into a triangular space in front of the iron gates of the palace some 200 yards away. There must have been at least 500 people present, mostly men wearing white Gandhi caps, with women in white saris carrying the Congress tricolour flag in the lead. The participation of women in processions was a novel phenomenon as was the appearance of white caps in Sarila. The overwhelming majority of the crowd were Congress sympathizers from neighbouring British India.

Then I heard the crunch of boots on the gravel below and saw the Crown Reserve Police double march towards the tower gate on the right side of the palace, through which my elephant used to pass. From there they could wheel left towards the secretariat to which the protestors appeared to be heading. I could not see the mêlée that followed because of the trees, but could hear loud shouts of *Inqalab Zindabad* and then some incoherent noises. A little later I saw men and women racing back helter-skelter through the space beyond the iron gates and retreating into the narrow street from which they had emerged. In less than half an hour the Crown Reserve Police came marching back.

Sarila was not the only princely state afflicted by trouble that summer. The Congress Party's overwhelming success in the elections to the provincial legislatures in 1937 had galvanized political leaders in the princely states to start demanding people's rule in them too. Even Gandhiji found it difficult to continue to screen the princes from the agitation gripping the British provinces. Meanwhile, the Congress Party's radical wing, led by Pandit Jawahar Lal Nehru, pushed through a new resolution on the party's policy towards princely states, which completely reversed its earlier position. The Congress as a party was to offer no more than moral support and sympathy for the people of the states, thus placing the burden of carrying on the struggle against the princes on the subjects of the states. However, the resolution permitted Congressmen from British India to participate in these agitations in their individual capacity. Gandhiji separately warned the princes that Congress might abandon its policy of non-intervention if the rulers failed to cultivate friendly relations with the organization he claimed would soon replace the paramount power. All this opened the floodgates for the start of agitations in the princely states with the help of agitators from the outside. Disturbances erupted in

23. Group photograph of the rulers with the viceroy Lord Linlithgow at the 1937 meeting of the Chamber of Princes. Some rulers mentioned in the book can be identified as follows: sitting: fifth from the left, Alwar; sixth Jaipur; seventh Nawanagar (next to the viceroy); tenth Kotah. Standing in the first row, fourth from the left, Patiala; fifth Dungarpur; eighth (with the flowing moustache) Bikaner; fourteenth Panna; and fifteenth (the last but one) the author's father.

most states, large and small. In an outbreak of lawlessness in Ranpur state in Orissa, the British political agent was killed.

London realized that unless radical reforms in favour of representational government were introduced in the Indian states it would only be a question of time before Congress Party pressure against the princes became overwhelming and the viceroy, Lord Linlithgow, was advised accordingly. On the other hand, the political department in New Delhi was against the rulers being hustled on the matter and advised that the question of constitutional reforms be tackled through the Chamber of Princes. The political department also felt that, with the exception of a dozen or so, the overwhelming majority of states were too small for representational government without being grouped together and their rulers surrendering their powers, which they, however, could not be forced to do without violating solemn commitments made to them. The princes, on their part, neither in nor out of the chamber, made any serious attempt to introduce reforms or head off the agitation in any other way; they continued to depend on British power to sustain their rule.

Sarila was an enclave in the United Provinces where a Congress government had assumed power in 1938. Though it enjoyed peace throughout 1938, it was fully exposed to the howling winds of change blowing around it. Bihari Lal, the leader of the Sarila Praja Mandal (people's forum) was away in Panna on a carpentry contract and the other leaders in Sarila felt unable to organize a demonstration in his absence, but agitation in several other states of Bundelkhand began that year.

The other political leaders in Sarila were Nanhoo, Bharat, Girdhar, Shiv Pershad Goswami, Jawaharlal Rajak and Dr Beni Pershad. The first three belonged to the Lodi community. The Lodis, noted for being hard-working and prosperous farmers, were spread around and within the state and had had a lot of influence in the area before the Bundelas ousted them in the eighteenth century. Goswami was a Brahmin, had attended high school and was a minor functionary in the state administration. Jawaharlal was a washerman and thus belonged to one of the lowest castes; he was unusual in the sense that at that time people of the lowest caste had not become politically conscious. Beni Pershad belonged to the trading community, had a medical degree and worked as a doctor in a nearby town in British India. His wife, who had been to university, was also politically active. What is interesting about these six people was that they came from such a wide range of different castes and sections of the community, except that there was no Kshatriya or Muslim among them.

Bihari Lal was a carpenter and, unlike some of the other politicians, had no land, so nothing to fall back on other than his craftsmanship. His courage and energy cut him out for leadership among the people of Sarila. When I started to write this book Bihari Lal was still alive and, though in his nineties, in full possession of his faculties and as blunt as ever. Answering my questions on the events of more than half a century ago, he said that from 1938 he had started to receive urgent calls in Panna from Sarila to return home, but could only do so in March 1939 after completing his contract to build furniture for the maharaja's brother there and collecting his wages. On reaching Sarila he said he had immediately called a meeting to launch a non-violent demonstration against my father's rule. Its purpose was to kindle awareness in the population of the advantages of representational government and to put an end to certain injustices. He said that soon after the meeting he heard that a criminal case alleging conspiracy to destroy state property was in the process of being mounted against him, so he left Sarila to avoid arrest. He did not therefore participate in the demonstration that took place in the state in May 1939, though he remained in touch with the leaders who did.

Bihari Lal described to me how the Crown Reserve Police had dispersed the crowd on 14 May. Beyare Lal, the son of the agitator Bharat, who as a schoolboy remembered taking part in the march with his father, corroborated the description of the events. The procession had nearly reached the state secretariat, which was about 100 yards from the palace's tower gate, when they found their way blocked by Sarila and Crown Reserve policemen carrying *lathis* (long metal-tipped staffs) in their hands. The *diwan* of Sarila, Pandit Pratap Narain was also there. He said that this was no way to make demands for reforms and asked the marchers to disperse. When the leaders of the procession refused to budge, he ordered the police to disperse the crowd and arrest the leaders. The *lathi* charge that followed left several people, including women, injured and lying on the road; Dal Singh from Chhiboli in British India was so badly hit that he later succumbed to his injuries. The men and women of the Praja Mandal stood their ground for a while, but under the onslaught of *lathis* they fled and Nanhoo, Bharat and the other leaders were taken into custody. Bihari Lal said that on the following day an angry crowd entered the *diwan*'s residence; he was away at the palace at the time, so they beat up his wife. This resulted in a house-to-house search of the town by the state police to catch those involved and in the process some houses were ransacked.

The harsh response to the protest was what apparently led to the collapse of the agitation. No banner of revolt was raised in Sarila thereafter, right up until independence in 1947. Nanhoo, Girdhar and one or two others were sent to the Nowgong prison for a year, which was under the political agent's charge, to keep them away from Sarila. The other leaders absconded to evade arrest, some joining Bihari Lal in British India. Bihari Lal said that the only satisfaction they got from it all was from beating up the *diwan*'s wife.

I asked people who could recall that era, including our hero, what specific goals the Praja Mandal had in mind when it launched the agitation in Sarila in 1939. Were they unaware that representational government was impractical in small principalities? The reply I received was that all they aimed to achieve was the removal of certain officials like the *diwan* and police chief and the reduction or abolition of certain taxes. If this were indeed the case, their demands differed from those of agitators in the larger neighbouring state of Charkhari, where local politicians wanted power to be handed over to them.

They said they wanted the land revenue (the tax on agricultural produce) to be reduced in Sarila to the level charged in the neighbouring British provinces, though Bihari Lal said that when one added to the officially decreed tax in British India the extractions by the *zamindars*, the farmers in Sarila, where there were no middle men, did not actually pay more. Their second grievance was that adequate wages were not paid to workers for various services such as grinding grain, repairing state government property or cleaning prisons and police stations. Furthermore, each shepherd's family had to weave and supply the state with one free blanket a year for prison inmates; basket weavers had to supply a certain amount of baskets free of charge as a sort of tax; and cowherds had to supply milk to officials at half the going rate. State officials requisitioned bulls and bullock-carts for miscellaneous purposes at nominal payment. These burdens, they said, hit the lowest castes who were also the poorest.

My next question was: were their demands met after Sarila disappeared? They said that since independence land tax had not been raised to the extent it was periodically in British times, and was automatically adopted across the border in the state. This was the main economic benefit they had received after independence. In the British days the major source of income for the government came from land revenue, besides the tax on opium and salt. In fact, no industry was prosperous enough to be taxed; the import duties on British goods were minimal; there was no middle class from which to yield income tax; and revenue from the export of Indian raw materials was depressed because of the world recession. The rising cost of British civil and military expenditure more or less forced the government to periodically raise land revenue. The experiences of the defence of the Indian Ocean area, including the Middle East, was largely borne by the Indian exchequer, namely by the Indian peasant. Farmers were now better off also because fertilizers, diesel, kerosene oil, cooking gas and electricity were subsidised in one way or another.

Moreover, the imposition of a ceiling on the amount of agricultural land that could be owned in this area (27 acres of irrigated and 45 acres of unirrigated land per family) had yielded land for distribution to some landless peasants, though many farmers evaded the ceiling by putting holdings in other people's names and continuing to exploit them as before. Concessional loans were also now available to the lowest castes to dig wells and buy seeds and farm equipment, though when sanctioning the loans the officials of the state-run banks extracted on average 20 per cent of the loan in bribes. Also, there was now a minimum wage for daily rated *mazdoors* (workers) that kept rising 5–10 per cent each year in Sarila and matched yearly inflation. Furthermore, the value of farm products in real terms had quadrupled. The price of the farmers' land was appreciating by about 5 to 10 per cent each year, which was more than in earlier times.

Those engaged in cottage industries in Sarila like spinning, weaving, tanning, shoemaking, carpentry, pottery, toy manufacturing and dhurrie weaving had seen British imported goods wipe out their industries. Some could now at least move to seek

144

jobs in new industries in the towns, though living conditions there were deplorable. Also, the government had set aside 30 to 40 per cent of government jobs for the poorest and most backward castes and classes, except for certain occupations in which specialist skills were required.

I remember frequent famines in Sarila in the 1930s. Tanks would be dug and desilted as a way of distributing some money to the starving. When the men and women carrying baskets of earth on their heads reached the place where they had to be emptied, cowrie shells (then an acceptable tender) would be dished out to them. Such deprivation is now a thing of the past.

They pointed to the number of tractors, new shops selling agricultural equipment and consumer goods, and the new brick and cement houses in the town. The better clothes worn by people were also proof of improving living standards. Nowadays in Sarila mobile phones and TV sets are plentiful, and many people even have private cars.

The improvement in the social status of the lowest caste, now called Dalits, was particularly marked. With the Dalit population of India having increased from 6 to 20 per cent of the total since the 1930s (about 200 million out of a billion people), no politician can get elected without some Dalit votes. This forces them to bend before the outcastes. While the electoral system might exacerbate caste conflicts in the short term as political parties try to build up caste vote banks, in the longer term the growing political interdependence between the higher and lower castes is breaking up the caste system more effectively than any constitutional attempts to ban the practice, as well as all the efforts of the reformers.

I recall that my mother's maids of the lower castes had lighthearted names like Ujyari (luminous) Chhabili (playful), Gulab Rani (queen of roses), Gori Dulhan (fair maiden), Muliya (Sunday born) and Larli (lovable). The Dalit women of today have abandoned such names in favour of names that recall Hindu gods and goddesses, such as Ram Devi, Saraswati, Krishna and Paryati, which are used by upper-class women. This perhaps demonstrates a newfound confidence and desire to be part of the mainstream culture.

The people I questioned were, however, unanimous about law and order having greatly deteriorated in the past two or three decades and corruption having increased. No one is afraid to commit a crime because only 2 per cent of those charged ever get punished. Not only are the police officers careless or maladroit in preparing the charge sheets, but the courts also have no time to dispose of the hordes of cases descending upon them – 700,000 pending in Uttar Pradesh alone. Once the accused obtains bail, over the granting of which great laxity is practised, the criminal is as good as free. The court proceedings take place at district headquarters far from the aggrieved's home and criminal cases are not heard on consecutive days, which increases the opportunity to subvert witnesses. The procedures are endless and costly, which is very different from the princely judgements, which were sometimes given on the spot and because they were pronounced before an assembled crowd they could not be arbitrary or unjust.

Bihati Lal told me that Rajiv Gandhi, the late prime minister speaking once not far from Sarila, had said that 85 per cent of all the expenditure the government allotted to economic and social development was eaten away and that this was not an exaggeration. Unless politicians form links with engineers, contractors and civil servants to siphon off money, how, asked Behari Lal and his friends, were they to fight elections? To fight an election for a seat in the state assembly one needs to spend a minimum of Rs 50 lakhs to one crore (US$ 200,000) and to get into the central parliament costs four times that amount.

On the other hand, those on whose shoulders the entire administrative management of the country rested, the civil servants, received miserable salaries. How were they to survive when an officer's pay in the 1980s was often lower in real terms at retirement, after 30 or 35 years of service, than it had been when he joined the service? This was because the rupee had been devalued 50 times since independence and the government was reluctant to raise their salaries to keep up with inflation. (When this question was raised at a meeting the officers sought with Prime Minister Indira Gandhi in 1968, at which I was present, her answer was that the general public would not favour it.) The salaries of officers were revised steeply in the 1990s, but by that time the culture of a percentage of all funds allotted for development being routinely channelled into officers' pockets according to an agreed formula, had become firmly entrenched. The fact is that both Jawaharlal Nehru and his daughter were poor administrators.

Education and healthcare were neglected not because of lack of funds but because of administrative mismanagement and corruption. By bribing the inspectors, teachers at government schools could skip lessons and use the time to give private tuition for a fee. To encourage education, the government gave parents a monthly equivalent of US$ 11 and three kilos of grain for every child they sent to a government elementary school. However, a vast number of parents sent their children to private schools, which were proliferating because the teaching was better there, even though many were housed in ramshackle buildings or even under trees. The hospital in Sarila went without doctors, nurses or medicines for long periods and was in a much worse condition than it had been under the earlier dispensation.

New roads built around Sarila were in disrepair and bridges over streams remained half built. Power was unavailable for more than four or five hours a day (this went up to 12 hours in

2006). Crops suffered without electricity for the tube wells and small-scale industries could not be set up without power. Dirt and disease were spreading because of water pollution, lack of sewerage systems and a galloping population. There was no check on illegal hutments being built right next to highways and choking them. No town planning was being attempted at a time of growing population. Village tanks were getting silted up, thereby lowering the water levels in the village wells. But for the Hindu belief that all animate objects and human beings belong to the same family, perhaps even more trees would have been felled and birds and animals destroyed. As it is, forest coverage in my Hamirpur district has been reduced from 86 per cent in 1947 to 6 per cent today.

Bihari Lal said that the means by which abuses are perpetuated today are less visible than they were in the days of the rulers and the situation is therefore more frustrating. When I drew his attention to the Sarila town area committee, the elected local municipal body, he laughed. He said that few of the chairmen of the district boards or town councils in our area are sufficiently able or well enough educated even to draft the proposals required to apply for development funds. He said that the members of the state assembly and of parliament from the district did not wish these local bodies to flourish because that would reduce their own clout before the public.

Uttar Pradesh compares very unfavourably in economic development with the other states of India, particularly of western and southern India. We are discussing here one of the worst run states in India. Among the causes for this state of affairs are the frequent changes of government in the state because no one political party dominates the electorate; with a population of more than 170 million people, the sheer size of the state makes it unwieldy to administer; even those charged with crimes have succeeded in entering politics because to win votes parties prefer muscle to integrity. The ensuing political uncertainty has discouraged private investment in industry and in the infrastructure, thereby cutting the state off from possible sources of capital. A fairly recent UN survey (AD 2000) on the social and economic standards of member states noted that India ranked as low as 137th among the countries of the world, but with Uttar Pradesh and Bihar removed from the statistics, it jumps to 37th place!

Since India's GDP has started to rise yearly by between 7 and 9 per cent, some wealth has started to trickle into Sarilian pockets as well, but the poor management by the state government and neglect of the infrastructure, remain.

In 1997 A. M. Rosenthal, former editor-in chief of the *New York Times*, visited Sarila and wrote an article in *The Times* on conditions there, calling it 'The People of Sarila'. I quote below some passages from his article:

Sarila is a small farm town tucked into a corner of Uttar Pradesh, the largest of India's states stuffed with about 140 million people ... and it is not doing at all well. Nobody knows who is in political charge from week to week, or for what purpose other than power. High officials (and politicians) whip around the countryside in 20 car motorcades while the police clear roads and stop airport traffic for them. Highway bandits are so close to some politicians that it is hard to tell the difference between them, and barely worth the trouble. What the people here say they want most is water, water, and water. Their crops and businesses, their lives, depend on water for irrigation. ... In centuries of colonialism, princely rule and now 50 years of independence they have not received it. ... Roads are something else Sarilians want and need – to connect them to other towns, bring jobs and commerce.

On the other hand the openness of Sarilians is a tribute to India's freedom of speech and to their own insistence on expressing their mind. At a meeting of villagers one man bursting with questions demanded to know why the US let China get away with selling magnetic rings for nuclear weapons to Pakistan. I mentioned that Prime Minister HD Deve Gowda said he was absolutely sure the Chinese would never attack India as they did in 1962. Show of hands: four thought he was right. Almost all the 70 others voted that he was wrong.

Why were the villagers so apathetic about improving their lifestyle and failing to press for better municipal management? The answer I received to the first half of the question was that householders did not invest in good clothes, furniture and household articles, even when they could afford them, for fear that the children of the extended family might quarrel over the spoils and eat into the capital. Besides, they do not wish to excite envy or invite theft. It is true that in a society that does not have social security the extended family is a great hedge for the elderly, sick and incompetent, but it discourages enterprising family members from breaking away from their elders and moving forward. I received no clear-cut answer to my question about the people's apathy towards taking social responsibility, but given that the Hindu *dharma*, as popularly practised, places the accent on individual salvation, there is little incentive to show an interest in community enterprises beyond the age-old obligations to family, caste and temple.

The democratic form of government has proved a boon for India. To get votes and win elections candidates have had to accommodate the views and demands of castes, creeds and ethnic groups other than their own. This has helped to contain differences. Decisions taken on the basis of advice and consent have prevented arbitrary and hasty actions by government. It has provided the mechanism for a peaceful and orderly change of governments and shift of power. Elections have helped the masses to blow off steam. Without adopting a democratic form of government, it might have been difficult to hold the country together.

Admittedly, by the 1940s the princes and their states had become an anachronism and had to go. But, after disposing of them, did we have to adopt a democratic constitution so populist that it has put good governance and management in India at risk? Was it wise, for example to introduce universal franchise, thus jumping from a 14.2 per cent franchise at the time of independence to 100 per cent overnight, without first attempting to raise the level of education? Also, was it a good decision to adopt a parliamentary as opposed to a presidential system, which would have provided greater stability to the executive and avoided frequent elections, hung parliaments and coalitions? Or, indeed, was it wise to adopt a socialist or state-run economy without India having enough trained and efficient managers to run it? Socialist principles are now being jettisoned to raise the rate of the country's growth, but, as I stated earlier, the power the bureaucracy and politicians enjoyed under a system of state control has helped to entrench corruption.

The saddest thing is that the high cost of fighting elections and the criminalization of politics discourages honest and able men and women from seeking elective office. Some of the ablest men in the Indian cabinet in Delhi today, including Prime Minister Manmohan Singh and Foreign Minister Pranab Mukerjee, are not directly elected representatives of the lower house but nominees through electoral colleges to the upper house.

That three generations of the same family held the prime minister's portfolio in succession for the first 50 years of India's independence would appear to suggest that trust in hereditary succession has not died and that, even though the maharajas have disappeared, the people want to be ruled by leaders whose families they can easily recognize.

Of course the agitation in Sarila against my father's rule was not really about economic or social betterment or even enfranchisement, whatever Bihar Lal and his friends may have believed at the time. It was, above all, about pressurizing the princes into giving up their powers and states and integrating their territories into the Indian Union – it was about forging India's political unity. In this respect, the revolt I witnessed in Sarila can be said to have been successful.

Chapter 13
The Revolutionary

BIHARI LAL, who had organized the agitation against my father's rule in Sarila in 1939, had fled the state into British India. Immediately thereafter, at my father's request the British authorities issued an All-India warrant for his arrest.

He in turn lived underground in the adjoining British province for five years, moving from one village to the other and having many narrow escapes from the police. The peaceful Quit India movement against the British that Gandhiji had launched in 1942 failed to take off because he and other Congress Party leaders were arrested. Proponents of the violent overthrow of British power then took over the cause and it was these revolutionaries – locally called the *Garam Dal*, literally Hot Brigade – that Bihari Lal joined.

A few years back, when he was over 90 years old, I asked Bihari Lal what had prompted him to give up the Congress Party creed of non-violence to support violent action against British rule and why he had rebelled against my father in the 1930s. I had first set eyes on him from the elephant that in my childhood had served as a pram for my evening outings. He had then worn a haughty black moustache, but now, in 1995, he had a flowing white beard that gave him the look of a *sadhu* (sage). His answer showed that his mind was as alert as ever. He felt no rancour for the son of his chief antagonist even

153

though I, the raja's son, had risen to high office in free republican India while history had bypassed him, the old warrior, having to subsist on the small dole the government meted out to so-called 'freedom fighters' and on his work as a village carpenter. He was affectionate towards me and when I visited him a few years later on his deathbed in his miserable cottage, he held my hand and wept.

Bihari Lal began by saying that he had already once told me that after leaving the Sarila state service in 1930 he was deeply disappointed when Gandhiji banned demonstrations against the princes (the ban was only lifted in 1939) because he said he saw no point in wooing princes who were totally sold out to the British. He said he first met the members of *Garam Dal* at a Gandhi ashram, ironically devoted to preaching non-violence and social enlightenment. This was at Rath, a town near Sarila. People came to the ashram mainly to spin and weave *khadi*, homemade cloth, as part of Gandhiji's campaign to displace imported English cloth and to give a fillip to cottage industries. At the centre he met one Ram Kishan Palia, who elicited his views on violent action to overthrow British power and the princes. When Bihari Lal expressed an interest, Palia introduced him a few days later to two other people. They, however, refused to enlist him in the *Garam Dal* because, as a married man, he was susceptible to blackmail.

Bihari Lal said he persevered and ultimately was taken to a *Garam Dal* hideout in the thick forests on the banks of the river Betwa in British territory 25 miles upstream from Sarila. The local Zamindar or landlord of that area, Diwan Shatrughan Singh of Maghrot, was the most important Congress Party leader of the region. Though a follower of Gandhian ways, this revolutionary hideout enjoyed his protection. Here Bihari Lal met Chandra Shekhar Azad of Basarka village situated near Kanpur city.

Chandra Shekhar had become known all over India for

24. Bihari Lal, who led the revolt against the author's father in Sarila in 1939. Shown here in 1995 at the age of 91.

having looted a train and railway station in Kakori in 1925 and the government had placed a huge price on his head. Since then he had lived underground, recruiting and training youth for violent action. Bihari Lal said that if the first milestone in his political career had been his quarrel with my father, and the second the elation he felt at being able to reach the doors of Nehru's home in Allahabad, the third was witnessing how Chandra Shekhar met his death at the hands of the British police.

I interrupted to ask him to describe the first two experiences he had mentioned, for they chronologically came before Chandra Shekhar's death. He said he would come to those later and continued his tale. In 1942 British intelligence officers had won over a close lieutenant of Chandra Shekhar's, Veer Bahadur Tiwari of Orai (a town west of Sarila). One day, shortly before noon, when Chandra Shekhar was sitting with some collaborators on the lawns of Alfred Park in Allahabad, Tiwari guided the police to him. A police squadron under an English captain accompanied by the British district magistrate of Allahabad, soon surrounded the group. An officer of the force, Netbawar (or at least that was how Bihari Lal pronounced his name) then advanced towards the small group and, to ensure that Tiwari had not misled him, asked in a loud voice in broken Hindi: 'Which of you is Chandra Shekhar?'

Chandra Shekhar at once understood that he was surrounded and tried to draw his Mauser revolver from the pocket of the khaki shorts he was wearing. Netbawar, seeing the movement, fired from a distance of about 20 yards and hit his right arm. Despite the wound Chandra Shekhar was able to take out his revolver and fire. By then the Englishman had retreated behind a tree a few paces behind. Taking advantage of the moment gained, Chandra Shekhar slid behind the trunk of another tree and both started to fire intermittently to get the other. At one point Netbawar's knee became visible and Chandra Shekhar immediately shattered it. Aware of Chandra Shekhar's prowess as a marksman, Netbawar asked his force to get down into a *nallah* (storm-water drain) that skirted the lawn on which they were and then move to surround him. This manoeuvre gave Chandra Shekhar's companions an opportunity to run away.

Behari Lal said that Chandra Shekhar spotted among the police Bishan Singh, from his own Badarka village. And he cried out: 'You are an Indian. There are enough of them to confront me. Do not join them.' To this Bishar Singh answered with some choice words of abuse, but before he could finish Chandra Shekhar shot him through the jaw. Amazingly, said Bihari Lal, he heard the English magistrate say, 'wonderful shot'. At this stage some of the Indian soldiers refused to advance further. (They were later tried and dismissed.) Others had reached behind the tree trunk and Chandra Shekhar was now fully encircled and exposed. He had by then three shots left and he used the last bullet to shoot himself.

The story of this confrontation, Bihari Lal maintained, spread like wildfire and inspired more fervour against British rule than Gandhiji's peaceful methods. Bihari Lal said he witnessed the action from afar because he had left the group to pass water a moment before it was surrounded. Something stopped him rushing forward to divert attention. 'It was pure cowardice,' he said, 'and perhaps that reluctance to risk death made me join the violent revolutionaries to redeem myself.' (The British government recently returned Chandra Shekhar's revolver to India and it is now in the Lucknow museum.)

About the same time, he said, another incident affected him: Bhagat Singh, the well-known revolutionary imprisoned in the Lahore Fort, was awaiting execution. One day Bhagat Singh was informed from the outside that a rescue operation to free him was being mounted. Bhagat Singh, however, rejected the offer by sending a message to them as follows: 'My time is ripe for the ultimate sacrifice. Such sacrifices alone will galvanize my countrymen to fight for India's freedom.'

Bihari Lal said that he had come to believe that to create an awakening and strong patriotic fervour among the masses, leaders should arrange events that depicted violent and heroic confrontations. In fact, he said that Gandhiji's methods and those of the revolutionaries complemented one another. People vary: some are aroused by the brutality perpetrated against those who turn the other cheek, like Gandhiji's peaceful *satyagrahis*, while others are inspired by violent acts of sacrifice undertaken against a mighty power. He said that the Congress movement, however peaceful, had helped create an environment of sympathy for the *Garam Dal*. Could he have survived as an outlaw in the early 1940s without being given shelter and food in the dozen or so villages in which he took refuge? He said that many Congressmen had contacts with the revolutionaries and quietly helped them. Even Gandhiji, the apostle of non-violence, had sought Bhagat Singh's release from Viceroy Irwin in March 1931.

Bihari Lal said that Gandhiji's thinking was very different from that of people like Chandra Shekhar and Bhagat Singh. Gandhiji believed firmly that there is a God and when we are ready to sacrifice our lives to resist oppression or injustice peacefully, we have completed our work and the one who keeps the world going will take care of the rest; He, not we, should be the final judge of the right punishment to be meted out to our oppressors.

Bihari Lal said that in his quest to elevate India he was influenced first by religious impulses, then by Gandhiji's *Satyagraha* philosophy and finally by the revolutionaries. He told me that between 1941 and 1945 he committed 355 armed robberies, some of government treasuries, to collect funds for the revolutionaries. 'Now in old age,' he laughed, 'having lost my way, I have become a sort of a Trishanku [the character in Indian mythology who remained in suspended animation].'

At subsequent meetings I asked him about his early life. The notes I took reveal that Bihari Lal was born in 1901, so he was three years younger than my father. He belonged to a family of craftsmen and was educated at the state school of Sarila. Since he could write Hindi as well as Urdu and was intelligent, in 1923 my father asked him to join the Sarila state Public Works Department. In 1926 he had a quarrel with the overseer, his superior, and although my father supported Bihari Lal, which led to the overseer's resignation, he left the Public Works Department and started working as a freelance carpenter. Bihari Lal did not fear unemployment because he knew he was a good craftsman. Some of the intricate mouldings on the *almirah*s in my rooms in Sarila Palace are by him and are proof of his talent as a carpenter.

The electric generator on my father's Sarila property needed to be fixed, so my father sent Bihari Lal to train as an electrician and later appointed him as an electrical engineer. There was no supply of government electricity then and our private generator was used only for a few hours in the evenings until my father retired to bed. Some time around 1930 my father asked Bihari Lal to work in the state carpentry shop during his free time. When Bihari Lal responded by asking for extra wages on the grounds that this was an entirely different occupation, my father became very annoyed. And Bihari Lal left the Sarila state service.

In 1928–29 Bihari Lal came under the influence of a Hindu revivalist movement called the Arya Samaj, which introduced him to abstract, theological thought, after which he gradually started to toy with political concepts like freedom and equality. When he left the Sarila state service he went on a journey that took him first to the holy town of Chitrakoot in a forest 150 miles east of Sarila (where Rama is supposed to have spent some time during his wanderings) and later to Allahabad.

Prayag (or Allahabad, the name given to the city by Akbar) is situated at the confluence of the Ganga and Yamuna rivers and is considered holy by the Hindus. During the British period its importance grew with the founding of two institutions – Allahabad University, then north India's main centre for Western higher education, and the high court of the huge United Provinces, which attracted lawyers from many parts of north India. One who came to seek his fortune there and became famous was Moti Lal Nehru, the father of Jawaharlal Nehru. The Nehru Brahmins had left the valley of Kashmir for the plains of India in the eighteenth century.

Moti Lal Nehru, like Mohammad Ali Jinnah, an even more famous barrister from Bombay, made his money at the Bar. If Jinnah ordered his suits from Savile Row, Moti Lal was reputed to send his dirty shirts to be laundered in Paris. People in the villages used to say that he gave up this practice as his sacrifice to the national cause, but nobody asked why he had engaged in this wholly unnecessary extravagance in the first place. In the late 1920s Moti Lal built a villa in Allahabad from which one could see the distant Ganga and named it Anand Bhawan, the abode of happiness. It was a two-storeyed curved building in the Sarsenic style bounded by deep verandas and with a large domed round canopy placed on a raised platform on the roof. The canopy not only increased the beauty of the edifice but also provided an ideal spot for young Jawaharlal Nehru to sleep in during the summer when he was not in prison or travelling. Moti Lal, intellectually a moderate nationalist, joined the Gandhi mass movement after his son joined it. Mahatma Gandhi once remarked that Moti Lal's love for his only son was the reason why he threw himself into the freedom struggle.

Though Allahabad is not very far from Sarila as distances in India go (about 250 miles), at the time a world divided the two places. One was in British India, an intellectual centre and a hotbed of democratic ideas; the other was in princely India, where places like Allahabad were considered to be breeding grounds for sedition. It was thus surprising that Bihari Lal, an ex-electrician from Sarila Palace should have been standing outside the gate of Anand Bhawan in Allahabad on that day in 1930. For six long hours he stood there hoping to get a glimpse of the Nehrus. Then finally, in the late afternoon a chauffeur driven car descended from the portico 20 yards away and the gates opened. Vijaya Lakshmi Pandit, Jawaharlal's sister, was in the back seat in a cool sari and she did not even raise her eyes from the newspaper she was reading.

The simple act of reaching the gates of Nehru's house had nonetheless given young Bihari Lal a sense of fulfilment. The knowledge that going there would be looked upon as sedition in Sarila excited him. He wandered off from the gates of Anand Bhawan towards a nearby Victorian bungalow, Moti Lal's home before he moved into Anand Bhawan and now the headquarters of the Congress Party. It was here that he learnt that the Congress Party had passed a resolution forbidding agitation in the princely states. This came as a shattering blow. Gandhiji was of the view that at this stage nothing should be done to push the princes further into the arms of the British.

On his way back to Sarila after visiting the Nehru house at Allahabad, he was so fired with zeal to strike a blow at the British raj, that at Hamirpur, a town in British India, he raised slogans against British rule and got beaten up in the process by the police. It would be many years before he joined the violent revolutionaries and only in 1939, when the Congress Party withdrew its ban on agitation against the princes, did he organize a revolt against my father's rule.

After India's independence Bihari Lal was made responsible for organizing and strengthening the Congress Party in the territories of the former princely states in our area. Ever the loner, he soon fell out with his bosses and, with no revolution immediately in sight, he gave up active politics.

Chapter 14
The Nawab Misses a Tiger

W E WERE about to leave for Mussoorie in the summer of 1943 when my father received a letter from the Maharaja of Panna, my mother's maternal uncle, inviting him to a tiger hunt in his state to which Nawab Hamidullah Khan of Bhopal, the new chancellor of the Chamber of Princes, was coming. My father was reluctant to brave the heat but since the new chancellor was bound to have news of the great goings on, he went, taking me along with him.

Nawab Hamidullah Khan was a Muslim prince of a middling state about 250 miles southwest of Sarila in the Vindhya hills of central India. He was a short, dapper man with high cheekbones and hair brushed back off a rather square forehead; in his khaki breeches, high boots and arms akimbo he cut the figure of a central Asian chieftain; only his flashing eyes betrayed his Indian mix. His ancestors had migrated from central Asia via Afghanistan in the early eighteenth century and the Mogul emperor had given them land near Bhopal. In the chaos that followed the disintegration of the Mogul Empire they had established their kingdom in the area.

Even the least educated Muslims in India are more aware of

the wider world than their Hindu compatriots. In that they are taught to regard themselves as part of an international, inter-racial brotherhood spread over the world, the names of places like Mecca, Jerusalem, Baghdad, Damascus, Istanbul and even Cordoba in Spain are familiar to them. Hindus are content to remain wrapped up in the lap of mother India. Despite his wider sweep and undoubted charm and energy, Hamidullah was, according to my father, 'rather jumpy'. At the Round Table Conference in 1930 he had argued eloquently in favour of an All-India Federation, but in 1947 the same Hamidullah threw in his lot with Pakistan and worked actively to wreck India's unity. A few months before the Panna meeting he was elected to replace the Jam Sahib (Maharaja) of Nawanagar as chancellor of the Chamber of Princes, thus becoming the princes' spokes-person before the British viceroy and Indian political parties. In 1943 his switch to Jinnah's camp was still incomplete.

Also attending the Panna meeting were the young Maharaja of neighbouring Chhatarpur, the heir apparent of adjacent Ajaigarh and the Maharaja of Panna's two sons, who had been my seniors at the Mayo College. Our host insisted that, while awaiting the arrival of the rest of the princes and before delving into other matters, we get down to the serious business of tiger shooting. So, after lunch we left for the jungle in a convoy of cars loaded with *shikaris* in khaki coats and turbans, guns and ammunition from the Panna armoury, and thermoses in leather cases filled with lemon juice and tea. To get to the forest of Sri, where the beat was to take place, we drove first on a curvy *pukka* road and then on a bumpy track through the bush.

Panna state was situated on one of the ridges of the Vindhya hills (in central India) before they flatten out towards the east. We drove through a deciduous forest in which teak, sal, mahua and khair abounded and in which there were numerous deep ravines, watercourses and plenty of small game – in other words, ideal tiger country. Because tigers gravitate towards water sources in summer, they are easier to locate and hunt at that time of the year. In those pre-Jeep days, American Cadillacs, Fords and Chevrolets, which had high clearances, were used on rough roads.

Within an hour of leaving the palace we found ourselves walking in Indian file towards our *machans*. One *shikari* had been assigned to each hunter and, as we approached the line of *machans*, the party split up; I was to sit with my father. Our *machan*, which was 18 feet high and onto which we climbed with the help of a ladder, consisted of a village rope cot measuring about five feet by four feet; it was comfortable enough to accommodate the two of us, as well as the *shikari* who was carrying the guns. To camouflage us as much as possible, cut branches had been tied on the side from which the tiger was expected to come.

About 50 yards to the right I could see Hamidullah and my maternal grand uncle trying to settle down in their *machan* and they waved to us. We could not see the other *machans* because they were in a straight line beyond them, but Chhatarpur's was on our left. The dry forest, some of which had been cleared to give us an adequate field of fire, started about 15 yards from the line of *machans*. Low blue ranges were visible on the horizon beyond the dry brownish and fairly dense scrub.

The art of beating lies in anticipating the tiger's most likely line of retreat and placing the *machans* accordingly. Stops – flags or men on trees – are used to prevent the tiger slipping away to the right or left. After some time we heard a shot fired from the direction of the beaters, about a kilometre away, and some noise; the beat had begun. As the beaters started to move in our direction the idea was to drive the beast towards us. My father pointed out to me a depression, which ended about 30 yards in front of the chief guest's *machan* and whispered that the tiger was most likely to emerge from it. Tigers naturally like to take advantage of as much cover as possible. After some time the sound of the tom-toms and beaters' calls increased; looking left and right, sweeping the forest and the clearance, I waited with bated breath.

Suddenly, there was the sound of a rifle shot from the right and, as I turned to look, I saw a huge tiger bounding at great speed past the nawab's *machan* at some distance to his right. Then there was another shot, but by then the tiger had disappeared into the jungle behind. My father said, 'a miss'. Later he told me that the sound of an impact of the bullet on the animal is different from that of a miss.

I was somewhat lost in my disappointment when the *shikari* gave me a nudge from behind and pointed to the left. And 50 yards away right in front of Chhatarpur's *machan* I saw a tiger trotting to get past the clearing. His was the same gait as that of a cat, except that his powerful body and large head made him look menacing. At the same time there was a loud report followed by another and then an incredible sight. The tiger roared and jumped several feet high almost like a fish leaping up in the air from water, and then crashed immobile to the ground. Two more shots were then put into him.

Soon the beaters were visible under the trees in front of us and then there was a loud cry from the left, which my father said must be from one of the stops, possibly indicating that a third tiger had been sighted. By this time the bugle had sounded to announce the end of the beat, after which no shot may be fired. The beaters were local villagers in ragtag clothes and they were collecting at some distance to gaze at us.

My maternal grand uncle's *shikari* was the first to jump down and disappear into the jungle behind the nawab's *machan*, but it soon became clear that the nawab had missed his second shot too. My maternal grand uncle told us later that he had withheld firing immediately after the nawab to give the chief guest another chance and then it was too late. Soon we were collecting around Chhatarpur's trophy, while he concealed his emotion. At this point an excited beater appeared and announced that a tiger had mauled a stop's leg and people were rushed to give him first aid and take him by car to Panna.

A third tiger was evidently about to pass this man's tree and break through the line of stops. The man growled to turn it back, but the noise had a quite different effect. The tiger bounded up, and, although the man shot upwards towards the top, the tiger caught his foot and crunched it. Fortunately, at this moment a branch next to the one from which the stop was hanging broke and fell onto the tiger's back and it then bolted away with a rough growl. The branch had saved the stop's life, though a part of his leg was lost.

Back in Panna that evening we relaxed on the lawns in rattan chairs under the cooling breeze of electric pedestal fans. Behind us loomed the palace, its deep-pillared veranda running the length of the handsome mansion and a broad flight of steps, as in Sarila, descending from the landing. By then the maharajas of Orchha and Nagod had arrived to join us. Orchha, it may be remembered from an earlier chapter, was the maharaja who liked to live in a house built of beer bottles and was more interested in golf and books than in ruling. The sporting nawab was not in the least fazed by his failure that afternoon and over whisky and soda took up the topic he had come to discuss.

The nawab's mission was soon made clear. Though the immediate object of Sir Stafford Cripps's mission to India (in 1942) had been to obtain the support of the Congress Party for the war effort, Cripps had also met the princes and two questions had emerged during their discussions. The first was whether the states could seek independence individually or collectively after Britain's departure, as the British provinces were being promised and to which the British minister had given an affirmative answer; and the second was how were the states to be fitted into any new All-India constitutional scheme given the vast disparities in their sizes, resources and rulers' power? A large number of states consisted only of a few villages, and the larger ones were as big as the Netherlands or even France, with armed forces and the paraphernalia of proper governments. Cripps's advice had been to group the smaller states into viable units and to encourage popular representation in such units. The chancellor was touring the states to sound out the princes on both these issues.

Hamidullah began by saying that a couple of weeks earlier he had had a long discussion in Delhi with the viceroy's adviser on the states, Sir Conrad Corfield. Apparently, the British were envisaging a weak centre for the All-India Federation, with most power residing in the federal units. In such a setup and with the Congress and Muslim League at each other's throats, the princes, if they could organize into a third force, could insert themselves between the British, the Congress Party and the Muslim League and hold the balance of power. The nawab said that, at the very least, such a policy would give them more bargaining power with which to protect their interests. He said he had good relations with the viceroy and his advisers and with Mohammad Ali Jinnah, the Muslim League leader. He was now going to sound out the Congress Party leaders' views on the princes' role in the future. Mr Nehru was ideologically opposed to the princes, but was a much easier person to talk to than the other Congress *dhotiwallas* (as the nawab disparagingly referred to the Congress Party members). Chhatarpur interrupted to say that Nehru would be more open to a Muslim than a Hindu prince and the nawab smiled at the young man's perspicacity. Nehru had little time for princes but Muslim princes were special: they had to be kept away from the snares of their Muslim League coreligionists.

The nawab then sought the views of the rest of the company. Panna said straightaway that it was highly unlikely that the British were considering leaving just yet or that Congress or Muslim League leaders could run a democracy in India, which in any case was unsuited to such a form of government. He felt that Cripps wanted no more than to placate the Indian leaders into supporting the war effort and that not much attention need be paid to what he had told the princes. He would rather watch and wait. Orchha, the other senior prince present, chose to continue to puff at his pipe and take sips of whisky.

Bhopal then said that on his mission Cripps had mentioned the possibility of a separate (either confederated or independent) Muslim union and asked why princely India should also not think of a similar separate union. It would, he said, at least allow us to adopt reforms in which we, free from Congress pressure, determined at what pace our subjects participated in our state governments. At this point Chhatarpur asked whether large important states like Hyderabad would join such a princes' union given that they had refused to join the Chamber of Princes. To this the nawab had no answer.

Bhopal went on to say that if the small states grouped together to form larger units they could generate the resources necessary for economic development. The princes of smaller states, however, were generally against mergers or attachments to larger states because that would mean an immediate end to their rule, whatever happened afterwards. Since he had been elected by their support he was not in the best position to promote the idea of grouping.

My father said that a senior official of the political department, Sir Arthur Lothian, had told him that for the state system to survive the number of states would need to be reduced to fewer than 20 viable units (from the present 350) and each with a yearly revenue of no less than one crore (then roughly £750,000). My father added that he did not think that London would agree to such an extreme policy, but asked for the nawab's view. Bhopal said that Lord Linlithgow had assured him that even if some believed that small states were anomalous in today's world, no radical reform would be pushed down the princes' throats, especially while the war continued and in the face of 'unrealistic' Congress agitation and demands.

Orchha suddenly woke up. He said that the viceroy had also said earlier that the British wanted the princely states to join the All-India Federation in 1935, but that his political department had by and large sabotaged the idea. Therefore, he did not know what to make of Cripps's or the viceroy's views, and the Congress too was speaking with two voices. Then, raising his voice said, 'Let us drink to double speak.' He then produced a shabby cutting of an article written the previous year by Pyare Lal, Mahatma Gandhi's secretary. Orchha began to read: 'The Congress wished to restore to the States a reality and vitality which, on their own admission, Pax Britannica had robbed them of.' This means, Orchha interjected, that even small states are to be upheld; there is no suggestion of grouping. He then raised a finger, said 'But now comes the rub,' and read on: 'Nationalist India would welcome them into partnership with itself, on a basis of absolute equality, provided they came as free agents, representing the will of their people.' 'Now,' asked Orchha: how will the will of the people of Orchha be ascertained? Will not the Congress Party's view on the future of my state and my future be presented as the wishes of my subjects? Who will be there to judge? And for the Congress to suggest that they will accept Orchha, if democratized, as equal to a British province fifty times larger, proves the insincerity of this statement. He then relapsed back into his reverie.

The others who spoke showed little anxiety about the future, taking shelter in the belief that the British were not going to leave. There was ample time to reflect on the matters the chancellor had raised. Chhatarpur and one or two others also said that an active role by the princes might provoke all sorts of adverse reactions in British India, so perhaps silence was golden. The nawab, conceivably feeling unsure about future developments, did not press matters and the princes rose for dinner.

Panna later told us that Bhopal appeared to be a bit too excited about the possibility of positioning himself to play a mediator's role between the various parties on the larger canvas. On the other hand, Bhopal could only have gone back with the impression that the Bundelkhand princes were unforthcoming about both a Princestan and about merging their states and joining an All-India Federation.

On reaching Mussoorie we never again talked about the ominous Panna meeting. The princely states and the nawab continued to drift and toss as the storm gathered force.

The ebullient and engaging Nawab Hamidullah met a sad fate. Faced with the prospect of losing his power, he drifted into the hands of Sir Conrad Corfield, the head of the political department then bent on blocking any settlement of the problem and hoping thereby to give the largest states an opportunity to declare independence (and remain tied to Britain). Then, in 1947, he fell into the hands of Jinnah, who promised Bhopal autonomy and him high honours in the new Muslim state if he acceded his state to it and lured the Marhatta and Rajput princes – Indore, Baroda, Jodhpur, Jaisalmer and others whose territories lay between Bhopal and West Pakistan – to throw in their lot with Pakistan too. Their chancellor's drift towards Pakistan alarmed the Chamber of Princes and, after several princes had denounced him, he resigned from his high office.

Soon the British also gave him up. After Jawaharlal Nehru and Sardar Patel agreed to accept Pakistan, the viceroy agreed to deliver the princely states into their hands and obtained a protesting Hamidullah's accession to India.

Hamidullah's tragedy was that, in panic, he turned to Muslim separatis for protection, forgetting his family's integration into India, this tolerant rule over his subjects of all faiths and his standing in the country. And once again he became the rootless wanderer his forefathers had been in central Asia 200 years earlier before they settled in central India. Faced with the same dire prospect of losing their kingdoms, his Hindu brother princes, even the direst of diehards who hated the Congress Party's democratic and egalitarian philosophy, nevertheless remained irrevocably tied to their old country. Their children, after a time, were able to adjust and came to occupy high positions in the republic, some even becoming chief ministers of federal units and central cabinet ministers. The nawab might have lost the tiger in Panna that day, but in the upheaval of independence, he also lost his country – India.

Chapter 15
The Charkhari
Succession

I N 1942 I participated in the coronation of my brother Jayendra Singh to the Gaddi of Charkhari state. He was two and a half years younger than I was and Charkhari was a larger state than Sarila. Its maharaja, besides being addressed as 'His Highness', had the title of *Maharaja-dhiraj, Sipahidarul-Mulk* and enjoyed an 11-gun salute. Charkhari's capital was 50 miles from Sarila as the crow flies and 90 miles by road.

The state of Charkhari originated in the eighteenth century when one of Chhatarsal's grandsons, Khuman Singh, was sent there from Jaitpur to build a fortress on a precipitous hill, which rose from otherwise flat terrain, to defend Chhatarsal's conquests from the north. Khuman Singh was assigned areas from which he could collect land and other taxes to finance the administration and defence of the territory, establish law and order, dispense justice even-handedly and make himself and rule of the Bundelas popular with the people.

The crowning ceremony took place in the *durbar* hall of the City Palace situated at the foot of the 300-metre high hill on which the fort was located. The gold leaf mouldings on the palace doors sparkled against the smooth white areolas on the walls. Wide French windows connecting the hall to a surrounding gallery in which hung a fine collection of old arms – swords, guns, daggers, shields, pieces of armour, helmets and other tools of war. The ruggedness of this display offset the mellow majesty of the hall. Colonel Fisher, the British Resident for central India, had travelled from Indore to preside over the ceremony and Humphrey Trevelyan, the then political agent for the Bundelkhand states, assisted him. After independence Trevelyan joined the British foreign service and served as British ambassador at Cairo during the Anglo–Israeli attack on Suez in 1956. He later served as ambassador in Moscow.

Since my brother was not adopted and succeeded to the throne by a decision of HMG, there was no religious ceremony. Once the assembly was seated Colonel Fisher made a speech and my brother then read out a brief statement. He was then in his fourteenth year. The maharajas of Panna, Chhatarpur and Orchha and a few other rulers whose names I forget, witnessed the ceremony. They were seated in chairs in the gallery with a good view of the proceedings through the wide-open French windows. They were witnesses to the ceremony without being part of the *durbar*, for the ruler of one state did not sit in the *durbar* of another.

The state spanned approximately a thousand square miles and had a population of about 100,000. Surrounded by orchards and gardens, its capital was possibly the most pleasant of all the Bundelkhand states. One could see the reflection of the Mangalgarh fort in the waters of the huge tanks with masonry embankments and topped with parapets that girdled the town. There were many impressive buildings in the town. Besides the huge City Palace at the foot of the hill, there was the Rao Bagh palace where the ruler lived, and the Tal Kothi, the state guesthouse that had a pagoda type roof that jutted into the water and looked from afar like a huge houseboat.

25. Enthronement of the author's younger brother as Maharaja of Charkhari, 1942, with the viceroy's resident representative presiding. The author is seated second in the front row, beside Mrs Humphrey Trevelyan, the wife of the political agent (in striped dress).

The former ruler Arimardan Singh moved to the Rao Bagh palace, in a park on the edge of the town, in the early 1930s. General Maharaja Mohan Shamsher, prime minister and *de facto* ruler of Nepal, built it and presented it to him on the occasion of his daughter's marriage to Arimardan Singh. It was in classical European style, with columns, parapets and cornices. However, all important ceremonies continued to be held in the City Palace.

To me, Charkhari's most attractive feature was the Imaliya forest at the edge of town, a renowned *cheetal* (spotted deer) reserve maintained by the state. It was about a hundred square miles in area with a hill, from which it took its name, at the centre. The state forestry department had created watering

26. Gate of the City Palace in Charkhari with the British Resident arriving for the enthronement of the author's second brother in 1942.

holes (filled by wells and canals) to prevent the animals moving away from the reserve in search of drinking water in the dry season. Driving through Imaliya one could see hordes of *cheetals* – 50 or more – some with majestic heads, any day of the week. In the summer, from camouflaged lookouts with sunken paths leading to them, one could watch the animals as they came to the watering holes. Spotted deer, wild boar, hyenas, jackals, an occasional sambar and many other species would come to slake their thirst. If one saw the animals stampede, a panther was surely approaching, for there were panthers aplenty in the forest. In the cold season it was a wondrous sight, if one had the luck, to see a panther basking in the sun on a high boulder on the Imaliya hill.

Three features of my brother's succession to the Charkhari

Gaddi are worth noting. First was the dissolute and irres-
ponsible behaviour of some maharajas of that time, including
that of Arimardan Singh, whom my brother was succeeding.
The second was that the principles by which the paramount
power decided matters such as successions were never
authoritatively formulated. The British felt that the situations
were too varied and complex to be brought under the purview
of rules. Precedents did count but the viceroy largely trusted
his officers in the field to recommend action based on their
own judgement, bearing in mind the best interests of the state
and dynasty concerned and, of course, overall imperial
interests. And third, my father's understanding of how
Englishmen and the political department worked was spot on.

In October 1941 a childless maharaja, Arimardan Singh,
lay dying in the Maidens Hotel in Delhi at the young age of
38. On a stool next to his bed a fair, willowy young lady with
slanting eyes sat gently rubbing his feverish palms. She looked
central Asian, but in fact came from no farther than the
Almora hills. Though she called herself the *Swayam Maharani*
(personal queen) she was the maharaja's favourite concubine,
which distinguished her from the real queens, of which the
maharaja had two – first the princess of Banswara in Rajasthan
and then the daughter of General Maharaja Mohan Shamsher
of Nepal, mentioned earlier. Though they were in Delhi at the
time, Arimardan Singh would receive neither; childless
themselves, they kept busy receiving claimants to the throne.

Despite a handsome brow and forehead, the maharaja's
cheeks were ashen grey as he lay prone with his head on a
pillow and his aquiline nose protruding. On hearing a firm tap
on the door of the hushed room, the personal queen whispered,
'come in' and an official of the maharaja's entourage, recog-
nizable as such from his khaki closed-collar coat and khaki
turban, entered the room. He was a slight wiry man with the

glassy eyes of a drunkard. 'Have you brought it?' the lady asked, and Pyare Raja produced a packet containing a wad of notes. He then took out some papers from an inner pocket and gave those to her too. She examined them carefully and, smiling, handed them over with a pen to the sick man, indicating where he had to append his signature. It took a few moments for the maharaja to collect his strength but he then scrolled his signatures where required without looking and Pyare Raja retreated. All this was part of an ongoing intrigue for the succession of the next ruler of Charkhari.

Later the same day two visitors called and the guard passed their names on to the *Swayam Maharani*. One was a senior official of the Maharaja of Ajaigarh, a sister Bundela state, and the other, Vijay Singh of Jigni, a distant relative of the maharaja. They told the guard that they merely wished to touch the maharaja's feet to salute him, but the maharaja shook his head slightly to say no, and the lady told the guard to tell them that the doctors had prohibited the maharaja from receiving visitors, even close relatives.

By tradition, Arimardan Singh could adopt any Bundela from among Chhatarsal's descendants. This left the field wide open and, as the maharaja began to sink, claimants and their sponsors started to gather in Delhi to press their suit. They concentrated on consulting lawyers and trying to win favour with the queens and the maharaja's entourage. None consulted the fountainhead of all power concerning the princes, the political department of the government of India.

Arimardan Singh's extravagances as a young man were common knowledge – he loved women and cars. With the first of his collection I had no acquaintance but some of his cars were beauties. He had two Rolls-Royces, one a 1921 model convertible with aluminium mudguards and radiator and sky-blue bodywork. He also had two 1932 convertible

Lancia Lemdas in bright yellow with narrow bodies and boat-like behinds. Low slung, they had coil springs that were rare at the time. It was the same model my father had fallen in love with but refrained from buying.

Arimardan Singh always travelled long distances at night, at which time in those days there was hardly any traffic. The two Lancias would race, one after the other, at great speed through the night, the maharaja sitting in the first car with the convertible hood down, wrapped in an overcoat and wearing a tweed stalker's cap. He once told me that he used to cover the 400 miles from Charkhari to Delhi in six-and-a-half hours. (To maintain an average of more than 60 miles an hour, he would have had to travel between 80 and 100 miles an hour, which was very fast for Indian roads.) My father frowned when Arimardan Singh told me this, for he feared that it might stimulate my imagination for fast cars.

The British required the Indian maharajas not only to be loyal to the king emperor, but also to act with prudence within and outside their principalities. But of this Arimardan Singh was incapable. His illustrious predecessor, Maharaja Ganga Singh, who was also childless, had adopted him to the Charkhari Gaddi from the tiny state of Jigni. Ganga Singh had hoped that a boy from a humble background would be more likely to turn out prudent and responsible, but that was not to be.

In 1933 he tried to get close to a well-known Bengali stage actress at the Corinthian Theatre in Calcutta. When the theatre manager refused to let him meet the lady, Arimardan Singh bought the company that ran the theatre lock, stock and barrel, and transferred the entire establishment, including of course the heroine, to Charkhari, where he built a theatre with a stage fitted with the latest equipment. This gesture did not escape the notice of the political department. It fell to Jardine, whom we have met, to inform the maharaja that the viceroy was contemplating taking away his powers and asking him to reside outside the state unless he became more disciplined.

My father was the Maharaja of Charkhari's closest confidant among the Bundela princes, not only because Sarila was near Charkhari but also because Arimardan Singh used to need his help to intercede with the political department when he got into trouble, which was often. So on this occasion too Arimardan rushed to Sarila to ask my father to speak to the British resident for central India, Jardine's boss, on his behalf. He added as a palliative that since his doctors had told him that he was unlikely to father an heir, he would like to adopt my younger brother, Jayendra Singh, then three years old, to succeed him. He also gave my father a letter to this effect. The Resident, Sir Kenneth Fitze, whom my father met, told him that he would advise the government to agree if Charkhari got rid of the Corinthian Theatre and its actresses forthwith. Fitze also put the letter the maharaja had written about my brother on record.

The maharaja did give up the Corinthian but so enamoured had he become of watching the latest Indian plays and pretty women frolicking in them that he persuaded the Corinthian management to leave some of its sets behind in Charkhari and he started to put together a company of his own. On one of our visits to Charkhari in the late 1930s I went to a performance at this theatre and still remember the striking scene when the curtain rose. It was Chowrangee, the main street of Calcutta, and with wrought-iron lamps on the pavement and all. With the help of side curtains and a cyclorama an effect had been created of it stretching into infinity.

In 1938 Arimardan Singh faced another crisis. Charkhari was on the verge of bankruptcy, the theatre had been long closed and the Praja Mandal campaign for representational government in the state was in full swing. The maharaja was absent; he was busy with other pursuits, this time in Lucknow, where there were courtesans galore.

The courtesans of Lucknow became famous in the eighteenth century when the town blossomed under the Shia nawabs of Oudh; in fact, courtesan culture and tradition even survived the British conquest of that city. The more renowned courtesans maintained palatial establishments, which one could visit during the day to discuss the latest poem, hear recitations of *shairs* (Urdu couplets) full of wit and penetrating analysis and, indeed, get an informed response from a well-educated lady on any subject under the sun. Their comportment was considered so impeccable that aristocrats would send their sons to them to learn *tehzib* (manners). Alternatively, one could have one's head massaged to get over a hangover or just relax – away from the family prattle.

In the evenings the courtesans would entertain privileged guests to *nautch*. The spectators would sit on carpets, or recline on cushions or bolsters on the floor, and convey their appreciation of the dancing and singing by throwing silver or even gold coins at the dancers' feet. Wine passed around in goblets would augment their sense of satisfaction. Only special patrons were permitted to visit the courtesan in her *kotha* (room) for sophisticated lovemaking. Society at that time did not consider it a vice to seek favours of such ladies in moderation.

The political department again considered whether enough was not enough. However, once again, on the intercession of my father, it offered Arimardan Singh a reprieve if he retuned home to his state forthwith, which he did. This time Arimardan Singh, in thanking my father, wrote to him that since my brother was of school-going age and as he had decided to adopt him, he would like to pay for his education. Since the maharaja's health was deteriorating my father also handed over this second letter to the British Resident.

The axe fell on him in 1941 and he was banished from his kingdom. A political department minute recorded on 2 July 1941, which is available in the Oriental and India section of the British Library in London, expressed the situation as follows:

The real cause of Arimardan Singh's retirement from Charkhari State was not ill-health but his persistent mal-administration of state affairs, on account of which he was required by the Crown Representative either to submit to a Commission of Enquiry or to withdraw from the state and live outside Central India. He chose the latter course, and a public announcement was made to the effect that he was taking this step on account of his indifferent health.

It was only after his banishment that he fell seriously ill and lay on his deathbed in the Maidens Hotel in Delhi.

The political secretary in Delhi who advised the viceroy on princely affairs in 1942 was none other than Sir Kenneth Fitze, earlier Resident to the central Indian states. He knew everything about Charkhari.

Over whisky and soda in his pleasant bungalow at 2 York Place, Fitze told my father that, besides my brother, there were nine claimants to the *gaddi* (throne) – four of them nobles of Charkhari, then the issues of the maharajas of Ajaigarh, Panna and Datia, a young man from Jigni and finally a boy whom the Nepali *maharani* claimed she had adopted. Fitze said that, except for one, the Charkhari claimants were too poor to come to Delhi, but the rest were trying to curry favour with either the queens or the concubine. He further said that the Maharaja of Datia had obtained a letter from the sick ruler that he wished to adopt his second son. This he had achieved by bribing the concubine. (Was this the letter the maharaja had signed at *Swayam Maharani's* behest at the Maidens Hotel?)

The maharaja had a secretary named Madan, the son of a well-known Delhi lawyer, B. B. Tawakley of Darya Ganj in Old Delhi. To neutralize Datia's intrigue Tawakley advised my father to get Arimardan Singh to sign an adoption deed reaffirming his commitment to my brother. Madan then approached Pyare Raja, the Bundela *thakur,* who was the maharaja's man Friday and also reputed to be the *Swayam Maharani's* favourite.

He said that Pyare Raja could swing the lady at will. It was only on 6 November that the *thakur* was prevailed upon to accompany Madan to the concubine for he had first to be weaned away from his commitment to Datia. Fortunately, on 6 November, the maharaja felt a bit better, as terminally ill people sometimes do before they die, and the secretary obtained the signatures.

At this stage my father sent for my brother from the Mayo College. On 2 or 3 November 1942 the house master, W. H. Bradshaw, told me that he was required to be in Delhi in connection with his adoption to the Charkhari *gaddi.* Accompanied by our tutor, S. P. Khare, he left for Delhi by train the same night. But, as it turned out, there was no adoption.

After the maharaja's funeral my father saw Fitze again. The political secretary advised that he should not insist on adoption based on the letter he had got Arimardan Singh to sign. This would give a say in the succession to the senior *maharani* (the one from Banswara) who would have to perform the adoption ceremony and 'who was quite mad and unreliable'. The viceroy could very well recommend a succession of my brother to the secretary of state in London on the basis of known facts since 1933. In such a case his son would not become legally separated from the Sarila family, which he would under Hindu law if another family adopted him.

I was able to see the secret file on the Charkhari succession in the British Library in London much later. My brother's claim is supported on the basis of:

Letters written to successive Political Agents in Bundel-khand from 1933 onwards which indicated his clear and consistent intention rather than the oscillations of a dying man. In addition, the Sarila house, through Jaitpur was the nearest legitimate branch to the Charkhari family by descent from the Raja Chhatarsal, a common ancestor.

The political secretary extricated my father from the diffi-culty he had placed himself in, by getting the letter of adoption signed by the dying maharaja, as follows:

There is the question of the letter left by the Maharaja on the adoption of Jayendra Singh which he is reputed to have signed on his death-bed on 6 November, 1941, and the validity of which was contested by his two Maharanis after they had left Delhi and gone back to Charkhari (and there had been subjected to Panna, Datia and Ajaigarh influences). Any investigation into the circumstances in which the will was made and signed as desired by the *maharanis* would undoubtedly give rise to an orgy of perjury on the part of the disreputable parasites who surrounded the late Maharaja and it was in the last degree unlikely that an investigation could lead to anything except a great deal of unpleasant scandal. Fitze's note con-tinued: By the time the senior *maharani* was willing to go through with the ceremony (of adoption of Jayendra Singh) the Rajah of Sarila was unwilling for his son to be

184

adopted and as at this juncture the question of whether or not the adoption was made could have no possible effect upon the succession to the Charkhari Gaddi – as the Sarila candidate would have been selected anyway – the senior *maharani* should be told if she returned to the charge that His Excellency the Viceroy was no longer interested in the question of adoption.

My brother never ruled Charkhari, as the state was wound up within six months of his assuming ruling powers.

Chapter 16
Mussoorie

FOR ALMOST their entire length, the first Himalayan ranges rise almost perpendicularly from the plains of north India to about 2000 metres. Then, they ascend towards Tibet in folds each higher than the last, with those above 5000 metres covered in perpetual snow. Himalaya in Sanskrit means 'waves of snow', which is how the snow covered ridges of the inner Himalayas look from an aeroplane. Finally, one comes to the great peaks, which are twice as high as Mont Blanc in the Alps and, like mighty ramparts guarding the approaches to India from the north, stretch in an unending line for 2000 miles.

With fewer lakes and dales, the Himalayan landscape is less varied than that of the Alps, but its snow caps are more dramatic, its gorges steeper and more mysterious and the air more invigorating. The most magnificent view I know of in India is from Tiger Hill in Darjeeling. One day, long before daybreak, I trotted up on a pony to this point and waited looking north, as I had been advised to do. Shortly, a tiny pink triangle, like some celestial body, became visible above me in the night sky at a 75-degree angle. As I watched, it grew bigger and brighter, and appeared to come closer. Although it remained pitch dark at 8000 feet where I stood, I was seeing the rays of the rising sun lighting up the peak of the 28,000 foot high Kanchanjanga towering above Darjeeling.

Indian *rishis* used to retreat to the Himalayan heights to study and speculate, but it was the British who first founded the hill stations on the lower ridges for rest and recreation. These ridges are high enough to have summer temperatures similar to those of Gstaad or Aspen, enabling one to escape the summer heat of the Indian plains for a while among pine trees, coniferous woods, wild poppies, bluebells, bubbling brooks and falling waters. In the last century ponies were used to reach these stations and the journey took a day or two, but with the winding motorable roads that came thereafter, the journey was reduced to an hour or so.

As the summer capital of British India, Simla was the most famous hill station. The viceroy, commander-in-chief and entire secretariat of the British government would shift to Simla for seven months, coming down to Delhi for the five winter months only. It was from its cool heights that Curzon and other British viceroys earlier in the nineteenth century played the great game against Russia in central Asia and in my youth Wavell and Mountbatten planned the British retreat from India.

There were a dozen other hill stations besides Simla in the Himalayas, and several more in the western and south Indian mountains. Among these, for example, were Dalhousie, Dharamsala, Darjeeling, Nainital, Mussoorie and Kulu in the Himalayas; Shillong in the east; and Ooty (Outacommund) and Munnar in the south. Mussoorie is about 100 kilometres to the east of Simla as the crow flies. I know it more intimately than any other hill station because it was where my parents had a house – Mar Lodge. It had four rooms in a row on the ground floor and four above, a glazed veranda on each floor across the front of the house and bathrooms at the back. There was also had a cottage for guests. The house was built on a steep slope with a grand view of the plains below. The

Ganges was visible as a blue ribbon emerging from the hills far to the east and at night one could see the twinkling lights of Dehra Dun 4000 feet below, not to mention those of other towns up to 100 kilometres beyond. Here I spent most of my summer vacations.

The British government purchased the Mussoorie ridge, which is about ten kilometres long, from the Maharaja of Tehri in 1820 and, as the story goes, paid only 50 rupees (about a dollar) for it. Mussoorie derives its name from the Mansoor shrub (*cororiana Napalensia*). The Mall, the main road, runs along the southern side of the ridge overlooking the distant plains and the Camelsback road, so named because of a loop in it, has views of the northern snow ranges. These are often veiled in summer but tantalizing glimpses are sometimes revealed towards sundown.

In my scrapbook I found the following description of a storm over the Doon Valley, which I watched from the window of our house in April 1946:

As we were lunching in our glazed veranda the clouds came suddenly as they do in these hills and cold descended as noiselessly as fear does in wilderness. A curtain of grey and dark grey sheets of falling rain was moving from the spur of the mountain to the right across the slope to the spur to the left gradually obliterating the view of the plains like a curtain being drawn across the stage of a theatre. However, there remained a hole in this menacing veil through which a part of the valley was still visible. Through this aperture the blue river and green and yellow countryside could be seen flooded by sunlight and beyond purple low hills too, and a deep blue sky. This view in the enveloping darkness was like a glimpse into another world. But soon the curtain got fully drawn, as the rain and mist reached our mountain. And I heard the pit pat of big drops fall on the roof of the house. It had started to rain.

Dehra Dun had the famous Doon School, a boarding school founded in the 1930s and run along the lines of an English public school with an English headmaster. It was for boys of the elite who could not enter the princes' colleges. It was to this school that Indira Gandhi sent her two boys – Rajiv and Sanjay – in the 1950s. In Mussoorie there were a number of private schools run by religious and secular societies and a little beyond, was Woodstock, the only American school in India at the time. It catered for the families of American missionaries in Asia and was an American cultural island in Anglo-Indian India. It was here that I first tasted chewing gum.

Some parts of Mussoorie resembled villages in the Lake District, Scotland or Ireland. It was not uncommon to see stone or white plastered bungalows with neat lawns, hedges, flower beds and roses climbing up to a thatched or tiled roof. Names like Mullingar, Shamrock Cottage and Killarny suggested Irish parentage; Scotsburg, Redburn, our own Mar Lodge and names ending with glen Scottish descent; Castle Hill, Hampton Court, Snowden and Teal Hatch undoubtedly English stock and Chenowyth, Welsh. Bungalow is an Anglo-Indian word derived from Bangla, a country house in Bengal.

Mussoorie's grand hotels, the Savoy and Charleville were spread over whole hillsides. They were at that time run mostly by Swiss managers, as were the two tea houses, Devico's and Wenger's, whose chocolate cakes were better than those I later tasted at Hansalmann's in St Moritz or Zurcher in Montreux. The Hakman's Hotel restaurant served fruit in bowls made of ice – a detail I have never encountered in postwar Europe or America. At Hakman's there were tea dances daily and of course more dancing at night with cabarets performed by touring east

27. Charleville Hotel, Mussoorie. Snows in the background.

European artistes. My parents would take me to Hakman's on the nights that jugglers formed part of the cabaret. The first film I ever saw was at the Majestic cinema in Mussoorie around 1935. It was *Tarzan the Ape Man*.

Mussoorie had two indoor skating rinks and several tennis clubs. In one of these, the Happy Valley club, the British tried to confine membership to their own race, but failed to exclude the maharajas and senior Indian civil servants. The Savoy hosted the all-India summer tennis tournament in June. Skating for an hour or two gave one an enormous appetite and then one could order 'American drink', which was nothing other than a strawberry milkshake. American soldiers who started to arrive in 1943 to reinforce India's air defences against Japan had introduced it to India. From Mussoorie the war looked distant, as if being fought on another planet.

A military or police band played music each afternoon on a wrought-iron bandstand in a flat space on the ridge across from

28. Society ladies at the Hakman's Hotel in Mussoorie in 1943, with
several ranis and maharanis among them. The Maharani of Rajpula,
the author's aunt, is sitting in the centre.

the municipal library, and this provided a popular outing for
nannies and their charges. In the shops further down the Mall
one could buy anything available in Bombay, Calcutta, London
or even Paris. Lilaram, the drapers and silk merchants, had two
distinguished cutters – Harrison for European suits and jackets,
and Beg for Jodhpur closed-collar coats and breeches. Also on
the Mall were the Army & Navy Stores, W. Fitch & Co.,
Whiteways Laidlaw, D. H. Evans, Fraser Co. and other English
stores, some housed in rafted Tudor style buildings. The Mall
was where the gentry sauntered in the evenings, as they do on
the esplanades of La Concha in San Sabastian or the Croizet in
Cannes.

The grandest house in Mussoorie was the Chateau
Kapurthala, complete with grey stone façade and black slate
turreted towers at both ends of the roof. Its terraced garden
descended in front to a patch of lawn surrounded by flower-
beds and shrubs. The large drawing room had Louis V pieces
and the servants there spoke French. The Maharaja of
Kapurthala's Sikh prince was at home for garden parties twice

in a season and guests could stay back for dancing and champagne. Other princes and *zamindars* from the United Provinces also had houses, which were large or small depending on their resources. In these there were parties galore, including fancy dress ones for the children. These were the days before Coca-Cola and we children drank wimto, a sweet brownish drink that has disappeared without trace.

Cars were banned on the roads of Mussoorie where one walked, rode with a groom trailing behind, or was carried in a rickshaw. Rickshaws were two-wheeled carts in which two people could sit comfortably while two men pulled from the front and three pushed from behind. Rickshaw-wallas were all poor hill people and their rags contrasted with the finery of the strollers on the Mall. The rickshaw-wallas of privately owned rickshaws, however, wore impressive uniforms and turbans, and those working for maharajas would often have their employer's state crest emblazoned on the bodice of their uniform. The old Maharaja of Rajpipla, prevented by the war from spending the summer in his house in Surrey in England, could be seen taking a rickshaw ride daily, dressed in dark suits, spats and gloves, a bizarre sight. His Maharani, a princess from Panna, was then reputed to be the most beautiful woman in Mussoorie.

Mussoorie was neither a British military station nor the summer capital of one of the British provinces, like Naini Tal was of the United Provinces or Darjeeling of Bengal. It was thus a place with less protocol and more room for play. Most people went to Mussoorie to escape the heat and enjoy its invigorating climate. Many went to be near their children in the excellent hill station schools. There was also the allure of a smart resort. Mussoorie had acquired a certain reputation and this attracted playboys. The British coined a word for gentlemen on the loose in Mussoorie who went after single or attached ladies – 'poodle-fakers' they called them. They were said to go down from the hill fighting rearguard action against the husbands (on leave) coming up. At the famous Charleville Hotel, or so we used to be told in whispers, a bell would be rung at around 4.00 a.m. to awaken those who were not in their proper beds.

According to Ruskin Bond, a long-time resident and historian of Mussoorie, the hill station's reputation for 'adultery under the pines' was well established by the 1880s. In *Roads to Mussoorie*, he claims that 'Mussoorie was probably at its brightest and gayest in the 1930s and 1940s. Ballrooms, skating-rinks and cinema halls flourished. Beauty salons sprang up along the Mall. An old advertisement in my possession ... recommends Holloway's Ointment as a certain remedy for bad legs, bad breasts and ...'

Our *jhampanis* (rickshaw pullers) used to tell us about a witch that haunted the motor road near the point at which it descends from Mussoorie into Dehra Dun. They affectionately called her *Bhoot* (ghost) *Aunty*. They said she troubled car drivers and passengers but never rickshaw pullers or their passengers. In all my summers in Mussoorie I never saw the witch, who was said to wear white but then we hardly ever drove down to Dehra Dun after dark. Ruskin Bond writes:

Ganesh Saili, Abha and I were coming back from Dehra Dun late one night when we saw this woman in white sitting on the parapet by the side of the road. As our headlights fell on her, she turned her face away. Ganesh being a thorough gentleman slowed down and offered her a lift. She turned towards us then, and smiled a wicked smile. She seemed quite attractive except that her canines protruded slightly in vampire fashion.

'Don't stop!' screamed Abha. 'Don't even look at her! It's Bhoot-Aunty!'

Ganesh pressed down on the accelerator and sped past

her. Next day we heard that a tourist's car had gone off the road and the occupants had been severely injured. The accident took place shortly after they had stopped to pick up a woman in white who had wanted a lift. But she was not among the injured.

Everyone has seen her at one time or the other. To give her a lift is to court disaster. Many accidents have been attributed to her baleful presence. When people pick themselves up from the road (or are picked up by concerned citizens) Bhoot-Aunty is nowhere to be seen, although survivors swear that she was in the car with them.

In those days there seemed to be many more ghosts than there are today. Have they disappeared, like our tigers, with the galloping rise in human population? I do not believe in ghosts and have never seen one, but was nevertheless very frightened of them when I was young.

The guards at the tower gate of Sarila Palace used to tell us that on certain nights an apparition in white would rise from the grave of a Muslim schoolteacher (*maulvi*), which was some 100 yards away. One morning a youth was found lying dead by the grave with his shirt torn. Enquiries revealed that another boy had challenged him to go to the grave at night and plant a nail in it, if indeed he was so fearless of ghosts. The nail was to prove he had been there. The boy reached the *maulvi*'s grave and drove the nail into it with a hammer, but as he was moving away someone caught hold of his shirt. He struggled, ripping the shirt, but then fell down dead with fear and shock.

What was discovered was that in the dark the boy had driven the nail through his own shirt into the grave, which tore as he moved away. But people asked: did the wily *maulvi*'s ghost contrive the accident? On me the story had the same effect as when I read *The Canterville Ghost* by Oscar Wilde; it helped to banish my fear of ghosts.

The following episode has, however, shaken my scepticism about ghosts. Back home on a holiday while I was serving as the Indian ambassador to Libya in the late 1970s, I invited the Libyan ambassador to India to accompany me on a visit to my old school, the Mayo College in Ajmer. There we were put up in a bungalow called Twiss House. In my school days more than thirty years earlier, the house, which a Colonel Howson who looked after the college grounds occupied, was reputed to be haunted. If we were alone at night, we would make loud noises or sing as we ran past the house.

For breakfast next morning the school principal joined us. I happened to ask him whether the house was still haunted. As I said this I noticed the Libyan ambassador stiffen in his chair. 'I saw him last night,' he said. Having never heard of the Twiss House phenomenon, what he said could not but be taken as the absolute truth. He said he suddenly woke up at around 1.00 a.m. to see a man in a white shroud standing at the foot of his bed. When he challenged him, he did not respond, so he sat up in bed and started to recite the *Kalma* (the Muslim prayer). The apparition then vanished, so he lay down to sleep. After a while he woke again and saw the same phantom. He then got up from the bed and sat in a chair where he remained all night reading the *Quran*. The apparition vanished when he got up and did not reappear. After daybreak he dozed off for an hour and then took a shower. All those present were stunned and so was I.

೮ට೧

Most days I skated in the morning and played tennis in the afternoon. In 1944 at the annual all-India tennis tournament held at the Savoy Hotel courts I was placed in the very first round against Ghos Mohammad, who was then India's best player. He generously allowed me two games in each set. It was in the Happy Valley Club that I had my first sexual encounter, if it can qualify as such. As I was walking to the changing room after a hard game of tennis I noticed an attractive young brunette sprawled on a deck chair taking in the sun. She was wearing a white tennis skirt, which she had pulled up well above her knees. I could not help but look between her parted thighs where I saw a tuft of black hair contrasting with her light skin. She wore no panties. Our eyes met as I walked past. Unperturbed, she kept looking ahead – was it at me or through me?

From Mussoorie it was possible to take excursions towards the snows in the upper reaches of the Ganges; the trek to Simla, where game abounded on the wooded hillsides and oak, birch, deodars, pine, rhododendrons and ferns grew in the valleys, took a week. One summer I trekked from Chakrata, which is close to Mussoorie, through a forest called Deovan (Forest of the Gods) to a peak 4000 metres high. The trail led through huge cedar trees, called deodars in the Himalayas, and through the gaps in their pillar-like trunks one could glimpse the far away snow ridges dazzling in the sun under skies of the deepest blue. At the edge of the tree line at 3000 metres my porter cum guide found a hut with two rooms and a man to cook, but to wash one had to descend to a brook of freezing water 100 metres below.

We came across raw-boned hill men and their more substantial women. The men wore narrow brown woollen pyjamas, striped brown shirts, black waistcoats and skullcaps; the women wore horizontal striped skirts and giggled a lot, holding a bent finger across their mouths the while. I was told of panthers and other game in the valleys and regretted not having brought a rifle. I have walked in Switzerland, in the Arctic Circle in Norway, in Scotland, in Ireland, in the Rockies in the

USA and I have crossed the Pyrenees from France to Spain, but the memory of the Deovan hike, of its invigorating Himalayan air and of the grandeur of its views, outshines them all.

In Mussoorie I remember meeting two Nepalese Rana brothers called Jagat and Mussoorie, the latter named after the hill station at which he was born. They owned a castle on a hilltop 1000 feet below and used to ride up to their social engagements in Mussoorie in brown or grey rip-cord breeches and matching Jodhpur coats with their grooms tramping behind. They were so full of mirth and verve and had such good manners that I have always associated gaiety and nobility with the people of Nepal.

The father of these two had had a fight with his cousin, the then prime minister of Nepal, and was exiled from the kingdom. In those days in Nepal the senior Rana became prime minister and, all in all, against him the king was powerless and his virtual prisoner. In fact the Rana prime minister was called *Panch Sarkar* (five governments) but the king merely *Teen Sarkar* (three governments), a public assertion of the superior authority of the former. The exiled cousin was allowed to enter the treasury and help himself to as much as he could collect in 15 minutes before being thrown out. With the wealth he brought out in those few minutes he built a castle and his two sons never had to work for a living all their lives. There were other families of exiled Ranas living at other Indian hill stations, and no doubt adding to their vivacity.

The best cobblers in India in those days were Chinese and Lee Fa owned a shoemaker's shop in the Library Bazaar. Every time I passed it he would give me a paper bag to blow up and burst with a loud bang. The Chinese who had settled in the country spoke the local dialect, but it was in Mussoorie that I saw Chinamen from China for the first time. They carried bolts of silk on their backs and visited houses to sell their wares. This gave me the impression that China was a very poor country; why else would its citizens eke out a living by selling wares in far off lands? The fact that these itinerant salesmen showed enterprise and pluck somehow escaped me.

In Mussoorie I also saw Afghans for the first time – tall, long nosed, grey-garbed and bearded. They were employed to excavate the hillsides for stones with which to build houses. They were paid a pittance but held their heads high compared with our hill people. We were told not to go near them as it was said they abducted children.

The Nehru family used to come to Mussoorie to recuperate from the bouts they had spent in British prisons. However, they kept their distance from the hoi polloi of the station, from the maharajas, *zamindars*, industrialists, British officers on leave with their families and, no doubt, the 'poodle-fakers'. In a letter from prison to his sister Krishna in Mussoorie in the 1940s, Jawaharlal Nehru indicates why the Nehrus kept their distance.

As I read your letter [from Mussoorie] I was suddenly made acutely conscious of a contrast. ... I saw a procession of rajas and ranis ... dancing away in a veritable dance macabre for they danced on a seething mass of hungry and famine stricken humanity and their dance led to a sudden precipice over which they toppled, relics of a bygone age trying bravely to keep up appearances but doomed to inevitable extinction.

What used to strike me most about going to Mussoorie from the hot plains was the total change, within an hour of a car drive on a winding road, of air, vegetation and even the shapes and sounds of things. Before jet planes came to India, going to these mountains was the only way to transport oneself so quickly to a completely different environment. And when we drove back to the railhead in July to catch the train to school, the monsoon would have begun and it was like descending into a Turkish bath – again another world.

Chapter 17
The Last Delhi Durbar

AFTER OBTAINING my BA degree from the Mayo Chiefs' College in Ajmer in 1946, I had moved to Allahabad University to study for a master's degree in economics. Agitation in favour of what was termed 'responsible government' was increasing in princely states all over India.

In Charkhari this took the shape of rallies of a few thousand in which slogans were shouted, the most popular being *Inqalab Zindabad* (Long Live the Revolution). There were also efforts to disrupt the business of government by preventing functionaries of the state from reaching their offices. The Charkhari Praja Mandal (Charkhari People's Forum) organized the protest. Each and every princely state had a people's forum; they all took their cue from the All India State's People's Congress, a unit of the Congress Party, the head of which was none other than Pandit Jawaharlal Nehru. The leader of the Charkhari Praja Mandal was Kamta Prasad, about whom, and the agitation, more later.

As my brother was a minor, in 1947 the government of India's political department had appointed a *diwan* (chief executive) to administer the state. His name was Badri Prasad and he was a distinguished retired officer from the United Provinces provincial civil service. The government of India had appointed my father as regent.

Because of the turmoil in Charkhari, my father spent more

and more time there instead of in Sarila. He therefore wanted me to come back home. He felt that at such a critical moment Sarila should not be left without the presence of a member of the royal family. He wanted me ultimately to take the all-India Indian Civil Service (ICS) examination and thought that a spell in Sarila would give me an opportunity to familiarize myself with land revenue assessment and collection, how law and order were administered and the rudiments of civil and criminal procedures. My teacher would be our capable *diwan* Ram Chandra, another retired officer of the provincial civil service of British India.

I was reluctant to return because I was keen to play for the United Provinces in the coming Ranji trophy interprovincial all-India cricket tournament that year. In my last year in the Mayo College I had been selected to play for Rajputana (now Rajasthan) in this all-India tournament. Rajputana that year was matched in the first round against northern Punjab (now Pakistani Punjab). The Punjab team had famous players, some of whom had played for India. Having bagged a few wickets against such a team had boosted my confidence; though, of course, Rajputana was roundly beaten.

I was a fast in-swing bowler. My action, which was natural and not acquired, ensured a very late swing. Some lost their off stump while shaping to late cut the ball. In humid Allahabad the ball swung for many more overs than in dry Rajputana. This enabled me to take more wickets that year. The United Provinces was playing the first round against Bengal at Eden Gardens in Calcutta, the most beautiful and famous ground in the country at that time. My father said that if I were selected for the United Provinces team I could stay, otherwise I had to come back forthwith. I did get into the team and on the first day at Eden Gardens bagged four wickets for 54 runs (bowling 26 overs). The ball in Calcutta swung all day. The memory of the velvety turf, the myriad swaying palms around the field, the quaint, rafted, very English pavilion and pictures of me in the newspapers the next morning has remained forever vivid.

I finally returned to Sarila in April, abandoning my economics course. As the entire family was in Charkhari I was left to my own devices at home. Of course I attended the office in the secretariat every day, and studied the Indian criminal and civil procedure codes, but sitting for panther at night, stalking black buck and arranging beats of sugarcane fields to flush out wild boar sheltering in them during the day interested me more. There was hardly any agitation in Sarila, as Bihari Lal the leader of the Sarila Praja Mandal was away. Also, Pandit Nehru's States People's Conference was well aware that it made no sense to call for a representative government and constitutional monarchy in small states. The purpose of the pressure was to soften up the princes to accept the policies of the Congress Party government that would take over at independence. Now the target of this pressure – my father – was not in Sarila at all but in Charkhari, thus the concentration was on the latter. In Sarila it was indeed the calm before the storm. There was no communal tension in the state; we did not even know of the fear that was starting to grip those who would find themselves on the wrong side of the line of demarcation 1000 kilometres away in the Punjab.

I had been certain for at least a couple of years that India's independence was coming. Until 1947 neither my father nor any of the princes or gentry we met ever believed the British would go. I used to tell my father that there could not be democracy in half of India and autocracy in the other half and therefore the rulers' powers were bound to go. Seeing my enthusiasm for 'freedom', the Diwan of Sarila asked me one day whether I would be willing to lose Sarila if that were the price I would have to pay for India's independence. Unhesitatingly, I said 'Yes'. Of course I was unclear what precisely might happen thereafter, but at that age I did not care. If worse came to worse, I used to fantasize, I could always earn my living as a tennis marker (coach) at a fabulous resort in Cannes or Monte Carlo on the French Riviera, which was of course a very immature reflex. However, I did not have to worry because my future took care of itself, thanks to the intervention of that most important factor in our lives, chance.

In July 1947 my father announced that there was to be a meeting of the Chamber of Princes in New Delhi on 25 July, which the new viceroy, Lord Louis Mountbatten, was going to address. Since he could not go, he asked me to deputize on his behalf. He said that Shaffat Ali (the senior official who would be representing Charkhari state) would accompany me. I accomplished the 600-kilometre journey from Sarila to Delhi in ten hours in my brother Charkhari's convertible Sunbeam Talbot.

There were no trucks on the roads in those days, so none of the unending lines that make driving such a hazard in India today. The roads were well maintained, albeit untarred and rather narrow. Forests stretched north from Bundelkhand right up to Agra. The somewhat hazardous ferry crossings on the great Betwa and Chambal rivers gave one a feeling of being out on an adventure. We skirted two remarkable buildings – the five-storeyed rigorously square Bundela palace of Datia built on a rocky rise in 1620, and the immense Gwalior fort stretching for a mile along the main north–south axis road of the subcontinent on the last outcrop of the central Indian hills before the beginning of the unending Indus–Ganges plains. The Kachhwaha Rajput clan built the great fort in AD 900 and since 1754 it has been the seat of the Scindias, the Maratha warriors from the western coast. Although we drove through Agra, we missed the Taj Mahal by the Yamuna River because it was too far from our road.

It was dark when we drove into New Delhi. The British-built

Delhi had no fortified city wall or gates, as had all the earlier seven (or nine) cities of Delhi built on the same site since 1000 BC or earlier. We drove from the Agra highway past some Mogul monuments and right into a lush park in the new city Edwin Lutyen had planned to the south of old Delhi; it was spacious, symmetrical and green. I was eager to see the massive majestic buildings of the new imperial capital, begun before the First World War but completed in my youth, so waited with bated breath for the following day.

The Chamber of Princes, as well as the Legislative Council and Legislative Assembly, were housed in the huge new circular Council House designed by Herbert Baker. The rotunda was on one side of a rise in the ground called Raisina hill, on which both wings of the central secretariat were situated with the Viceroy's House at the far end. As I approached the Council House I was struck by how massive it was. It had a circular parameter of high foundation in red sandstone, with the round building above it decorated with 144 sandstone pillars, 'which gave it an impersonal and imperial quality'; porches that led to the interior broke the uninterrupted sweep of the lofty foundation. It was surrounded by lawns and flowering trees. When on my return to Charkhari I excitedly described the Council House to my father, he told me how his friend Gaya Prasad Singh, a member of the old Legislative Assembly, had described it on its opening day in 1931: 'Situated on a lower level than the secretariat [which housed the executive branch] it is in the form of a zero which signifies its political significance.' This changed in 1947.

The seats in the semi-circular Chamber of Princes, which one approached from one of the porches, descended in rows like in an amphitheatre. From the back row where I sat I had a grandstand view. The room was relatively small with no more than 150 seats (108 for princes who enjoyed 11 or more gun salutes and the rest for those who were elected to represent the non-salute or smaller princes, of which my father was one). A rostrum on which the viceroy was to appear faced the seats and, behind it on either side, were the balconies for officials. The walls and benches were of carved dark wood and the panels and pillars were in glistening black, white and coloured marble. Shields containing heraldic escutcheons tinctured in enamel and golden mantling and set against dark panelling formed a colourful frieze. The upper galleries were screened with pink marble *jallies* through which the maharajas' consorts could observe the proceedings without being seen. It has been described as, and indeed was, 'a jewel-box like chamber'.

The maharajas who were now filing into the room were dressed in long or short closed-collar jackets of cream silk or white cotton and white breeches. Some wore turbans. There were 25 senior maharajas and 75 state representatives at the meeting. Shaffat Ali drew my attention to the absence of the Nawab of Bhopal, the former chancellor of the Chamber of Princes. We did not know it then, but the nawab had persuaded many other princes to boycott the meeting. Also absent were the rulers of the biggest states – Kashmir, Hyderabad, Mysore and Travancore. Of course, the Nizam of Hyderabad and Maharaja of Mysore never attended the Chamber of Princes, for they considered themselves more equal than other princes. Among the representatives who sat in my row were some distinguished administrators. Although it was the hottest and muggiest time of the year in Delhi, the chamber was cool and restful.

We had no idea in Bundelkhand, or at least I did not, that the Congress Party and viceroy had already struck a deal on the princely states, namely that as a quid pro quo for the Congress Party accepting partition and independence on a dominion status basis, the viceroy would persuade princes with territories contiguous to India, to join India. And also, that if the Congress Party agreed to limit the states' accession to India to three subjects – foreign affairs, defence and communications – leaving them otherwise autonomous, he would deliver 'a full basket' of them to the free Indian government.

Suddenly there was a hubbub and I saw a tall handsome man with black hair mounting the rostrum in an English admiral's white uniform and an imposing array of military and civil orders and decorations that would have outshone even the most jewelled potentates who confronted him. For a few minutes Lord Mountbatten was caught in a blaze of flashbulbs as photographers took pictures; he was very upright, but moved his head slightly to the left and right in perfect showmanship. Then he started to address the gathering in a loud and clear voice. 'Your Highnesses and gentlemen,' he began. Speaking extempore, Mountbatten made two main points: first, that the princes were being provided with a political offer that was unlikely to be repeated, for under the proposed instrument of accession they were conceding rights (on foreign affairs, defence and communications) they had never enjoyed anyway; and second that, after 15 August, he would no longer be in a position to mediate with the government of India on their behalf as the representative of the king emperor. He succeeded in creating the impression that he was a friend who was trying to help the princes and his bearing and enthusiasm were infectious.

The speech was followed by a question and answer session. The questions showed that most of those present had failed to grasp the dramatic shift of British policy towards the states. This shift was from the old policy of withdrawing British suzerainty over them and freeing them to choose their own future, perhaps even independence, to a new policy of shepherding them into accepting the suzerainty of one of the two dominions – India or Pakistan. An amusing scene then took place. The Diwan of Bhavnagar said that since his ruler was abroad, he could not obtain instructions on whether to sign the instrument of accession to join India. Mountbatten immediately picked up a glass paperweight from the rostrum and said: 'I will look into my crystal ball and give you the answer.' There was an absolute hush while he looked at the glass for several seconds and then announced: 'I see that His Highness asks you to sign the instrument of Accession.' Mountbatten's reply brought the house down. The browbeating I was to observe over the next few days had begun.

On 20 July I was invited to a reception at the Viceroy's House. It was my first visit to this famous building designed by Lutyens. What struck me most was the contrast between the daunting, imperious exterior and the cosiness of the drawing room into which I was shortly ushered. The French windows on the level of the garden terrace, with lawns and foliage beyond, made one feel as if one were in a country house rather than an immense palace.

The business for which we were there was being relentlessly pursued. Princes who had not yet decided to sign the instrument of accession were taken in batches to sit with the viceroy for a friendly chat before V. P. Menon ushered them to Sardar Patel sitting at the other end of the room in his white dhoti and shirt, his droopy eyelids half closed, conveying the impression of lofty detachment. Pandit Nehru, in his pronouncements on the future of the states, had been drawing attention to the artificiality of the barriers the British had erected between the princely states and the rest of India. He argued flatly that it was impossible for islands of autocracies to survive in the midst of the new democratic India. What I saw that day in the Viceroy's Palace was how Patel handled the princes. He first flattered them as the scions of a race that had fought for centuries to protect India's integrity and honour and then asked abruptly whether they would let India down now when it was approaching freedom after centuries of subjugation. Simultaneously, he offered them assurances along the same lines as Mountbatten had done – leaving it to the latter to take care of the details.

I was not required to take part in the proceedings so enjoyed observing the cut and thrust of statecraft in such venerable surroundings. I was struck by the smooth performance of the viceroy's staff. For example, an ADC introduced each one of us by name and title – and we were more than 150 guests – to the viceroy without referring to any list or paper. I wondered how this British naval officer (Captain Peter Howes) whom I had never met came to know my name. Some months later, after joining the governor-general's staff, I picked up the trick.

In Delhi the game of 'herding in' the princes was in full swing and, on 2 August, we attended a meeting at Bikaner House. We reached this fine mansion by driving for a while on Kingsway, the great procession way flanked by lawns and pools that ran from the Viceroy's House to India Gate, Lutyen's *Arc de Triomphe*, around which the princes' houses, including that of the Maharaja of Bikaner, Sardul Singh, were situated. As early as February Bikaner had promised Pandit Nehru that he would stand by India. K. M. Panikkar, the prime minister of Bikaner, had brought the two together. Panikkar acquired international fame when, after India's independence, he was the Indian ambassador to communist China. Chou En Lai chose to convey the warning to the West that China would intervene in Korea if General MacArthur's forces approached the Yalu River through him. Panikkar is now blamed in India for not having been more wary of Chinese intentions towards Tibet. The truth of the matter is that Nehru passionately believed in Chinese good intentions and Panikkar had served too many princes not to become a bit of a courtier. My father's story of how Panikkar acquired his Lenin-like goatee beard illustrates the point. When appointed foreign minister of Patiala, Maharaja Bhupendra Singh thought that Panikkar looked too boyish and dispatched him to Paris to a famous coiffeur to suggest the correct cut of a beard for him. 'And don't come back until you have got one,' he had told Panikkar.

The 35-year-old Colonel Yadavendra Singh, Maharaja of Patiala, Bhupendra Singh's son, was prominently there. The tall Sikh prince had only a few months back replaced Nawab Hamidullah Khan of Bhopal as the chancellor of the Chamber of Princes. The nawab had lost the princes' confidence when he inclined towards Jinnah and Pakistan. Patiala had already made the choice to lead the Sikh princes (and the Sikh community as a whole) to go with India.

The Jam Sahib of Nawanagar was known to have an equanimous temper, as many fat men do. He sat calmly through the harangues of princes who opposed accession. Some expressed doubts about the viceroy's assurances that accession on foreign affairs, defence and communications would prevent the future government from interfering in their internal affairs. Others expressed the view that by holding out they might improve their terms. For example, they wanted the Congress Party leaders and viceroy to give them firmer guarantees that the government would not instigate revolutions in their territories and, in the event of such agitations taking place, come to their rescue, as the British used to do. Nawanagar then spoke to them in a low voice: 'Without your highnesses entering into some kind of an organic relationship with the future central government you would be even more vulnerable to the Congress Party inspired agitations.' Face to face with reality, the euphoria among the rulers that they would become independent on British withdrawal to do as they wished was visibly evaporating.

About this time Shaffat Ali happened to run into Colonel

Zaidi, the prime minister of Rampur. Like Bhopal and Hyderabad, the ruler of Rampur was Muslim but his subjects were largely non-Muslim. The state was located in the United Provinces (presently Uttar Pradesh), far away from territories earmarked for Pakistan. Zaidi told Shaffat Ali that Liaqat Ali Khan had threatened his nawab with serious consequences if he deserted Pakistan and joined India. Liaqat Ali, who also hailed from the United Provinces, was the number two to Jinnah in the Muslim League. Zaidi said that he had replied that he would gladly advise the nawab to accede to Pakistan if, by magic, Rampur could be transferred to a position of contiguity to Pakistan. He asked how Pakistan would help Rampur if there were a showdown with India. Liaqat replied: 'By moral support,' and then added, 'after a corridor is established between East and West Pakistan through Indian territories, Rampur would become a part of it.' According to Zaidi, Rampur's stand infuriated Liaqat Ali, who then instigated riots by Muslim Leaguers against the nawab, thus leading to a lot of damage to property and loss of lives in Rampur state.

Sahibzada Yakub Khan was the only member of the Rampur family to migrate to Pakistan and, in the 1980s, he became the foreign minister of Pakistan. In 1947 he had been a captain in the Indian Army and adjutant to the viceroy's bodyguards in Delhi. His brother Yunus, who was also an officer in the Indian Army, told me that Yakub had left India reluctantly. Field-Marshal Auchinleck, the commander-in-chief, had pressed him to take over as the commandant of the governor general of Pakistan's bodyguards in Karachi because he said there was no suitable officer in Pakistan with training for such a post. Mountbatten told me in 1972 that he was proud of his ex-adjutant's conduct in Pakistan. Yakub, who by 1971 had become a general, was appointed to command the Pakistani forces in rebellious East Pakistan. He disagreed with the Pakistani military junta's decision to suppress the Bengali rebellion with brutal force (which caused the East Pakistan breakaway) and was replaced. Later, as foreign minister, with his aristocratic manners that bowled over the Americans, he became a thorn in India's flesh. What were these uprooted Muslims to do but, as honourable men, serve their adopted country with loyalty, even passion, preferring not to ask *a quoi bon?*

Before returning home I went to see Nagendra Singh, the youngest brother of the Maharawal of Dungarpur who was married to my mother's first cousin. At that time he was an officer in the elite ICS (Indian Civil Service) and posted in New Delhi. If Shaffat Ali had not been with me and taken notes I could not have recalled for the reader the wealth of information Nagendra Singh gave us that day.

He said that most princes were going to join India but some, despite Patel's and Lord Mountbatten's efforts were holding out. For one, his father-in-law the Maharaja of Panna and Panna's friends the rulers of Dholpur and Bharatpur were unwilling to sign the instrument of accession. They believed that those with divine right should have no truck with elected representatives. Then, said Nagendra Singh, there was the case of Muslim princes like the Nawab of Bhopal. He was busy persuading princes whose territories lay between Bhopal and the proposed western wing of Pakistan to stand out and later join Pakistan. These were Yashwant Rao Holkar of Indore and the Gaekwar of Baroda, two important Marhatta princes, and the Rajput rulers of Jodhpur, Jaisalmer and others in Rajputana. The Maharawal's brother said that if all these states were to follow Bhopal, almost a continuous corridor of independent and pro-Pakistan states would be formed linking the western wing of Pakistan with Bhopal in central India – a dagger pointing at the heart of India. This was indeed dramatic news coming on top of the stands taken by three large states not to accede to either dominion.

These were Travancore on the southwest coast of India, Hyderabad in the centre of the Indian peninsula, and Kashmir on India's northern border abutting Sinking and Afghanistan.

But before I go on, let me quote what Maharaja Hanumant Singh of Jodhpur, who was with me at school, told me some time later about the approaches made to him to keep out of India. 'In July 1947 Jinnah Sahib sent word through a prominent Muslim of Jodhpur inviting the Maharaja of Jaisalmer (a state that also bordered Pakistan) and me to his house at 10 Aurangzeb Road in New Delhi.' Hanumant Singh said:

Jaisalmer did not go but sent his *Maharajkumar* [heir apparent] with me. Zafrullah Khan [soon to be Pakistan's first foreign minister] was also there. Jinnah Sahib told us that if we joined our states to Pakistan he would transfer the border districts with Rajput populations from West Pakistan's Sind province to our states, give us free access to Karachi port and complete autonomy. And [he] pushed across the table a blank paper with his signature on it, saying that we could fill in our other terms for acceding to Pakistan. Expecting trouble from the Congress *wallas* after independence, Narendra, I was frankly tempted. But M. K. Jaisalmer suggested we first consult my mother, the dowager Maharani. So I thanked Mr Jinnah for his offer and told him that we would think about it and then return. As soon as I said this Jinnah pulled back rather brusquely the blank paper with his signature that I held in my fingers. The bloody fellow probably thought I was going to run away with it. When we returned to Jodhpur to consult my mother, I found the old lady and the sardars [Jodhpur's powerful feudal lords] adamant on the Rathors [Jodhpur's clan] linking ourselves with the Islamites. So I dropped the idea.

212

In fact Jodhpur did not drop the idea until almost the eve of independence. When Mountbatten finally virtually forced him to sign up with India, it was not before indulging in the theatrics I have described in an earlier chapter, which demonstrated his confusion.

The next thing Nagendra Singh told us was that Maharaja Hari Singh of Kashmir, whom the political department had earlier encouraged to seek autonomy with British protection, was now in a quandary. The British government wanted him to join one or the other dominion. The maharaja did not want to join Pakistan. He was also opposed to joining India because he feared that, once he did so, Pandit Nehru would force him to accept Sheikh Abdullah, his enemy, as his prime minister. Abdullah was the leader of the political party in the Kashmir valley that was affiliated to the Congress Party and a friend of Nehru's. Abdullah had been agitating for representational government and had wanted to end Dogra rule, namely the rule of the maharaja's family, for some time. Their hatred of each other was intense.

Nagendra Singh said that if the smaller states had followed the suggestion of his brother (the Maharawal of Dungarpurs) a year back, that is grouped into larger units and drafted the constitution of each unit with its subjects' cooperation, they could have kept the ball under their feet. Now the initiative had passed from them. (The princes of the Orissa states, however, did form a union with the support of the leaders of the political parties in their states, but this did not prevent the free Indian government from dissolving them in 1948 and merging them into neighbouring provinces and groups of Delhi's choice and on Delhi's terms.)

On returning to Sarila, Shaffat Ali and I reported all the information we had collected about the last Delhi *durbar* to my father and younger brother. My father had already decided that there was no alternative for him but to sign the instrument of accession to India. He signed two of them – one for Sarila and the other for Charkhari, as its regent on behalf of my minor brother. My father did not still believe that the states were about to disappear. I remember his telling me that his immediate priority was to arrange for the coronation ceremony of my brother so that he could start to rule Charkhari.

On the other hand, I had no doubt by this time that sooner or later my father would lose his powers and, in any case, that I would never rule Sarila. When on our long drive back from Delhi I told Shaffat Ali that the Bundelkhand states now had a chance to merge together and recreate Chhattarsal's pre-British dominion, even though it would now be ruled by elected representatives instead of by the Bundela knights, I recall his dry comment: 'What does it matter who rules what, once you have lost your princedom and powers?'

Chapter 18
The New Order

THE DAY India became independent, 15 August, was a subdued one in Sarila. Apart from hearing Pandit Jawaharlal Nehru's 'India's tryst with destiny' speech on the radio. I felt no elation on that day, but that was because of partition.

I have already described my trip to Delhi in July to represent my father at the last meeting of the Chamber of Princes. There I had got my first glimpse of Lord Mountbatten. Legally, on signing the instrument of accession, Sarila and Charkhari had acceded to the Indian dominion on three subjects only – defence, foreign affairs and communications – leaving them internally autonomous. However, this was a mirage because we were surrounded by provinces on which we depended for our day-to-day needs – for canal water for irrigation, for electrical power, for the purchase of essential commodities and for marketing our produce. The centre's control of the roads and railway lines that crossed our territories, and of the post and telegraph services gave it a further stranglehold on us. Most important of all, 90 per cent of the princely states were small and their rulers depended on the centre to uphold their authority. The states had been autonomous under the British also, but only to the extent that the imperial power let them be. The British supported the princes because they were politically useful to them. Free-

215

India leaders were ideologically opposed to princely rule and their states had no use for them. Therefore, it was uncertain how much rope Delhi would give the princes, despite accepting them as autonomous entities.

The amount of autonomy that the government under the new order would allow the states was soon to become apparent to us in Charkhari, with my father and brother in the middle of the imbroglio. It is also a story of our family's brush with free India's government.

As described in another chapter, on succeeding to the Charkhari *gaddi*, my brother had been installed as the maharaja in a resplendent ceremony on 7 September 1942. He was then 14 years old and rulers were normally only invested with powers at the age of 19. In June 1947, shortly after his nineteenth birthday and three months before independence, my father approached Sir Cecil Griffin, the political secretary to the viceroy, to request that my brother be invested with ruling powers. But with the political department in turmoil and shortly to be wound up, no action was taken. The question that arose after 15 August 1947 was what was to be done about his assuming powers. My father's view was that there was no obligation under the instrument of accession to obtain the prior permission of the new government of India to be invested with ruling powers and that it would be sufficient to inform them immediately after the investiture ceremony had taken place. My father worried that if more time were lost my brother might never assume ruling powers. Other princes of Bundelkhand whom he consulted agreed with him.

The ceremony was held in the same white and gold *durbar* hall of the old palace in which he had been placed on the throne five years earlier, witnessed by the maharajas of Panna, Orchha and Chhatarpur. After independence the British political agent for Bundelkhand in Nowgoing had been replaced by the regional commissioner of the new ministry of states in Delhi. His name was Mr Chaturvedi. He was informed of the investiture the same day, but only after it was over.

Soon after, the secretary of the ministry of states Vapal Panguni (V. P.) Menon sent my father a telegram asking him to come and see the home minister, Sardar Vallabhbhai Patel, as soon as possible in connection with 'a ceremony of investiture which was reported to have taken place in Charkhari'. The wording suggested that the government had not recognized the investiture. My father wired back that he was unwell but would come to Delhi to see the home minister as soon as he recovered. His calculation was that if things were allowed to cool down there might be less trouble. In three or four weeks it would become clear to the government of India that this investiture had not given rise to any defiance of the central authority by the other princes in our area, which, in my father's view, was the centre's main worry about my brother's investiture.

Accompanied by V. P. Menon, my father saw Sardar Patel at 2 Aurangzeb Road, the home minister's residence at the time, in September 1947. Sardar Patel was the government's most able and feared minister. As always, he was laconic and gruff. My father explained that there was no question of any defiance and that his concern had been to terminate the regency and get back to Sarila now that his son had become a major. Menon interjected to say that he should have 'approached them and not acted unilaterally'. My father said that he was sorry and then kept quiet. No one spoke thereafter. After a minute or so of pin-dropping silence, Sardar Patel suddenly jerked his chin slightly forward in a gesture that could be interpreted either as his having taken note of my father's explanation or that the meeting was at an end. My father interpreted it as both and got up to take leave, as did Menon.

My father first met V. P. Menon in a lift at the Savoy Hotel in

London during the Round Table Conference in 1930. Menon was then a clerk in the viceroy's reforms commissioner's office, but his ability would carry him to great heights. In May 1947, as reforms commissioner to the viceroy, he proposed to Mountbatten and Patel the compromise formula that all sides accepted and that cleared the way for independence and partition. In 1948, as secretary of the newly created states ministry, he negotiated with the princes for the integration of their states into the Indian dominion. Indeed, he helped to draw the map of political India as it is today.

After I entered government service, V. P. Menon once told me with a wink that he had calmed down Sardar Patel on the Charkhari investiture issue by telling him that a reprieve could make an ally of my father who was fairly influential and that this would help during the forthcoming negotiations for the takeover of the powers of the Bundelkhand princes.

To return to Charkhari, in Sarila soon after this episode I received a letter from my father by special messenger. He asked me to come to Charkhari forthwith and to bring enough clothes for a prolonged stay. I learnt the reason for this summons soon enough; I was to be installed as the chief minister of Charkhari. I was then a few months short of 21.

The Praja Mandal's campaign for representational government in each state intensified after the transfer of power to Delhi. The Congress Party's States People's Conference wanted to increase pressure on the Indian princes with a view to getting them to accept the new government's plans for their future. There had been quite a few instances in some states of deaths occurring as a result of police firing on the protesting mobs. In Charkhari the police had felt impelled to *lathi*-charge crowds quite a few times and to imprison the Praja Mandal leaders. As the trouble continued, my father decided to attempt a diplomatic solution. He asked my brother to release Kamta Prasad, the leader of the Charkhari Praja Mandal, and his colleagues from prison and invite them for talks.

The Praja Mandal's demands were for the removal of the *diwan*, the maharaja's appointed chief executive, and the installation of an all-Praja Mandal ministry to administer the state. Once it had been decided to remove the *diwan*, however, Kamta Prasad agreed to a cabinet of three, in which he alone would represent the Praja Mandal. Of the other two ministers, one would be a nominee of the maharaja and the other a neutral person, jointly chosen by the two sides, to head the cabinet. On the choice of a neutral person there was an impasse, but eventually, quite out of the blue, the Praja Mandal agreed on me as a compromise candidate. Perhaps Kamta thought he would be able to manipulate an inexperienced young man who was reported to hold 'advanced' views. It was also a measure of his ambition not to let this opportunity pass to become a minister.

There were several reasons for the Praja Mandal's strength. First, the establishment of elected governments in neighbouring provinces had made educated people in Charkhari want to take part in running the state's affairs, a demand the Praja Mandal voiced. Also, the Praja Mandal was making it known that if it gained power it would reduce land tax, which was higher than in British India, and provide more funds for irrigation, roads and other infrastructure. The Praja Mandal's slogan 'Charkhari for Charkharians' (or the removal of officers imported from outside the state) appealed to officers belonging to the state who thus hoped to get higher posts. Their silent support for the Praja Mandal was a big factor in whatever success it met. This background is important for what happened later.

The installation ceremony of the new government was held in the large forecourt of the City Palace, which had ample space for a large crowd to participate in this 'popular' function. The only people to show any enthusiasm, however, were Kamta Prasad's supporters and friends. The supporters of the other Praja Mandal leaders, those who had been left out in the cold, clapped perfunctorily. The 'loyalists' (the maharaja's men) seemed uncertain about how much enthusiasm to show.

If I believed that the days of princely rule were over, I also believed that the Charkhari Praja Mandal had no future and would, along with my brother's rule, be wound up. Also, however legitimate some of the Praja Mandal's ideas, the time had run out for the state to consider and implement reforms.

Charkhari's new ministers' salary of Rs 800 each a month (Rs 40,000 at present-day values) was a considerable sum in those days and was probably the main inducement for Kamta Prasad to have entered the cabinet and accepted the compromise formula, which, despite the reservations of some of his followers, had placed me in the driving seat. The ousted *diwan*, Badri Prasad, was getting Rs 1200 a month (about Rs 60,000 today) and the same salary was offered to me, but I decided to work for my brother in an honorary capacity. However, I accepted for my residence the Tal Kothi, which, as I described earlier, had a pergola shaped roof and jutted into one of the lakes so that from some of its rooms you felt as if you were floating on water. In the Tal Kothi there was an exceptionally beautiful dining service for 100 guests and some of its plates were mounted on the walls. The service formed part of the Banda loot retrieved in 1858 when Maharaja Rattan Singh of Charkhari, the same friend of the British who had betrayed Parichat (see Chapter 2), looted Banda at the instigation of the British after they had quelled the uprising of 1857–58, also called the Great Mutiny in which the Nawab of Banda had taken up arms against the British.

How then did a Muslim state come to exist among the territories of the Bundela Rajputs? Well, in 1737 Chhatarsal,

29. Part of the Banda loot.

the conqueror of Bundelkhand, had sought the help of Baji Rao Peshwa, who headed the powerful Maratha confederacy from Poona at that time, to help him to resist a Mogul army sent against him. After Chhatarsal and Baji Rao had driven back the invaders, Chhatarsal, who was by then 80 years old and anxious to secure the future of his conquests, gave territories on the periphery of his domain to the Marathas to ensure that the mightiest power in central India at that time would automatically get involved in any future inroads into Bundelkhand. In the west he ceded Jhansi, whose famous Rani's fight against the British in 1858 has become a legend. And to the east, at Baji Rao's behest, he gave Banda to the son of Mastani, Baji Rao's Muslim mistress, who became the Nawab of Banda.

When I was ambassador in France I showed a piece of this dinner service to the director of the famous Sèvres factory to find out where and when it had been manufactured. The

221

director, after making enquiries on a visit to England, informed me that it had been made in Davenport in 1850, and exported to India in 1852.

৪০০৪

I took over the old *diwan*'s office outside the gates of the City Palace. Much of the administrative work could be disposed of with the help of past precedents and common sense. However, criminal and judicial cases on appeal posed a problem. I did not have a legal background or any experience of judicial procedure, so I used to take the files of the cases back to Tal Kothi to study at leisure and to discuss with a judicial officer from Sarila whom my father had assigned to my staff for just that purpose. Despite my duties I continued each weekend to take off by train (five hours) to Allahabad to play cricket for one of the teams there.

In mid-December newspaper reports appeared to the effect that Sardar Patel had gone to Cuttack in Orissa to persuade the rulers in Orissa and Chhatisgarh to hand over their powers to the central government and merge their states into a larger political unit that would be formed after this merger. In return, the government would pledge to respect their existing privileges and private properties and grant privy purses for their upkeep. Patel had told the rulers that unless they listened to his advice, they might find themselves uprooted by the people; on the other hand, if they agreed to give up their powers, this act of abnegation would gain them their people's devotion in perpetuity.

Thus, 500 square miles of the territory of the states of Orissa, with a population of eight million, gross revenue of two crores (now worth more than Rs 100 crores) and immense potential in minerals and forest wealth, was brought under the direct administration of the Indian dominion. What I had anticipated earlier had begun to happen. To me this made the demands and campaigns of our Praja Mandal all the more irrelevant.

Towards the end of December some senior officers warned me that the Charkhari Praja Mandal had received a message from Delhi to launch a campaign. Immediately afterwards Kamta Prasad started vehemently to seek an expansion of the Charkhari cabinet by bringing in two more Praja Mandal ministers. Until then, the cabinet meetings, which I held in the dining room of Tal Kothi, had been relatively friendly and without dispute. Kamta Prasad also insisted on cutting the maharaja's privy purse to secure more funds for the development of roads and other infrastructure. I told Kamta Prasad that I expected the government of India to intervene shortly to merge the state with some larger unit and that there was no point in discussing reforms of any kind that had no chance of being implemented, let alone of benefiting the people. He did not believe me, saying that the establishment of people's rule in each state would be the first step before any other was taken. Shortly thereafter he renewed his campaign.

At the beginning of January we received a telegram from the regional commissioner that the governor-general, Lord Mountbatten, had called a meeting of rulers on 10 January 1948 to which the Maharaja of Charkhari was invited. My father felt I should represent Charkhari state because if my brother went he might be asked to sign some document that could harm him, whereas if I went the matter would have to be referred back to Charkhari, which would give us time for reflection.

Mountbatten addressed the assembled princes and their representatives (of which there were more than 50) in the old Viceroy's House, now called the Governor General's House. He had already addressed the bigger princes on 7 January. It was

223

soon clear that he was advising the rulers to hand over their powers to the government of India and to merge their territories to form larger units or join neighbouring provinces. He gave the example of what had happened to his family's principality of Hess in Germany. He said that in 1804 Napoleon had passed the Mediatization Act under which the rulers of the numerous principalities of Germany were asked to give up their powers in return for guarantees of their titles, private properties and privy purses. He said that the rulers of those principalities, like his own Hess, who had agreed to merge their territories at the time did not lose their castles or properties, but that those who refused lost everything, some even their lives, when the 1848 revolution swept through Germany. He said mediatization had saved his family. No decisions were taken at the Delhi meeting but what was coming was now clear to everybody.

On retuning to Charkhari my father, brother and I discussed what Lord Mountbatten had said. My father was shocked that Mountbatten, who had asked the princes to sign the instruments of accession a few months earlier, had not revealed at the time that this was to be a stepping stone for the elimination of princely rule and the states. However, unlike some other princes of Bundelkhand, he was realistic enough to accept the inevitability of it all.

The Praja Mandal was making strenuous efforts to provoke the state administration. Its leaders were making fiery speeches and calling for strikes. In some outlying villages its supporters had even attacked police stations. One fine morning my brother and I decided to proclaim Section 144 of the Criminal Procedure Code, which prohibited assembly of more than four people and provided for arrest of those violating it. (In the princely states, the civil and criminal procedure codes prevalent in British India had been adopted *mutatis mutandis*.) We felt that with the rabble-rousers out of the way, it would be easier to enjoy peace in the short life span left to us to rule the state. Soon enough Kamta Prasad insisted on holding a meeting and was arrested. The Charkhari prison was not far from where we played tennis in the evenings and sometimes we heard shouts of protest from those imprisoned there, with perhaps the voice of my cabinet colleague swearing at me among them. The disturbances simmered on but there were no untoward incidents and soon the next stage of the drama unfolded, making the Praja Mandal's protest pointless. This was the arrival of V. P. Menon in Bundelkhand in March. He had come to persuade the Bundelkhand princes to give up their powers and states. However before proceeding further, let me note the following.

∞⊃⊂≪

For some months uncertainty about the future had been growing in Bundelkhand, with contributory factors being the trouble in the Punjab, the war in Kashmir, Hyderabad's moves to secede from India and unrest in the princely states. For example, some distant members of our family asked me to lend them two of our Charkhari state Jeeps to transport ammunition from the thick forests on the Vindhya mountains that lay 100 miles south of Charkhari town. During the Second World War this terrain had been used to train US and British troops for the Burma campaign and at the end of the war tons of 303 bore bullets (the standard bore for the army at that time) were found abandoned in the forest, some packed in cardboard cases. My interlocutors asked for the loan of two Charkhari state Jeeps to haul some of this ammunition to their homes. They said the police would not check state vehicles. With revolutionaries and dacoits scouring the jungles for the ammunition, they (our clan members) had to take steps to protect their properties and themselves. They feared a collapse of law and order. We did not give them our Jeeps.

However panicky their assessment may seem today, the times were indeed far from normal. The elevation of an inexperienced 21-year-old youth to chief minister of a state was in itself proof of abnormality. In such an atmosphere, a revolutionary move to topple the princely states seemed less extraordinary than it might have done in normal times.

Mahatma Gandhi was assassinated barely a month after my mother and I had attended his prayer meeting. We heard of it on the 6 o'clock news. As his last act the Mahatma had fasted to force the Indian cabinet to reverse a political decision. The government had decided to delay the payment of Rs 55 crores (the equivalent now of about $500 million) to Pakistan that India owed it as part of the partition arrangements. This decision was made on the grounds that Pakistan was likely to use the sum to buy arms that would kill Indian soldiers in the war then raging in Kashmir. The fast had forced the government against its better judgement to release the money to Pakistan. The Mahatma's move had not been popular. I was wholly opposed to such vacuous gestures.

Charkhari bordered the United Provinces, which had been the hotbed of Muslim separatism. Some 20 per cent of the town's population was Muslim, against an average of 5 to 6 per cent in the other towns of Bundelkhand, so there was apprehension that the large Muslim population might show sympathy for Pakistan, which could result in communal clashes. Although some Muslims from Charkhari had quietly left for Pakistan, including my bearer Alauddin, Charkhari had always enjoyed communal harmony. The maharajas had appointed Muslim *diwans* to run the state for the same reasons as my father had explained, as recorded in Chapter 6. In fact, the prominent Abbas family had supplied *diwans* to Charkhari for generations. Fortunately, communal harmony was not disturbed during the uncertain period of 1947–48.

The regional commissioner, Mr Chaturvedi had informed us that V. P. Menon would meet the Bundelkhand princes on 13 March at the regional commissioner's house in Nowgong. Two days before the meeting a message was received from Chaturvedi that Menon also wanted to meet the Praja Mandal leaders of the various states, though separately from the princes and informally. It added that he had been informed that the leader of the Charkhari Praja Mandal was in prison and may be released so that he could attend the above meeting.

My brother and I felt that Kamta Prasad should not be released until he had been brought before a court and we informed the regional commissioner accordingly. The next day Issar, the assistant regional commissioner at the time, drove to Charkhari to explain that Menon's discussions were purely with the rulers, who alone had the right to decide on the future of their states, but that political considerations required the secretary to exchange a few words with the Praja Mandal leaders. So Kamta Prasad's release was important. Issar was a pleasant young man from the Indian civil service. When we remained adamant, he said he would have to report the matter to Secretary Menon and went promptly back. The same evening, Issar came back with a message for my father. This was a letter from Chaturvedi, enclosing a handwritten message from V. P. Menon asking Chaturvedi to seek my father's help to 'control the Sarila boys'. Thereafter my father, who had kept quiet so far, insisted that Kamta Prasad should be released. He said it was a pointless dispute and if we had any point to make we had already made it. Kamta Prasad was released the next morning and he reached the regional commissioner's garden in Nowgong just before V. P. Menon met the Praja Mandal leaders.

I accompanied my father and brother to the meeting. From the long glazed veranda of the house where the princes were collecting, I saw how quickly Menon disposed of the Praja Mandal representatives collected under a *shamiyana* in the garden and rushed to take our meeting. Almost all the Bundelkhand princes were there. The atmosphere was charged.

Menon began by saying that the establishment of representational government in the princely states was a government priority and necessary if popular revolts and chaos were to be headed off. Only if the rulers merged their territories into larger units would there be sufficient financial resources to sustain parliamentary forms of government and to develop the infrastructure so woefully

30. V. P. Menon, 1948.

lacking in the states, especially of our region. He said that unless this were done, people might rise and the government would not be responsible for what then might happen to the princes and their properties.

The tension now was palpable. However, no ruler entered into an argument with Menon, but instead asked questions. In response to one Menon said that the government was willing to guarantee to the princes their present privileges, titles and private properties and to fix privy purses for the upkeep of their families and themselves. He said that these commitments would be enshrined in the constitution of India now being drafted, so that no future government could renege on them. After the mergers, the rulers could utilize their talents on a much larger canvas by getting elected to the central or provincial legislature and formulating laws; and the younger ones could enter the civil and diplomatic services.

The tension eased when one ruler suggested the name Vindhya Pradesh for the new union of the Bundelkhand and Baghelkhand states, which Menon immediately agreed to accept. He said that Vindhya Pradesh would comprise the state of Rewa, as well as those of Bundelkhand and Baghelkhand, and that our union would have 36 seats in the constituent assembly of India. Of these, half would be from the Rewa state, which was larger than all the others combined, and the rest from the other states of Bundelkhand and Baghelkhand. To enable the government to guarantee them, the rulers would need to present inventories of their properties for clearance by the government of India, after which they would become theirs in perpetuity. For the amount of privy purses the same formula would be followed as adopted for the states of Orissa and Chhatisgarh. Menon's speech was both daunting and cajoling, and he kept the ball under his feet throughout the discussion that followed.

V. P. Menon was dressed in ducks, sandals and an orange bush shirt, the dress of the typical *babu* or clerk he had once been. However, with his clear exposition and the confidence and authority he exuded from every pore of his body, he quickly established his ascendancy over the meeting. The princes accepted his terms much more easily than might have been expected, failing even to insist that their privy purses be pegged to rises in the consumer price index. (Actually, in a quarter century or so, that is by 1972, an annual privy purse of Rs 100,000 when fixed had been reduced to a mere Rs 5000 in real terms.) Menon then said that he had yet to go to Rewa to get the Rewa maharaja's signature and the Bundelkhand princes might consider affixing their signatures to the covenant that very day. With Orchha leading the pack – if I remember correctly – the assembled maharajas in Nowgong signed on the dotted line that very night. My maternal grand uncle, Panna, told me that it was not the end. The princely states would emerge once again as the sun does from an eclipse.

The next month N. V. Gadgil, a minister in the union cabinet, inaugurated the new union of Vindhya Pradesh. It had an area of about 25,000 square miles, a population of about 36 lakhs (3.6 million) and an annual revenue of approximately two-and-a-half crores (in present terms US$ 2.8 million).

As a result of these happenings, I became unemployed. It was a relief in the sense that I had more time to indulge in my favourite pastime – cricket – even though it was too late to enter the United Provinces team for the Ranji trophy tournament that year. My father hoped I would combine cricket in Allahabad with study under a tutor to prepare for the competitive examination for the newly formed Indian foreign service. Here again, as the next chapter will show, chance intervened to give me a helping hand.

I might add that soon afterwards Kamta Prasad became a minister in the Vindhya Pradesh union. However, the responsible leaders indulged in so much corruption that in 1950 Sardar Patel had to persuade the rulers to rescind their earlier agreements, abolish the Vindhya Pradesh union and merge their states in the Central Provinces (now Madhya Pradesh), with some like Sarila and a part of Charkhari going to the United Provinces (Uttar Pradesh). This, however, did not affect the government's guarantees to the princes.

Chapter 19
Why the Princes Collapsed

I AM SOMETIMES asked why the princes, who loomed so large on the Indian horizon at the beginning of the twentieth century, were nowhere in the picture as the country approached independence in the 1940s – ignored by the British as well as the Indian political leaders. The short answer, of course, is the one given by Lord Linlithgow, the viceroy, who said: 'We [the British] have emasculated them.'

The longer answer is that there were two watersheds in the princes' fortunes during the British period. The first was the great revolt of 1857–58, before which the princes were Britain's potential enemies, with their territories in danger of being gobbled up by the British East India Company as it advanced into the heartlands of India. Once the British had crushed the 1857–58 insurrection and assumed direct responsibility for governing the company's conquests, British policy changed. At that point the British left any unconquered territories in India, amounting to more than one-third of the country, to the rulers and chiefs who controlled them, so long as they did not threaten Britain's imperial interests. The British drew up treaties with the princes of the larger states and issued guarantees (*sanads*) to the smaller ones, some of which were no bigger than the island of Manhattan, promising non-interference in their internal affairs and a solemn commitment to protect their dynasties. By abandoning the policy of war and annexations, and providing security instead, the British succeeded in turning potential enemies into potential friends. A political department was set up in Delhi, and resident British officers were posted in the princely territories to offer friendly counsel and to keep a watch over their new allies. Boarding schools modelled on Eton and Harrow, like my own Mayo, were founded to educate the future rulers, nobles and their families, and to integrate them into the British system.

The peace and order following the mutiny ushered in an age of unimaginable splendour in which Muslim, Sikh and Maratha princes joined Rajput rulers in the British cavalcade. In 1875 Queen Victoria assumed the title of Empress of India. In this land of stark contrasts, vivid colours and love of theatre the British race finally found full scope for its genius in organizing grand *durbars*, meticulous parades and colourful ceremonies that married with such *élan* the British and Indian aristocratic traditions.

To be allies, however unequal, of the greatest power that then existed on earth, was heady stuff for the Indian maharajas. They built new palaces and beautified their capitals, learnt to entertain the scions of British royalty in their homes 'the English way', organized memorable hunts, vied with each other to buy the latest Rolls-Royce and get Cartier and Henry Wilson to reset their old jewellery. They began to frequent the Riviera and mingle with the 'fast set', to be entertained by European royalty and to race horses at Ascot. The British monarch showered them with honours that made some companions, others knight commanders and yet others grand knight commanders of the British orders, old and new, creating escalating hierarchies of fidelity to the crown.

In the process most of them failed to notice that their positions were being undermined. Many had become vassals of the Moguls too, but Mogul control had been haphazard, based as it was on the shifting whims of despots. The situation required the princes to remain ever vigilant in the physical defence of their territories, not only from Delhi but also from their neighbours. To wage wars successfully it was necessary to ensure the goodwill and support of their subjects and to practise thrift. But with a world power guaranteeing their position, the princes had less need to depend on and look after their subjects, or indeed to control extravagance. These were the main reasons why the Indian princely order became disoriented, and alienated from the masses and the new developments unfolding in India. Those whose main function had been to defend the integrity of their country and its ancient ethos had nothing left to defend but their properties and pleasures.

The second watershed for the princes, and the one that finally finished them off, was their failure to enter the 1935 federal constitution of India. This aimed to push them to the forefront of the Indian political scene. As I mentioned in an earlier chapter, the representatives of British India were to be elected to the federal legislature, while those representing princely India were all to be nominated by princes – 33 per cent in the lower house and 40 per cent in the upper one. If the princely nominees could only have worked together they could have outvoted the elected representatives, who would in any case be divided among the various political parties, and thus have dominated the federal legislature and, indeed, the government of India.

But the princes hesitated to join the federation. They feared that to do so might prove to be the thin end of the wedge for the introduction of democracy in their states and therefore the end of their absolute rule. They thus failed to take advantage of the political opportunity the British had placed their way. By the beginning of the Second World War, HMG realized that its policy to build them up as the bulwark of the raj had failed and sidelined them in future political and constitutional negotiations, shifting their attention to M. A. Jinnah, the leader of the Muslim League. Meanwhile, the princes' closeness to the British had created a gulf between them and the nationalists.

The princes and their nobles never had a realistic chance of providing a viable government for India. They lacked the unity, the dexterity and a realistic view of the country's future and how it should be organized. Before India could start to move forward it would have to await a resurrection of the masses and the adoption, chapter and verse, of the philosophies of the invader.

Chapter 20
The Viceregal
(Government) House

I RECEIVED a telegram in Allahabad from my father saying that the military secretary to the governor-general in New Delhi wanted to see me as soon as possible. I could not imagine what this could be about, but abandoned cricket and returned to Sarila to proceed to Delhi.

I saw the military secretary, Colonel Douglas Curry, in his office at Government House. Without wasting words, he told me I had been chosen for appointment as an aide-de-camp to the governor-general and asked whether I could suggest a prince with state forces who would be willing to appoint me an honorary captain. He said I would have to wear a captain's uniform as an ADC. I suggested the name of my maternal grand uncle, the Maharaja of Panna, who had a force called the Chhatrasal Infantry. Colonel Curry said he would take care of the matter and asked me to see Captain Jim Scott, another ADC who had been instructed, he said, to brief me about my duties. He then ordered his peon to escort me to the ADCs' room.

The meeting had not lasted more than five or six minutes. Colonel Curry, who sported a moustache, was of middle height and appeared to be around fifty, had been the military

31. The author in his ADC uniform, May 1948.

secretary to the previous viceroy, Lord Wavell, and Mountbatten had asked him to stay on. As private secretary to the
viceroy/governor-general he looked after all the political
aspects of the work, whereas the military secretary was
concerned with the entire *bandobast* or administrative arrangements, including security. Colonel Curry's office was at the
southern end of the building, well over 100 yards away from
the ADCs' room in the northern part of the building.

The ADCs' room was large and airy with a wide French
window opening onto the Mogul Garden. The other three
walls were fitted with bookshelves. The walls and bookcases
were painted pale green and near the French window two

had done with India. In his country they had created Ulster and here, Pakistan. Tall, slightly stooped and with a long nose, de Valera did not like the English. Frank Aikin, his companion, later became the foreign minister of Ireland. Rarely in my life have I met an Irishman with a good word to say about the English, but then did not a Roman senator once say that the hatred of those closest to you is the most violent? The distance between India and England may explain why the two have largely been able to get over their mutual antipathy.

Jim Scott told me that ADC-I had to read out to HE his day's appointments at exactly 9.00 a.m. wherever he may be – even if in his toilet. The form was to knock and enter, without further ado. I had been told that one saluted HE by dipping the chin to touch the chest, while standing at attention. On the first day I was ADC-I, I found that at 9 o'clock Lord Mountbatten was still in his bathroom (after returning from a fairly long ride on his horse). As advised, I knocked and did not hesitate to enter. At that moment Mountbatten was getting up from the bathtub and had no clothes on. When he saw me – a new face – he instinctively bent down a little to hide his nakedness. I kept my eyes on the arrangements pad and read out his programme. After I had read it all, he said 'Thank you,' and I retreated.

After a bath he used to lie down on his bed and cover himself with a blanket. In cold climates people do this to avoid catching cold, but probably it had become a habit with him. I often read out the programme while he was resting in this way, or at the breakfast table on the veranda overlooking the Mogul Gardens, with Lady Mountbatten and his daughter Lady Pamela at his side. He did not generally dress before breakfast, remaining garbed in a thick white towel bathing gown.

Curry had advised me to consult the *Dos and Don'ts* book, which I would find in the ADCs' room; it contained good examples of English *savoir-faire*, one of which I recall below.

Because the entrance to the ADCs' room was near the entrance to the house from the north court across the principal corridor, people sometimes came into the ADCs' room by mistake. Should this happen, according to the *Dos and Don'ts* book, the person in question should not be led out by the same door but asked to come in and, to avoid him or her any embarrassment, led out through the other door on the other side of the room that led to the same corridor.

Other advice concerned how to present guests to HE and Her Ex without reading from a list; this entailed a lot of work, especially for large luncheons and dinners. Well-known figures were easy to identify, but aides-de-camp were unlikely to recognize all, if there were 60, 70 or more invitees. We first had to memorize the names of the guests and their calling and then, to learn to recognize them, we needed to attend large receptions or meetings at which they were likely to be present. If they were from outside Delhi we would consult their biographical data against their photograph. As the guests would arrive about ten minutes before HE and Her Ex were announced, efforts continued in these last few minutes to match the guests to the list in one's head. As the guests lined up to be presented the trick was to try to ensure that wives stood with their husbands, for this simplified the ADCs' task by half. Even so, one was bound not to remember the names of all the guests and in such cases one had to resort to mumbling and murmuring.

Curry told me that since each ADC had charge of a department in the governor-general's household, I would be in charge of the garage, stables and library in the ADCs' room. I had to ensure that all the cars were in perfect working order at all times and had enough fuel. Jim later introduced me to a roly-poly sardar who would be under me for the detailed *bandobast*. The establishment had one Rolls-Royce (for HE), a Humber for

Her Ex, nine other cars and three lorries. There were eighteen drivers, ten cleaners and two clerks.

The Government House stables could take up to 44 horses. They included the personal horses of the governor-general, the horses of his staff, the aides-de-camps' chargers and horses for nine carriages. There was an eight-horse carriage for HE, a four-horse carriage for Her Ex, as well as victorias and barouches for guests and staff and two brakes for luggage. Mountbatten and his daughter Lady Pamela often took a morning ride. There were riding tracks on the hilly ridge behind Government House on which one could continue in those days right up to Old Delhi. The bodyguards' polo ground, which had been excavated from the ridge on the west of Wellingdon Crescent, had a riding school at one end on which we could canter in a figure of eight.

Apart from horses, the governor-general also had aeroplanes. In addition to the Dakota, which Lord Wavell had used, Lord Mountbatten had persuaded Prime Minister Attlee to allow him the use of a four-engined York. The viceroys also had at their disposal two special trains – one for broad-gauge and one for narrow-gauge tracks. The carriages of both trains were painted white on the outside. Besides the commodious saloons for their Excellencies, the trains had more than enough compartments with bathrooms attached, for their guests and for each member of their personal staff. For viceregal train journeys, the villages near the railway lines would be combed for strangers and suspicious characters and every inch of the railway track scrutinized to ensure that no landmine had been placed anywhere near the line. A guard would be posted every 100 yards along the route, which on a journey from Delhi to Calcutta meant a force of 16,000 men. The first aeroplane bought for the viceroy cost the same as three train journeys from Delhi to Calcutta. When Mountbatten did away with train journeys and used his York instead, the ADCs lamented the lost respite from the hectic schedule that the long train journeys had provided. Jim told me that 'in the good old days' the speed of the trains would be reduced in the mornings to allow HE to have his shave.

Around this time Prime Minister Pandit Nehru, who had been housed at 17 York Road (now Moti Lal Nehru Road), moved closer to Government House. When Field-Marshal Auchinleck left at the end of 1947 Mountbatten had wanted Nehru to move into the sandstone-faced commander-in-chief's house on the Teen Murti Circle. This house was only second in majesty to the viceregal palace in Delhi and Nehru was reluctant to move into it on the grounds that such a large house would cost the exchequer too much. Mountbatten then suggested that the cooks and servants could be supplied from the governor-general's establishment and kept on the Government House payroll. This helped assuage Nehru's conscience. But he still felt uneasy and ordered quarters for members of parliament to be built nearby on the spacious South Avenue that led from Teen Murti to Government House. The buildings in brick and plaster that came into existence were so shoddy that they had to be concealed from the processional way by hedges and trees.

Among the 2000 people employed to serve the governor-general, 166 worked in the private secretary's office and the press, 61 for the military secretary, 346 for the comptroller's establishment, 418 in the garden, 27 in the garage, 37 in the stables and more than 100 in keeping the compound clean. The comptroller's establishment, which was very large, looked after cooking, serving at table, the wine cellar, silverware, cleaning rooms and furniture, store keeping, tailoring and laundering. Then there was a surgeon's establishment of over 100, which functioned as a fully equipped dispensary. And of course there were the grooms and chauffeurs mentioned earlier.

By the time I arrived, Lord Ismay, who had been chief of staff, had left. Many of the senior officers had served with Mountbatten while he held the South East Asia Command. A conference secretary (Lieutenant-Commander Vernon Erskine-Crum) was an innovation. A 15-minute gap was provided after each important meeting during which, immediately the visitor left, he would rush into HE's office and Mountbatten would rapidly recount the conversation he had had with his visitor, which, by the time the next visitor had left, Erskine-Crum would have put together in draft form. Each day several pages of cipher messages were sent to London, which today are available (but not all) for inspection. The ADCs did not of course see these telegrams. The appointment of a press attaché was also a first at Government House. Rather than depend wholly on the government's press information bureau, Mountbatten had his own confidant, Alan Campbell Johnson (of *Mission with Mountbatten* fame) to fulfil the vital task of keeping in touch with the media. In later years he became a friend and some of what he confided to me is in my book *The Shadow of the Great Game: The Untold Story of India's Partition*. The most senior officer, the private secretary to the governor-general, was a naval captain called Brockman, a taciturn man whom I never got to know well.

The above-mentioned personnel did not include the governor-general's bodyguards composed at independence of half Jat Sikhs and half Punjabi Musalmans of the Tiwana, Awan, Mogul and Rajput tribes. When I was there the Jaipur cavalry had been brought in. They tied their turbans in the Rajput style. All personnel were over six feet tall. The horses were Indian bred bright bays with no white points, averaging 15 hands, equivalent to five feet in height. Their manes were worn on the near side instead of on the off side – a distinction held only by units of household cavalry. The clattering of the bodyguards' horses' hoofs with the men in splendid uniforms bumping on

245

their mounts holding aloft the mast of the flag absolutely straight, was a sight one can still enjoy because the presidents of India have retained this ceremonial guard. Let me add that it is composed of fighting units.

The commandant of the bodyguards was Major Thakur Govind Singh (Gomji) of Khatipura. He was from Jaipur and was the only person in Government House I knew from before. Until a few months before I arrived, this dashing soldier with Ronald Colman looks had under him as his adjutant, Captain Sahibzada Yakub Khan. He was from the Nawab of Rampur state's family and, as I mentioned in an earlier chapter, was to become foreign minister of Pakistan 30 years later.

ಬಿಂಬಿ

Before I start to give an account of my life as an ADC based on my diary, let me say something about the splendid viceregal house, now the governor-general's house, which it was my luck to inhabit for a short while.

Sir Edwin Landseer Lutyens, its architect, had sworn to create an edifice that would evoke both awe and majesty. Being 600 feet wide, 530 feet deep (from east to west), nearly two-thirds of a mile in perimeter and covering more than 200,000 square feet, including internal courtyards, it is larger than the Palace of Versailles and its size is awe-inspiring. Set 1000 feet back from the tall iron gates and grill, the approach roads to it dip and then surface 100 feet before the gigantic lengthy colonnade of the dodeca-style porticos with the ever changing light and shadow and the massive 180-foot high dome. The façade is indeed majestic. Nehru described this pillared façade in his *Discovery of India* (p. 220) as giving 'the edifice an air of standing at attention, eyes front, heels together'. This was a witticism, for he has said elsewhere in the same book that

32. The Viceroy's House, view from the front.

Lutyens's work in Delhi depicted 'What is true and beautiful and good in her [Britain's] own heritage'.

The only architectural language able to represent 'the ideal of British Empire', the architect believed, was 'of course classic'; it would be 'better, wiser, saner and more gentlemanlike than the sham imitation of Indian styles'. He felt that:

> universal classical principles were quite capable of comprehending within their framework the exoticism of Indian ornament. But such decoration could not be allowed to seize command and actually determine the architectural outline and profile as in the popular Indo-Sarsenic style. Rather in the manner of the Palladians, decoration had to be within reason ... its novelty and luxuriance modestly displayed.*

*R. G. Irwin, *The Indian Summer*, p. 170.

These concepts are at the heart of the viceregal house design. Lutyens resisted official pressure for the four-centred Hindu arch and the tip-lifted Mogul arch and used the Western classic arch based on the true circle. And he adhered to geometrical shapes. Nevertheless, in my view, the house cannot really be called a Western classical building. It is unique and with its flat horizontal lines can only be described as 'modern'. It was begun in 1914 and completed 14 years later.

Its dome reminds me of a Buddhist stupa. Its shape, the frieze surrounding it – like the one at Sanchi – and its flat top gives that impression. Was the dome Lutyens's concession to something Indian? If so, he placed it above all the rest. Irwin in *The Indian Summer*, on the other hand, laughs at Lutyens's dome, describing it as brooding 'over the city ... like the topied head of a British soldier, a district officer, missionary or viceroy, while great arms below grasp to subdue in their embrace an alien land and culture'. Was it so? Or had Lutyens bowed to Buddha? In any case, the black surface of the dome has the advantage of not dazzling the eye under the Indian sun.

The *durbar* hall is designed on a large circular plan under the dome and, with ceremonial steps leading up to it from the central colonnaded portico at the front of the building, it is the most majestic room in the house. Other staircases and broad passages paved with marble give access to it from inside the house. As sunshine streaks through the circular window at the apex of the dome, it fills the hall with brilliance. Soon after Lord Mountbatten left, C. Rajagopalachari was sworn in as governor-general and on that day I was the ADC in attendance. With the entire Indian cabinet present and the hall filled with leading personalities, I then saw how the grandeur of a room can increase the dignity of a ceremony.

The other great rooms, also on the first floor, are the 57 x 62 foot ballroom in which receptions are held (the days of dances

33. The *durbar* hall of the governor-general's house. Oath being administered to Shri C. Rajagopalachari as governor-general of India on 22 June 1948, the day after Mountbatten stood down from office. The author is in white behind Pandit Nehru.

were over) and the 108 x 24 foot dining room that can seat 100 guests. The ballroom ceiling is decorated with Mogul–Persian style paintings tinged with gold. In the early 1930s Lady Willingdon wanted the ceiling painted white to enliven the room, but London turned down her proposal. In 1948 the dining room still had full-size portraits hanging on its walls of past viceroys, some of whose posture and expressions reminded one of John Davidson's lines: 'It is with nations as with men; we must be first. We the mightiest, the heirs of Rome.' Both rooms look onto the magnificent Mogul Garden, which enhances their appeal.

Below them on the ground floor are the rooms used daily – the viceregal study, Her Excellency's study, the yellow drawing room, another dining room and a loggia. As mentioned earlier, the extraordinary thing about these rooms is that, with the greenery just outside their French windows, they give one the feel of being in a country house or even bungalow, the massive edifice forgotten, despite its 340 rooms, 18 staircases, 10 lifts, 500 yards of covered carriageways, mile and a half of corridors and spread over five acres.

The Mogul Garden is considered to be one of the great gardens on this planet and I reached Delhi when its flowers and flowering shrubs were in full bloom.

34. The Viceroy's House, Mogul Garden.

Two glistening channels of water run westward from the House and intersect with a pair of north–south canals. Circular fountains on 16-tiered lotus leaves carved from sandstone scatter water from their 12' jets. Two large fountains of 18-tiered leaves grace rectangular pools where reflections repeat with double charm the blossoms around them and the building.

In the centre of the garden, a 200-foot square plot of lawn is used as a place for providing entertainment. At the northern and southern edges are battlements with formal terraces and flowers alongside a path. On one entire battlement the colour scheme that year (1948) was of various shades of yellow against the green turf, produced by grouping together nasturtiums, pansies, yellow dahlias and, at central points, yellow roses. From the battlements one has a view of the park surrounding the Mogul Garden.

Perhaps the most beautiful part of it all is the circular

sunken garden where brightly coloured flowers are arranged in tiers around a large round pool; a high arched wall laden with creepers encloses the space further back. The fragrance of roses and mignonettes perfume the air as the sun sinks. It is no different 60 years on. Close by are situated tennis courts and a 30-yard long swimming pool with a patch of lawn enclosed by a wall alongside it. Over here Nehru used to be entertained by their Excellencies or simply by Her Ex.

One afternoon Jim Scott told me that the 'whirlwind' was arriving the next morning. By this he meant that their Excellencies were returning from their tour. The pace of life would quicken sharply and there would hardly be any time left to contemplate the beauty and comfort of the great house.

Chapter 21
Aide-de-Camp to Lord Mountbatten

HE 'WHIRLWIND' arrived back from South India at 4.40 p.m. on 28 April 1948 and immediately plunged us into a state of hustle and bustle. The personal staff members were lined up at the entrance of the north court where the Rolls-Royce stopped and their Excellencies alighted wearing jungle green safari uniforms. Shaking hands they had a remark or two for each of us. To me HE said: 'I am glad to see you here.' Her Ex gave me a smile. He disappeared into his office, she proceeding to hers further down the corridor.

At dinner Major Martin Gilliart, the tall, bald, merry deputy military secretary who had accompanied the Mountbattens on their travels regaled us with stories of the tour, which, if he were to be believed, consisted of one disaster after the other. For example, at one major temple in South India, Gaiky (Captain Gaekwar) had persuaded the *pujaris* to ring the temple bells with full force to welcome their Excellencies, but the untimely chant raised an alarm and the devotees stampeded towards the door, at the very moment that the Lord and Lady were making their entrance. These stories were Martin's way of conveying that everything had worked smoothly on the tour.

The day ended, as indeed each day did, with a film – the

Mountbattens very much there. According to my diary, it starred Bob Hope and helped to put more oxygen into my lungs than I had taken all day. That my diary notes that I was going to ride at 6.00 a.m. the next morning suggests that the 'whirlwind' had not totally swept me off my feet.

The next day was my day off. However, I attached myself to Jim Scott, who was ADC-I that day, to see how he went about his business. The following day (30 April) there was a lunch for a dozen princes at which I had to introduce them to HE. There were a few I did not know but by looking up their photographs I was able to name them correctly. The 1 May was my D-Day because I was to be ADC-I. It was on this day that the incident in the bathroom I have recounted in the previous chapter, took place. According to my diary, 'I was in the saddle from 8.00 a.m. to 12 midnight and could visit my room for 15 minutes only, towards the evening.' My diary records that I did pretty well except for stammering once rather badly. Bahadur Singh, the Maharaja of Bundi (who since his Mayo College days had fought in Burma and won the MC) had come for lunch. He whispered to me as he left: 'They are quite happy with you.' In the evening Pandit Nehru called and I escorted him to HE's office. I recalled that 'He looked very beautiful in his white attire and black Punjabi sandals. He was chummy with Their Excellencies. Came for ten minutes, stayed for 2 hours.'

Whatever impression I might have had that Mountbatten was a playboy disappeared very fast. He worked from 9.00 a.m. to midnight each day and scrutinized the minutest details. Lady Mountbatten had a more elusive personality. In my diary I record that I hoped to get to know her better as time went by.

2 May 1948

The lunch was lit up by a remark by N. V. Gadgil the Minister for Works and Housing (at which General

253

Cariappa, Sir Terence Shone, the British High Commissioner, Lady Shone and K. P. S. Menon, the Foreign Secretary, were the other guests). Lady Edwina used to smoke during meals using a longish cigarette holder. Gadgil sitting next to her was getting uncomfortable as the smoke from her exhalations swirled around him. Somehow the conversation turned to Hitler. 'Hitler at least had one virtue,' said Gadgil, 'he did not smoke.' Her Ex was the least dismayed and turning towards Gadgil with a seductive smile, said: 'You are right he didn't,' and blew more smoke onto his face.

On 4 May Lord and Lady Mountbatten left for a tour of Jodhpur and Bundi. Jim and I were asked to accompany them as ADCs in attendance. For me, going to Jodhpur was like going home, for I would be meeting so many friends from my Jodhpur House days at the Mayo College. According to my diary,

> We reached Jodhpur airport at 12 noon and were received by Hanwant Singh the Maharaja, Jai Narin Vyas, the leader of the Congress Party in the State, a guard of honour and a large crowd. We were to stay in the Maharaja's recently constructed huge Umaid Bhawan Palace, with its interior in the art deco style. In the late afternoon a game of polo had been arranged.
>
> Apparently HE had played polo here in 1921 while accompanying the Prince of Wales [later King Edward VIII] and wanted to recapture the lost moments of a quarter of a century back. His performance was quite impressive for one out of practice; and though out of breath after the second 'chakkar', insisted on playing another. Jodhpur had produced famous polo players that

included Hanut Singh who had nine handicaps. The polo personalities crowded round them after the game.

I noticed no resentment among the nobles for his role in helping to obliterate their 700-year-old kingdom.

In the evening there was a gala dinner in Umaid Bhawan given by the Maharaja. When we returned back to the palace there were barely five minutes left before their Excellencies' scheduled ceremonial appearance at the gala. Mountbatten, to my surprise, was able to change into dinner dress and appear perfectly groomed in exactly three minutes. (After all, it was he who is credited with inventing the zip to replace fly-buttons.) Lady Mountbatten had disengaged herself from the party earlier. She appeared at the top of the staircase as her husband emerged from his room in an impressively coordinated *pas de deux*.

In the morning HE had an hour's talk with Hanwant Singh. I learnt what this was about 50 years later when I was going through Mountbatten's papers at Southampton University. First, he advised Hanwant Singh not to favour the Rajputs (people of his clan) against the Jats (mostly peasants). He had to be fair and just; moreover, that would only push the Jats into the hands of the republicans in the Congress Party. Second, he upbraided the young maharaja for importing 21 women from Karachi (now in Pakistan) for his amusement. He said he had known his late father since 1921 and was sure he would give the same advice. Jodhpur promised to mend his ways. V. P. Menon had provided the above intelligence to the governor-general. The next day:

We flew in the York to Bundi and drove straight to Bundi's

'beehive palace' [as Kipling described it]. It is built on a rock that juts out halfway up a steep hill. While we were having gimlets before lunch, admiring the views of the white-washed town and the lake below from the palace *jharokas*, Maharaja Bahadur Singh announced that cars were ready to take us to the tiger shoot. Behind the hill on which the palace was situated was a thick dry forest, reachable by car within minutes. But I was not prepared for a tiger being shot between gimlets and the soufflé. It took a ten-minute drive and walk to the *machan*, a five-minute wait on it for the tiger to appear and five minutes more for the inevitable photograph with the dead beast lying at the Governor-General's feet, Bahadur Singh brimming with delight.

I was seated with some members of the staff in an old stone *burj*, watchtower, about 50 yards behind the *machan* of the principal guest. Soon after the beat commenced I saw a huge tiger moving from our left cutting across the beat, going slam bang for the *machan*. And soon enough [there were] two shots.

৲১৫৫

India is well known for the rope trick but there used to be a 'tiger trick' as well, though of a less magical stamp. I witnessed that day probably the 'last tiger trick' performed in India. What the trick was has to be left to the reader's imagination, so as not to spoil the romance of it all.

ADCs did not see any official papers or play a political role. It was much later that I discovered the background of the meetings with HE, to which I used to escort Nehru, Krishna Menon, then the Indian high commissioner in London, Sir Girja Shankar Bajpai, the secretary general in the Ministry of External

35. A tiger shoot in Bundi state in Rajasthan. The author is behind and between Lord and Lady Mountbatten, 5 May 1948.

Affairs, General Roy Bucher (a British officer still commanded the Indian Army), Sir Terence Shone, the British high commissioner, Gopalaswami Ayangar, who was representing India at the UN Security Council on India's complaint about Pakistan's aggression in Kashmir, as well as Sir Walter Monckton, QC, adviser to the Nizam of Hyderabad, Hyderabad ministers Laik Ali and the Nawab of Chhatari, and most others who then wielded power in Delhi. V. P. Menon was Mountbatten's closest adviser and he was in and out of HE's office all the time.

Nehru had earlier vowed before the Constituent Assembly that India would be declared a republic. This posed a problem for Mountbatten who had vowed before his cousin, King George VI and Prime Minister Attlee that he would keep India in the British Commonwealth. Anglo–Indian differences on Kashmir had foreboded failure for Mountbatten on the issue. However, a letter from Nehru to Attlee of 18 April 1948 that I saw much later in the Mountbatten archives perhaps explains the *bonhomie* between Nehru and the Mountbatten that I witnessed at that time. Nehru wrote to Attlee:

It is remarkable what Lord Mountbatten, and may I add Lady Mountbatten also, have done to remove many of the old causes of distress and bitterness between India and England. I shall not say much more at this stage (on the Commonwealth issue) except to repeat the hope that India and England will be closely associated to their mutual advantage.

Panditji was always uncomfortable at having to disagree with people he liked. Having taken a decision on this tangled issue, he was more relaxed with them.

The two other political problems to occupy the governor-general's attention during the time I was with him that summer were (a) Hyderabad and (b) Kashmir. His other preoccupation was with the princes. The numerous meals offered to them – at least twice every week – and his visits to their capitals were attempts to rub balm on their injured feelings.

On 13 May the Mountbattens and Panditji took off for Simla, the summer capital of the raj, on a ten-day visit. Jim and I accompanied them.

We flew in the York to Ambala airport in the plains about 50 kilometres short of the hills. From Ambala we raced in a procession of cars towards the Himalayas. (We were heading for the viceregal cottage called the Retreat in Mashobra beyond Simla, 8000 feet above sea level facing the snows a hundred miles away.) As we passed Kalka and started to climb out of the 40°C plus heat of the plains, our spirits soared. HE drove at a tremendous pace and changed cars three times, finally reaching the Retreat gates at 7.20 p.m. in a small red Sunbeam with only Her Ex, Pammy and PM. Why this speed and changing of cars? Was it to impress Nehru?

Written that night my diary contains a longish description of our arrival. I was excited. Portions of this I give below:

Cars did not drive right up to the Retreat. HE, Her Ex and Panditji walked in front; Pammy and I just behind. The winding track and the surrounding deodar and oak forest grew darker and darker but in the great valley to our right and on the snow mountains beyond, the day still lingered. In the rear we would hear some noise; that was our baggage and paraphernalia being selflessly brought up by Jim.

At the gates of the cottage we were welcomed by Sohan Singh, the caretaker who led us up the stone steps of a terraced garden to a very English looking rafted structure, the lights within very inviting. Wooden floors with rugs and chintz covered sofas. My room was on the second floor, in the attic, to which I foolishly bounded up. Suddenly became breathless. I had forgotten we were so high up, but soon recovered.

The dinner was in a cosy dining room (the shadows from the fire licking the ceiling). Around the table were seated Lord and Lady Louis, Panditji, Pamela, M. O. Mathai (Nehru's secretary and confidant), Jim and myself The talk ranged from the merits and demerits of purdah to metaphysics, mysticism and telepathy. Lord Louis spoke of his exploits in battle. He said sailors who saw sea horses were reluctant to report the experience for fear of being accused of hallucinations that might harm their careers. But what was there to prove that there was no such phenomenon? He said that in the heat of battle one sometimes received premonitions of the coming danger, and gave examples. Panditji took off from here. 'Yes, we do get intuitions of things happening far away,' he said. 'Is it not that the atmosphere is charged with events

259

36. Sketch by the author of the Retreat, the viceroy's hideaway above Simla, showing Mountbatten working on the veranda.

taking place all over on our planet and even beyond? Why can't we, if we have the facility, tune into this knowledge like a radio tunes into wavelengths. I am not explaining away metaphysics with science; I am just setting up a chain of thought for you.' He continued: 'Light is the fastest medium known to man. It takes ten years for light to come from certain planets to earth. New planets may be formed but we wouldn't see them. Well, if we discovered some other medium that travelled faster than light we could become aware of them, before light revealed them to us.'

When the talk turned to political matters I note in my diary that: 'Lady Louis was particularly harsh on the Americans, alleging that they entertained hegamonic ambitions in Asia, with which sentiments Nehru appeared to agree.'

14 May 1948

Spent leisurely day. HE full of pep; he first placed the table on which he would work under a tree in the garden, then somewhere else and finally on the veranda. Sitting in the garden at a distance, I drew a sketch of the house with him working in the veranda. Meanwhile, Lady Louis was trying to make Nehru's sojourn as agreeable as possible. Pamela (or Pammy as we called her) took off for a walk in the woods. She is thoughtful of others with no trace of vanity.

In the late afternoon, we drove to the local bazaar where crowds engulfed us. Did we go to shop there or to show ourselves to the populace? My new shoes were nearly ruined as I tried to protect the PM from the mob. PM's popularity, yes, but also the emotionalism of the crowd and indiscipline.

That night after dinner Lord Louis made us play a game that is better described in M. O. Mathai's book *Reminiscences of the Nehru Age* (Vikas Publishers, Delhi, 1978) than in my diary.

One evening, after dinner at Mashobra, seven persons, Lord Mountbatten, Captain Narendra Singh, the Lady Pamela, M. O. Mathai, Lady Mountbatten, Jawaharlal Nehru and Captain Scott sat around a circular table sipping coffee. Mountbatten talked about the folly of believing rumours. He also said that truth could get distorted beyond recognition if it passes through several mouths. He asked all of us to join him in playing a sketching game that he called Dame Rumour. The figure to be sketched was that of a woman sitting down and playing with her dog in front of a chair. Mount-batten would start drawing one line at a time. This was supposed to be copied by the next person. The third person was supposed to copy from the second and not to look at any other person's sketch; and so on it was to be until the last person around the table had finished his sketch, line after line drawn at random and copied strictly according to instructions. I was the fourth person and my sketch turned out to be horrible; Lady Mount-

37. The game Dame Rumour. No. 1 by Lord Mountbatten, 2 author, 3 Pamela, 4 Mathai, 5 Lady Mountbatten, 6 Prime Minister, 7 Scott.

batten's looked like nothing on earth; and the last man, Scott's, was the horror of horrors.

(*Reminiscences of the Nehru Age*, p. 34)

15 May 1948

We travelled 31 miles on the Tibet Road to the 9000 feet Narkanda Pass, the foursome in the red Sunbeam; Jim, Inspector Pearce, Handa the photographer, summoned from Delhi to leave permanent imprints of the trip on the sands of time, and me, in a Jeep ahead; Sohan Singh bringing up the rear with the food and the *khidmatgars* in a station wagon. I was supposed to stage-manage the photo operation, so I got Handa to perch himself at suitable

38. Lord Mountbatten taking a nap on the Narkanda Pass above Simla on the road to Tibet, 15 May 1948. Photograph by the author.

places on the way to do his job. The trouble I ran into was that HE wanted a picture of Panditji and themselves with the milestones marked 'Tibet', which were along the hillside, while the PM wanted photographs with the background of the snow mountains. 'Why not both, Sir,' I asked. Nehru's response: 'You are not artistic enough.'

After the picnic on the Narkanda Pass HE lay down on the grass and took a siesta, while PM and Her Ex took a stroll. On our way back, we passed a village fair where again the crowds collected as soon as they recognized Panditji, who, standing up in the car made an impromptu speech.

He was so full of the Mountbattens by this time that most of the speech was devoted to praising their services for India.

Later in the evening we left the Retreat and moved to the viceroy's lodge at Simla. It replicates a Scottish castle, its

39. Lady Edwina and Nehru taking a stroll on the Narkanda Pass.
Photograph by the author.

terraced gardens occupying a whole hilltop. The hall had a huge weighing machine with a notebook in which you recorded your weight. I am 13 stone.

On 16 May 1948 I wrote in my dairy that 'Pandit Nehru left for Delhi at 7 a.m. He has a very attractive personality. What luck to pass a few days with such a noble soul.'

I continued to run into Nehru while I was private secretary to Sir Girja Shankar Bajpai, the secretary-general in the Ministry of External Affairs (1950–51), and during Lady Mountbatten's visits to India in the 1950s, for she stayed in his house, and on other occasions. Indeed, he was my benefactor.

With more experience and maturity I began to see his shortcomings as a foreign minister and diplomat. The British high commissioner in Delhi's top-secret quarterly report fell into our hands in 1950 and crossed my desk when I was private secretary to Sir Girja. After acclaiming Nehru's achievements in certain fields, the report said that as a foreign minister he was 'over idealistic, inexperienced in foreign affairs and far too vain'. These words stuck in my memory. It was, alas an accurage assessment. On the other hand, he remained the people's darling until almost the very end.

The story of how this top secret British report fell into Indian hands is worth recounting. A copy of the report was sent from London to the British governor of Uganda, Sir Andrew Cohen. He had earlier been colonial secretary in the British cabinet and perhaps therefore reports on Commonwealth affairs with strictly restricted circulation continued to be sent to him. At this time our commissioner in East Africa, Appa Pant, who was stationed in Nairobi, happened to travel to Uganda where he was a guest of the governor. According to Appa Pant he was woken up by an Indian in the middle of the night. The Indian, who was a Bengali said he was a clerk in the governor's office and had brought a top secret report to show Pant, adding that this was the least service he could render to his country. Pant immediately realized its importance and told the clerk to come back to collect it from him before daybreak. Pant then switched off his bedroom lights

40. Pandit Jawaharlal Nehru, Lord and Lady Mountbatten and their daughter
Lady Pamela in their red Sunbeam Talbot in the Simla hills on 17 May 1948.
The author is standing behind Nehru.

and, sitting on the toilet, spent all night copying the report in
longhand. On returning to Nairobi he sent it to India.

৪৩০৪

I said above that whatever his shortcomings, he remained the
people's darling. The story below may explain why this was
so. As a trainee in the protocol division in the Ministry of
External Affairs in Delhi, I was attached to King Tribhuvan of
Nepal as a liaison officer for a visit he was making to Kashmir,
among other things to address Gurkha troops stationed on the
Baramula front. In Srinagar the officer commanding the operations, General Thakur Mahadeo Singh, approached me to
intimate that he would be taking the king to the front by

helicopter and regrettably there would be no place for me. I said that was all right. He then said 'And we cannot take Sheikh Abdullah either.' When I said nothing he pointedly remarked: 'I am telling you because you are the liaison officer from the Ministry of External Affairs.' 'If you can't take him, you can't take him,' was my reply; and I forgot all about the matter.

When we landed back at Delhi airport, Pandit Nehru had come to receive the king. As I climbed down the gangway he saw me and immediately walked towards me. 'What happened?' he asked. 'What happened to what, Sir?' 'Sheikh Abdullah', he said. When I told him what General Mahadev Singh had told me, he agitatedly asked: 'What did you say?' 'I said that if you can't take him you can't take him,' I replied. 'You fool,' said the prime minister. 'It is fools like you who create problems between Sheikh Abdullah and me,' and he banged one fist on the palm of the other hand, stamped his foot on the tarmac and walked away. After going a few paces he wheeled round and said: 'It is not only the fault of you, you fool, but of the fools who sent a fool like you.'

By this time the king and others had moved quite a distance away. I hurried to join the king to escort him to Hyderabad House where he had been assigned to lodge. The thought did cross my mind that I might be replaced and sent back to the protocol division. However, nothing happened and I accompanied the king to the reception that Pandit Nehru was giving for him on the lawns of the prime minister's house (the former commander-in-chief's house). I had to stay close to the king to translate English to Hindi for him, for he did not speak English. All of a sudden I found that somebody coming from behind had caught my two elbows and was pressing them together so hard that I could not look back. 'Don't play the fool, Yaar [buddy], I am on duty,' I said, thinking it was one of my colleagues. Soon my elbows were released and, as I turned, I saw Pandit Nehru rapidly walking away.

ഇൗരു

The same day I was informed that I would have to pose as a dummy for the painting of HE's portrait commissioned by the government of India to hang in the Viceroy's House. He could not obviously spend hours sitting for the painting. As I explained in my diary:

> I was drafted in, dressed up in the full viceregal regalia with all of Lord Louis' numerous decorations – (and please remember, he was the most decorated Briton of the time), Lord Louis himself buckling my tunic, arranging the decorations and medals and correctly placing the purple band of the Order of the Garter on me.

The portrait painter was called da Cruz. (A man called Swamy had been commissioned to paint a portrait of Her Excellency.) I had the presence of mind one day to summon Handa to take my photograph while I posed as Lord Mountbatten.

19 May 1948

[There was] a grand dinner for 119 persons at the Lodge. It was said to be one of the grandest in Simla ever. I was required to present the guests to Lady Louis. I missed only four or five names, which pleased her. I had had to work very hard for the presentation; fortunately the previous day there had been a reception by the governor of the Punjab, Chandu Lal Trivedi, where I spent the whole time identifying the invited personalities. The workload during the party was too heavy to enjoy it.

41. The author as Mountbatten. Dressed in the viceroy's ermine,
with Lord Louis's decorations and garter.

20 May 1948

The main event was the play at the Amateur Dramatic
Club (ADC) Simla which had a cosy and well appointed
theatre. We sat in the viceregal box. People were better

dressed and behaved much more informally than in Delhi. HE was attracted by the lead actress, one Mrs Bhasin, who was then invited to the Garden Party to be held the next day at the Lodge. The Club served us a very good dinner afterwards. Premita Saigal sat next to me.

21 May 1948

In the morning I had to pose for the painting but in the afternoon was free and wandered on the Mall and attended parties being thrown for us. I heard from Brockman's Secretary that a letter had been sent to VP Menon about me. So my future career was in the mould.

22 May 1948

Over 700 guests came for the Garden Party – pleasant sight of women in saris moving up and down the terraces.

23 May 1948

Heavy day. At 12.30 at night a trunk call came for Her Excellency. Fortunately I was still on duty in the ADCs' room. I transferred it to her room. 'Are you still awake?' she said.

24 May 1948

The Mountbattens departed for Chail to be the guests of the Maharaja of Patiala. Chail is Patiala's summer capital, not too far down from Simla. This meant that we were left to our own devices. No cars were allowed on the Mall of Simla, except those belonging to the Governor-General and his staff.

25 May 1948

We returned to hot Delhi. I was late in getting up from

bed, delaying our convoy's departure and got a raspberry from Douglas [Colonel Curry] for it, the first such, which depressed me. At the next car stop Douglas went out of his way to be friendly, which bucked me up. Travelled by air from Ambala. Very hot.

26 May 1948

Accompanied Lady Louis to the Safdarjang Tomb refugee camp. There was a lot of misery there but clothing and food aplenty with many volunteers and the Red Cross helping.

Hasan Suhrawardy had an appointment with HE. He came early and waited in the ADCs' room – pock-marked, ungainly and furtive.

ഇ૭൫

I remember Hasan Suhrawardy today for two things. The first was the direct action he launched in Calcutta in August 1946 when he was premier of Bengal. This resulted in the deaths of thousands of people and frightened the Congress Party leaders into accepting partition. The second was when he was prime minister of Pakistan and his defence for Britain's membership of the Baghdad Pact – the other members were Turkey, Iran, Iraq and Pakistan – because, he said, '0+0+0+0=0.'

On the same day I had noted in my diary that 'Panditji accompanied by Krishna Menon came to dinner. Panditji kissed Her Excellency's extended hand several times, though when Krishna Menon tried to follow suit she withdrew it.' A few days earlier I had heard that Lady Louis was going on a tour to Kashmir and I requested her to take me with her, if possible, for I had never been there, and she kindly agreed.

Kashmir, 27 May 1948

We first flew to Jammu. The Maharani and Bakshi the Deputy Premier of Kashmir, with state officials, welcomed us at the airport. Her Ex immediately plunged into visits to refugee camps. Some were tolerable – especially one run by an Englishwoman from the Red Cross – others deplorable with lack of food, medicines and clothes, pale faced women, dull to their pain – they had had enough. Bakshi was rather short with the Maharani who accompanied us. Though rough and ready he was apparently popular with the masses. War planes were constantly taking off and landing and one saw a lot of war material and military trucks. The Maharaja's palace in Jammu commanded snow views and we had lunch and dinner there.

ॐ

The Maharaja of Kashmir had baulked at Mountbatten's hint to him to consider joining Pakistan. But he did not wish to join India either, because he hated Nehru and Nehru's friend Sheikh Abdullah, the popular leader in the Kashmir Valley, who was opposed to monarchy in Kashmir. The valley occupied less than 10 per cent of this princely state's territory but had in it over 60 per cent of its population. While the Maharaja dithered, Pakistan lost patience and two months after independence and partition, invaded the Kashmir Valley, using the North West Frontier tribesmen promising them loot as spearheads to avoid the accusation of committing aggression. The Maharaja then sought India's help to defend his territory and acceded Kashmir to India. The Indian troops that were flown in stemmed the Pakistani attack. In May when I visited Kashmir the fighting was going on in western Kashmir bordering Pakistan. (The Gilgit Agency in northern

negative.' When I conveyed this to Mountbatten he was furious: 'Tell Menon not to come tonight,' he said, and he immediately embarked on a plan of action. By this time Erskine-Crum had appeared. HE asked him to compose a message for Her Ex. The message read: 'When the premier is ready to leave, HE would like to say "goodnight".' I was instructed to take the message up to her. As a rule ADCs knocked and immediately entered HE's or Her Ex's doors. As I entered, my eyes first fell on Panditji's highly polished Peshawari *chappals* (sandals), neatly placed on the carpet. They were sitting on the Knole sofa facing each other, their positions revealing an extraordinary intimacy between them. I delivered the message and withdrew, receiving a forgiving smile from the premier and a nonchalant one from Her Excellency, for the interruption I had caused.

The plan was that as the lift, with Panditji in it, began to descend, I would alert HE. Sir Walter would then loiter in the corridor and encounter the prime minister, as if by chance. Pandit Nehru would naturally say something about the current Hyderabad negotiations to the nizam's constitutional adviser and the two would then enter the governor-general's study talking about a matter Mountbatten could not be blamed for bringing up. The stage-managed arrangement worked perfectly and the three remained closeted in the study for quite some time.

Judging from Erskine-Crum's demeanour that night all had not gone well. Mountbatten's plan, I learnt later, was to get the prime minister to accept the Hyderabad formula that very night and thus create a *fait accompli* before Patel's negative reaction could reach him and Nehru.

8 June 1948

HE is very keen to get a settlement on Hyderabad before he leaves. 1 heard him tell Erskine-Crum that he wants to go to Hyderabad after the matter is all settled and announce that petrol and other goods would again be allowed to enter Hyderabad [for these had earlier been stopped to pressurize the nizam].

9 June 1948

Today's conference with Sir Walter, Laik Ali, etc. must have enabled HE to extract further concessions from Hyderabad, because his mood improved after this meeting.

10 June 1948

The King's Birthday dinner, to which all the foreign envoys were invited (100 people) flopped because of the very bad Indian dance performance enacted after it.

Earlier, after a meeting on defence matters in which HE, the PM, defence minister (Baldev Singh), the C in C, General Busher, General Cariappa and V. P. Menon (the secretary dealing with the princely states) participated, I found a doodle by Nehru on the pad placed before him. (This I collected for my journal and it can be seen on the following page.) What does writing his name in Hindi and then writing it in reverse and doing the same in Urdu indicate? Ego? Do the patterns and drawing he made indicate a love for order and logic but also fear of unexpected bolts from the blue?

The Standstill Agreement on Nehru's doodle is a reference to the agreement signed with the Nizam of Hyderabad pending a decision on the state's future. The integration of the states' forces refers to the forces of the princely states – the larger states

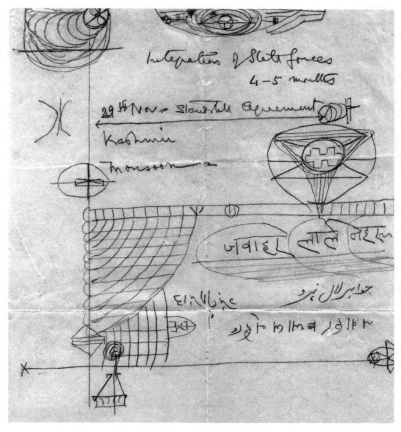

42. Nehru's doodle.

maintained armies – that were being amalgamated with units of the Indian army, subsequent to the princes giving up their territories and powers to the government of India. Obviously, Nehru was advised that day that the process would take another four to five months. Kashmir, where war was raging with Pakistan, and the monsoon, on which the Indian economy was so dependent, were also discussed or were on Nehru's mind. Only psychologists would be able to decipher the significance of

279

the designs he drew, but the doodle does certainly offer us a unique view of the workings of Nehru's mind.

11 June 1948

Her Excellency and Panditji have gone away to Naini Tal. I had an easy day with good squash at the Gymkhana Club. At the reception at the Roshanara [club] it was two or three degrees cooler, no doubt because of the park surrounding it.

The club is in a garden that once belonged to Roshanara, the daughter of Emperor Aurangzeb (1648–1707), and a few days earlier I had escorted Her Excellency there to see at leisure the Mogul rulers' apartments in the red fort. There the guide recounted a story of how Roshanara was with her lover when the arrival of the emperor was suddenly announced. There was nowhere for the half naked lover to hide other than in the *hamam* (Turkish bath) brimming with boiling water and exuding vapours, so that was where he was put and he got roasted. Her Ex's matter of fact response was that 'perhaps he would have met a worse death had he been discovered'.

13 June 1948

We went to Dehra Dun to meet Patel. [Lady Mountbatten had returned back from Naini Tal the previous night.] I sat in the jump seat of the Rolls-Royce. Panditji and Rajkumari Amrit Kaur were with us. Baldev Singh (defence minister), Gopalaswami Ayengar, V. P. Menon and H. M. Patel (secretary in the Ministry of Defence) reached Dehra Dun independently. [It was] a high-powered meeting.

After we reached Doon Court, where Patel was staying, I wandered into the garden to locate Mar Lodge, our house in Mussoorie. The hill station at 6000 feet appeared close

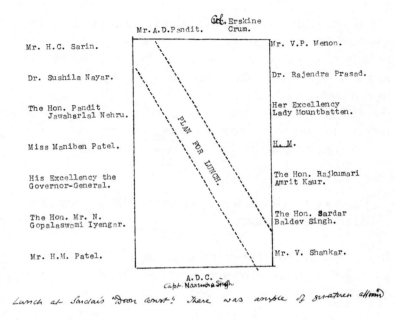

43. Table plan for the lunch at Doon Court on 13 June 1948.

from Doon Court at 2000 feet. But was hurriedly summoned to HE's presence. He asked me for his necktie, which, to loosen his collar during the drive he had given me and which I had forgotten to return to him on reaching Doon Court. Her Ex was with him using the same wall mirror to apply lipstick. 'You cling to him,' I heard him tell her. HE obviously did not want Nehru to be left alone with Sardar Patel. The vegetarian lunch was excellent. Patel, with his large bald head and severe mien, looked more impressive than Nehru. Have heard that HE got from Patel what he had wanted.

Later I learnt that Patel had remained adamant on the compromise plan, but in the final moments before HE's departure he accepted it, saying that he could not refuse an appeal by a friend just before he was about to leave India. According to V. Shankar, his private secretary, the sardar accepted the formula because he was absolutely certain that the nizam would reject it and that is what actually happened. (Patel had been bent on incorporating Hyderabad into India. When the Jihadis inside the state got the upper hand in late 1948 and chaos ensued, the Indian army moved in, the state forces surrendered after a couple of days' fighting, and the Nizam of Hyderabad acceded to India.)

15 June 1948
Today I was ADC-III, the day devoted to Mr de Valera who is staying at the House.

In the last chapter I mentioned taking him to the Anglican instead of the Catholic church by mistake. My diary for the day continues:

In the evening there was a press conference, which 50 correspondents, Indian and foreign, attended. They questioned him for one hour. He made the following observations: (1) North Ireland must join South Ireland. The division is a British creation and false. (2) Unlike Australia or Canada, Eire did not owe allegiance to the King of England but was in the Commonwealth purely for convenience. He said these remarks should in no way be construed as spoken to influence India's policy on the Commonwealth issue. All the diplomats in Delhi were there, the prime minister too. Later de Valera spoke on the All India Radio ending with 'Jai Bharat' (perfectly pronounced after my tutoring). No oily tongue. [He has] fixed convictions [and] bears his 65 years well.

The Indian national anthem 'Jan Gan Man' is taken from a poem by Rabindra Nath Tagore and ends with the line 'Jai Hey, Jai Hey, Jai Hey' (victory, victory, victory), which is not the last line of the stanza of Tagore's poem from which it was taken. The last line goes 'Bharat Bhagya Vidhata' (the Supreme Creator of India's Destiny), thus 'Jai, Jai' (victory) for the 'Supreme Creator'. If the last line from the stanza is removed, as it has been, 'Jai, Jai, Jai' hangs in the air – Jai, Jai, victory for whom? Mountbatten, not understanding the above and believing that the anthem should end on a high note as in European anthems, persuaded the Indian leadership to drop the last line of Tagore's stanza – 'Bharat Bhagya Vidhata'. One can forgive Mountbatten for his ignorance and activism, but not the Indian leaders who should have known better than to agree to mutilate Tagore's poem – a mutilation that has still not been corrected.

According to the Indian Council of Cultural Relations, from whom in 2006 I had requested more information on the subject of the origins of our anthem, Nehru had written in one of his periodic letters to the chief ministers of India's federal units 'that he chose Tagore's "Jan Gan Man" over "Vande Matram" (which had been the Congress Party's anthem during the freedom struggle) because he felt that the tune to which "Jan Gan Man" had been set was conducive to Western orchestration'.

17 June 1948

To have his face painted, HE had to find time for a few sittings. He got wild that Swamy, the artist, was late. To hurry things up, both the painters had been asked to work upon his portrait simultaneously. Impatient to know how they were getting on, he whispered to me: 'Tell me every minute what they are painting.' So every minute I would go and whisper to him: 'Da Cruz your nose, Sir and

283

Swamy your medals.' 'Which medals?' 'I do not know all of them, Sir.' More frustration on his face. After the sitting, while walking away from the room, he said to me: 'They have not got my face right and if they do not get my medals right, no one will recognize me.'

18 June 1948

The portions painted by da Cruz, including HE's face, showed an appreciable improvement today. Swamy is still in the doldrums.

19 June 1948

PM's farewell reception for them at the PM's residence [was] attended by all who matter. Her Ex and PM are getting infamous. They are all the time together. PM appears to be almost in love.

Received a letter from the Ministry of External Affairs asking me to appear for an interview on the 23rd. Another milestone crossed?

I was placed with the 1948 entrants for the foreign service and sent first to Magdalene College in Cambridge and later to Tours on the Loire in France to live with a French family to learn French.

20 June 1948

At 4 p.m. Rajaji arrived at Palam. I slow-marched with Parashar at the Guard of Honour ceremony.

A formal lunch for us – the personal staff – and then distribution of presents. An autographed, framed portrait and a silver cigarette case for each. It was great luck to have worked under such a dynamic and inspiring chief though for far too short a time.

have definitely made a huge impression in India. There was a sort of silence of sorrow at their departure. Before that there was an inspection of the guard of honour, a drive on the carriage escorted by the bodyguard to the gate, tears in his eyes and the final 'goodbye' at Palam. Nehru boarded the plane for a couple of minutes. Lord Louis when biding me goodbye said 'I am glad your father sent you to me. Remember me to him.'

Chapter 22
Epilogue

Serenely, Maharajah Strolls the Democratic Land

By John F. Burns

ALMOST A half-century has passed since India's independence began pushing the maharajahs into history, anchored in memory by images of pillared palaces and jewels the size of hen's eggs, by gold-plated Rolls-Royces and tiger hunts conducted on elephants' backs.

So when the maharajah of Sarila set off recently across a stretch of north Indian countryside that was once his family's private domain, history went before him.

As a modern maharajah – stripped of his forebears' powers and most of their land, but retaining their palace and a measure of their wealth – he has striven for a new place in an India where the vote of the poorest villager has counted as much as his own.

It is an uneasy balance, one that many of India's old rulers never achieved. But the maharajah here, Narendra Singh Sarila, scion of one of the 350 princely families that once held sway over a third of India, has not wallowed in regret.

For him, it has been enough that the new, democratic India offered fresh chances to the old elite, an opening he took when he served 35 years in the diplomatic service, finally as Ambassador to France.

'Some small princes who could not make the switch to something useful have sunk into the sands', the 68-year old Maharajah said as he headed for the wrought-iron gates of his 30-room palace on a crisp winter morning.

'But many of those had begun to sink a long time ago. The rest of us have tried to be as useful as we can. I've no doubt we'll still be flying our flags in the 21st century.'

For his journey into the countryside, the Maharajah left behind the Mercedes-Benz brought back from his years abroad. Instead, he walked, in a style not likely to be construed with a villager's. Along with a tailored hacking jacket and suede shoes, he carried a handsome cane.

At a discreet distance, a turbaned guard followed, with a stave topped by a scythe-shaped blade, not so much to ward off human marauders as to kill any cobra that might have slithered onto the pathways through the fields.

When the princely state of Sarila was established, in 1755, by the grandson of a Hindu warrior chief who pushed back the frontiers of the Mogul empire in India, it was part of a medieval kingdom, Bundelkhand, that covered an area almost as large as modern France.

Within the kingdom, there were more than a dozen maharajhas from the Bundela clan, each with his own state. Sarila, one of the smallest, accounted for about 100 square miles, more than four times the size of Manhattan.

Under the overall control of Britain, which succeeded the Moguls as the imperial power in India, the ruler of Sarila, like other maharajahs, raised taxes, levied his own forces and enjoyed what amounted to absolute powers, including the right to put offending subjects to death.

The powers lasted until India's independence in 1947, when

the princely states were merged, under bitter protest by some maharajahs, into the new nations of India and Pakistan.

Under the merger terms, the maharajahs lost their political authority, but hoped to save their luxuries. But before long, their economic base began to be eroded, too. In the 1950s, 'ceiling acts' passed by the Indian states sharply reduced the private estates left to them at independence.

In the case of Sarila, 400 miles southeast of New Delhi, the government of Uttar Pradesh State cut the maharajah's land to 45 acres, barely a tenth of what he previously owned.

In 1971, Prime Minister Indira Gandhi struck again, using a large parliamentary majority to push through a constitutional amendment stripping the maharajahs of the 'privy purses', or government stipends that were guaranteed in the Constitution when they lost their taxing powers.

With the stipends, amounting in the case of some of the larger princely states to as much as $330,000 a year in 1950, went the onetime princes' few remaining legal privileges, including exemptions from taxes, customs duties and gun licenses, and the right to use titles. In practice, almost all the maharajahs continue to use their titles, and to be addressed by other Indians as maharajahs.

Narendra Singh Sarila's career put him in service of leaders who combined to turn the maharajahs into museum pieces – as an aide-de-camp in the late 1940s to Earl Mountbatten of Burma, Britain's last Viceroy, who set the terms of the merger of the princely states into India; and later, as a diplomat, as an aide to Jawaharlal Nehru, India's first Prime Minister, and his daughter, Mrs Gandhi. It was Mrs Gandhi, hated by many maharajahs, who appointed him to a succession of ambassadorships, in Spain, Brazil, Switzerland and France.

Now, the Maharajah lives half the year in Montreux, Switzerland, and the rest at Sarila, with trips to New Delhi to conduct business on behalf of Nestlé's, the Swiss food and drinks company whose Indian subsidiary he heads as chairman.

Though not the pampered life of some of his forebears, it is luxurious, but apparently not so much so that it stirs resentments among the 10,000 residents of the town of Sarila, just beyond the palace gates, or among farmers in the neighbouring villages.

At Parcha, a settlement of immaculately whitewashed homes of brick and thatch, villagers poured into the dusty lanes to greet a man many seemed still to regard with awe.

'Things were better here under the maharajahs: there was never any law and order problem as there is now,' said Ram Singh, 60, a tailor who was one of many village men who kneeled to touch the Maharajah's feet, a traditional gesture of reverence.

'Yes!' others cried out. 'There was not such corruption then!'

In an orchard outside the village, the Maharajah demurred. As his staff set a white tablecloth on a stone table and served a sumptuous breakfast on china plates, he said villagers had exaggerated out of what he called misplaced loyalty.

'It is not a question of being nice, it's a question of being correct,' he said. 'Much of what they say about lawlessness is a result of the population growth, which would have overwhelmed any government. By most standards, there has been a tremendous upward swing since 1947.'

It was a view borne out later when, to celebrate the Maharajah's birthday, 200 Sarila men came to the palace for a gathering beside the lake the maharajahs caused to be dug more than two centuries ago.

As the sun set over an artists' vista of flaming red bougainvillea blossoms and curving palm trees, men sat in their turbans of white and yellow and red and debated amiably with their onetime prince.

'Is it not better to be a free man, but hungry, than a man in chains?' said Kashi Prasad Vishwakarma, 63, a doctor of homeopathic medicine.

The Maharajah and his wife, Shefali Kunwar, daughter of a Hindu Maharajah who lost his lands in Pakistan, spend much of their time in Sarila inculcating the responsibilities of a maharajah in their 16-year-old son, Samar Singh Sarila, who will one day inherit the palace.

They counsel discretion. 'We have to be part of the community where we have lived for 250 years, and help it where we can,' the Maharajah said. 'But we must never impose ourselves, because the people would never accept it. It is their India now.'

The New York Times
Thursday, 4 January 1996.

Glossary

achkan	long closed collar coat worn by gentlemen
akhara	square piece of ground prepared for wrestling
almirah	Anglo-Indian term for a mobile wardrobe or cupboard
alta	washable red body dye
angarkha	long flared dress for men
ankush	baton with iron spikes (used to drive elephants)
Ann Data	provider of sustenance
arak	distilled beverage
attar	perfume
babu	clerk
bahishti	water carrier
bandhni	tie-dye designs
bandobast	administrative arrangements
baradari	room on the roof with 12 doors
barat	chronicler
bhajan	Hindu devotional song
bhang	Indian hemp
bhangra	lively form of music and dance that originated in the Punjab region
Bharat Mata	Mother India
Bharat Varsha	Land of the sons of Bharat
bhed	creating internal divisions to weaken a country
bhopali leheria	zigzag stripes

burj	watchtower
chanwar	fly whisk, symbol of sovereignty
chapatti	unleavened bread
chappal	sandal
chauhatra	number 74 (to commemorate the suicide of Padmini of Mewar and her 73 companions)
cheetal	spotted deer
chowkidar	caretaker, watchman
crore	ten million rupees
Dalit	lowest social caste, formerly called untouchables
dam	currency, monetary inducement
dand	use or threat of force
dangal	wrestling tournament
darja or *darzi*	tailor
darshan	seeing a superior person or a diety
Dau	elder brother
devi	goddess
dhams	sacred places situated in India's four corners
dharma	underlying order in nature and life
dhobi	washerman
dhoti	long loincloth worn by men in India
dhurrie	flat woven cotton rug
diwan	chief executive
dobli	tie-dye designs with larger squares
durbar	court or government of a princely state
Dussehra	Hindu festival to mark the defeat of Ravana by Lord Rama
gaddi	throne
ganga-jamuni	blending together of gold and silver in handicrafts
Garam Dal	Hot Brigade

gari	a taunt in the form of a song specifically targeting the bridegroom's father
Garib Parwar	protector of the poor
ghungroo	ankle bell worn by dancers
gulmohar	flame of the forest or flamboyant tree
hamam	Turkish bath
haveli	town house with inner courtyards
ho gaya	it is done
Holi	spring festival
houri	nymph of paradise, alluring woman
howdah	elephant seat
hathpal	flat piece of jewellery worn on the back of the hand to link bracelet and finger rings
Inqalab Zindabad	Long Live the Revolution!
jagir	territory granted by the ruler with hereditary rights
jallie	stone-worked screen
jamadar	rank among non-commissioned officers
Jauhar	a sally by warriors from a besieged fortress to kill and be killed while their women folk commit mass suicide
jhampani	rickshaw puller
jharoka	balcony
kajal	mascara
kajari	romantic rain songs of Bhojpuri regions
kalgi	piece of jewellery for men
Kali	goddess of war
kaman	bow
katha	story
kathak	dance
khadi	handmade cloth
khanda	two-edged sword
khidmatgar	attendant

kotha	room
koyal	cuckoo
Kshatriya	member of the warrior caste
kumari	pre-pubescent girl, virgin
lahesia	shaded colours that merge with one another
lakh	approximately 100,000 rupees
lathi	long metal-tipped staff
leheria	straight stripes
machan	hideout on a tree in the jungle for observing or hunting wildlife
mahal	palace
Maharajkumar	son of a maharaja
Maharani	maharaja's consort
mahout	elephant driver
mand	melody typical of Rajasthan
mardana	men's part of the house
maulvi	Muslim schoolteacher
mazdoor	worker
mehndi	henna leaf
mela	gathering
memsahib	a form of respectful address for a European woman
mothra	check design, mostly in turbans from Jodhpur
mudra	gesture used in dance
murram	red earth used as a road surface
nai	barber
nallah	rivulet, storm-water drain
nautch	dance (in colloquial language)
nizam	title for rulers of Hyderabad
paan	substance made from the betel leaf that is chewed as a palate cleanser and breath freshener

pachranga	five coloured
pandal	temporary structure set up to hold a religious or secular ceremony
pankha	fan operated by hand
patta	low wooden platform
phag	songs from Bundelkhand
poodle-faker	ingratiating male, lounge lizard
Praja Mandal	people's forum
pugree	headdress
puja	worship
pujari	priest
pukka	authentic, genuine
purdah	separation of women from men
puri	unleavened bread
raga	Indian classical melody
rajpramukh	constitutional governor
Rajputs	those in India who belong to the fighting caste. Original word Kshatriya
Rana dynasty	Sisodia Kshatriya clan that held power in Nepal from the nineteenth century to the mid-twentieth century
rasa	mood, sentiment
Rathor	one of the Kshatriya (or Rajput) clans
rishi	Hindu saint or sage
sadhu	sage
safa	turban
sanad	guarantee
sanatan dharma	ancient ethos
sardar	nobleman, leader
Satyagraha	non-violent resistance
satyagrahi	practitioner of non-violent resistance
sepoy	Indian soldier

serpetch	crown-like ornament of precious stones for men's headdress
sirpench	brooch worn on a turban
shair	Urdu couplet
sham	goodwill
shamiyana	flat-topped marquee stretched over poles pegged to the ground and open on all sides
sharbat	juice prepared from fruits or flower petals
shehnai	aerophonic reed instrument
shikar	hunting (animals) as sport
shikari	hunter
stridhan	personal property of a married woman
taj	crown
takhat	low rectangular wooden platform
tehzib	manners
thakur	baron
thal	round tray
thumri	light classical song or instrumental music
toshakhana	treasury
tulsi	Indian herb closely related to basil
zamindar	landlord given the right to collect land tax from farmers for the government
zenana	the part of a dwelling appropriated to women